HOSTAGES OF COLDITZ

HOSTAGES OF COLDITZ

Giles Romilly and
Michael Alexander

PRAEGER PUBLISHERS
New York · Washington

BOOKS THAT MATTER

Published in the United States of America in 1973
by Praeger Publishers, Inc.
111 Fourth Avenue, New York, N.Y. 10003

First published in 1954 in Great Britain as
The Privileged Nightmare

Library of Congress Catalog Card Number: 72–11686

Printed in the United States of America

Contents

Contents—contd.

PART THREE
THE NIGHTMARE

Illustrations

(follow page 72)

PART ONE

THE ROAD TO THE TOWER

Chapter One

Narvik

Giles Romilly

A^T the beginning of April 1940 the " Daily Express " asked me to go from Stockholm to Narvik. It was another of many Northern journeys in the first winter of the war. I packed only a few things and settled happily into a first-class corner of an electric train which crept quickly northward, crossing the Arctic Circle and Lapland, for nearly a thousand miles, and descended from the Swedish-Norwegian frontier by precipitate tunnels towards the Atlantic seaboard. Above were mountains. Far below, a fjord in a canyon of cliffs, bisected by a sudden, ruler-sharp line: ice inland, blue water from here to the sea.

All that winter Britain and Germany were importing the Swedish iron ore, mined in Kiruna and Gällivare, which could reach them only through Narvik's ice-free port. The ore trains ran all night to the loading quay, and ore ships of the warring powers lay alongside each other scarcely a boat's length apart. Guns mounted on the sterns of the British steamers aimed themselves point-blank at the nearby Germans; their breech-blocks and ammunition were stowed under hatches under a heavy Norwegian seal. Crews had to stay aboard. Only the captains were allowed on shore. The captains, German and English, sat side by side in the waiting-room of the iron company's offices, puffing at pipes in steady silence, sometimes exchanging nods if they had known each other in days of peace.

At night the rattle of the trains, the jig-dance of iron boulders chewed up by grislies in the crushing plant, the recurrent throat-clearing rumble as the crushed ore was slid from the raised quay-side down chutes into the steamers' holds, and the great mass of frostily twinkling lights, offset the polar isolation and gave a friendly illusion as of ordinary city traffic. By day, too, Narvik seemed friendly and peaceful. Yet it declared plainly the dangerous function which had raised it from a forlorn fishing village. Iron was its master. A battleship could be made out of one day's work in Narvik. As soon as the ore-ships put out to sea, they faced destruction by weapons which their cargoes had helped to manufacture. The German ships could still creep safely down the gigantic Norwegian coast; but they were often sunk as they dashed across the Sound; and now came warnings of action by the Royal Navy to deny them the immunity of Norwegian territorial waters.

Expecting disaster, fearful of the counter-warnings and threats which poured from the Third Reich, the Norwegians braced their spirits with pessimistic, melancholy courage. In Narvik they said: "We must make the best of whatever comes." The town's garrison was strengthened, anti-aircraft batteries erected at points on the hills. The "Norge" and the "Edisvold", elderly armoured light cruisers, were stationed in Narvik harbour, and there were two tiny submarines.

Sunday (7th April) was a day of rest and silence and peace. The younger officers of the "Norge" went skiing into the mountains, hurtling down headlong slopes thirty miles beyond the Swedish frontier. They gave a party afterwards in the Royal Hotel. Wet skis parked against the walls, they sprawled in deep chairs wearing thick sweaters, glowing with zest and health. It was the last holiday they ever took. Less than thirty-six hours later they lay dead, one and all, at the bottom of Narvik harbour.

In the late night of Sunday to Monday, while all were abed, the Royal Navy laid minefields at points along the Norwegian coast. Thenceforth no German ship would be able to pass without going outside the territorial limit and making herself lawful prey. The news of this action struck terror into Narvik. Friendship to England did not waver; she was reproached as a friend who had been inexplicably inconsiderate. The ships in the harbour, forbidden to leave, lay about low in the water with tens of thousands of tons of iron in their holds. Loading went on in an atmosphere of dread darkened by rumour. In the early evening a huge grey shape glided into the cliff-walled pool and stationed itself retiringly among the ore-steamers. It was the "Jan Wellem" of Wesemunde, a German whale-factory ship, heavily loaded.

"Probably the first German taking refuge here from your blockade," guessed the Norwegians gloomily—and wrongly.

I telephoned to London, and was instructed to try to go by sea down the coast to Bergen. Afterwards I learned that it would be possible to leave next morning at eight o'clock. The coastal traffic was to be resumed, British ships providing escort through the minefields. Tension apart, I was thankful for the chance of leaving Narvik, sunless, isolated, enclosed, where the snow still shook itself out of the sky in an endless frenzy.

A sound sleeper, I was surprised when I woke to find that it was only twenty minutes to five. Through half-drawn curtains I could see the usual dense unhurrying snowstorm and a leaden half-light, neither of night nor dawn. The window banged shut loudly—strangely, because there was no wind. The irregular, friendly rattle of the trains and the hoppers was missing; the pall of silence seemed wrong. Then came two abominable, insulting bangs. Lifting the receiver of the room telephone I heard blurred sounds of distress and confusion; the voice of the hall clerk: "Yes. Yes. It is trouble in the river." I dressed fast and ran downstairs. On the landings, at the doors of bedrooms, were officers of the Norwegian garrison, in flowing nightshirts, in pyjamas of thickest flannel, buttoning shirts over hairy chests, fumbling with boots, buckling belts, some standing as though rooted, picking sleep off their eyelids. The hall, a mass of dressing-gowns and tousled heads, looked like a country-house party surprised by fire.

Outside, soldiers were tumbling helter-skelter, rifles clutched anyhow, down the steep, slippery slope that led towards the harbour. The slope ran out into a straggling square, bounded on the right by the railway, sunk in a bridge-spanned cutting. On the left was a covered market. In the centre, to the right of the road, stood a small, lighthouse-shaped kiosk, and near it some trucks were parked. Directly below, a few hundred yards further but invisible, lay the harbour. The heavy, whitish mist, leaving only a ragged, snow-drenched clearing between sky and land, made all beyond a region of mystery, now also of menace.

Some of the soldiers climbed on to the trucks and levelled their rifles along the tops of the hoods, others got behind the kiosk. A few took up positions on the bridge. The majority stood or crouched in bunches completely exposed in the centre of the square.

A sound cracked the almost palpable silence. There emerged, statically sudden, as if the sound alone had set it on the mist-screen, an oblong panel of forms kneeling on one knee, elbows supporting the weight of aimed guns, lines from knee to ground as close, straight, and fixed as altar-rails. Minute against the endless front of the mist, this green-grey tableau suggested, in some sickening way, an appeal for forgiveness. Not more than thirty yards divided it from the Norwegians. Already all was too late. The Norwegian soldiers whispered together, and one of their number ran out of the ranks, pulling a white handkerchief from his pocket and waving it aloft. The tableau sprang to life.

"Fly, fly, sir!" cried a young American to the British consul and his men, who stood doubtful on the hillside.

"But I hate to go! All our ships are here!"

"You can do nothing, you must fly!"

The consul and his men turned slowly away towards the steep mountains.

It did not occur to me that I, a reporter, would be affected by these events. Intending to see more of them, I walked back up the hill and was surrounded at the entrance of the hotel by an in-tramping posse under a great-coated, purple-ferret-faced sergeant who, thrusting forth a pistol like an obscene, small extension of his hand, was screaming, "Wo ist der britische Konsul?"—a question that nobody seemed inclined, or able, to answer.

All day fresh companies of German soldiers, humped like tortoises under enormous packs, struggled up the slope, and halted by the hotel. A swastika flag was run up on a near-by mast. I watched from the window of my locked bedroom, outside which stood a soldier who had said, pleasantly, "Das ist Pech für Sie."[1]

Towards evening I was visited by an English-speaking German lieutenant with a forage cap, yellow-white eyeballs, which rolled horribly, and the face of a scraggy bird of prey. His manners were agreeable. He ordered coffee for both of us and food for me, and gave a cup of his coffee to the guard.

"I never thought that I should live to see another war between Germany and England," he said. "I lived in France ten years, I became so fond of it. But I suppose the truth is, a great country like Germany could not be held back for ever. It was a mistake of your statesmen. We pay for it, you and I sitting here, and for us to discuss it is perfectly useless. We think we know that we are right to fight against the Jewish capital and against plutocracy."

In overcoat and black Swedish fur hat, carrying a brown suitcase, I, at his request, followed the lieutenant downstairs. The hall seethed with German officers. There were a sprinkling of majors and colonels, Iron Crosses and monocles, and a dash of claret-collared, hawk-featured general. A rolling-gaited German harbour-captain, seamanlike and seaworthy, in black, gold-edged uniform, was talking in a rich, dripping, Falstaff-like voice.

As we worked through this crush, a motley, derelict party of

[1] "This is bad luck for you."

men shuffled in through the hotel's swing-door, and was marshalled into unruly order by a tall, haggard man with fine, dark eyes, who tried in English—pronouncing his words very slowly and carefully—to explain himself to a thin, elegant major.

The forage-cap lieutenant hurried forward, put his hands on his hips, and inquired in a loud, vague, stern, yet not alarming tone: "What do you want?" Having heard the explanation of the Englishman, the lieutenant turned to the major and reported: "They are part of the crew of an English steamer. They want to make themselves prisoners, Herr Major."

This revelation rasped a happy laugh from the assembled Germans. The fiercer-looking men of the steamer's crew glared, and vented threatening mutters.

The major spoke to the harbour-captain, who was rolling himself massively towards the dining-room.

"Part of a crew!" cried the harbour-captain. "Where's the other part?"

"They have rowed to another district of the town, Herr Hafenkapitän."

"Ha! We catch 'em! We shoot 'em and hang 'em!"

Uttered in English, these dreadful jovialities seemed to restore the spirits of the captive seamen.

After a lot of waiting, I trudged under escort across the snowy town to a large building and up stone staircases to a guarded landing. A door was unlocked, I was pushed inside, a light was switched on. Grunts, exclamations, oaths rent the air. A mass of men tossed on a wooden floor, their coats over them as blankets, their jackets under them as pillows. It was a class-room. Desks, jammed together in one spot, were littered with shabby hats and suitcases. The teacher's dais under a blackboard, whence rose only profound, decent snores, seemed to have been reserved by the senior prisoners. On the floors there was no spare inch of space.

A voice: "What ship are you off, brother?"

I answered that I was a journalist, and the word seemed to mock me.

"Room for you here, journy!"

So, by miraculous compressions, there was. The light went out, the chatter dwindled.

"This new type of feather bed's a bit —— hard for my liking."

"Well, we shan't be in this long, anyhow ... "

The white light of early morning was coming in through the classroom's tremendous, uncurtained windows when we were woken by a cannonade, varied with detonating claps. It grew louder and nearer till first the windows and then the whole building quaked. A paintpot of white mist hid the harbour, not even flashes could be seen. The noise could not be too loud or too near for our ears. Confidence in the power of the Royal Navy was unlimited; some of the seamen put their coats and hats on, their suitcases by their side. We listened hard for the rifle and machine-gun fire which would mean a landing. But suddenly silence fell. I slept again, and woke to hot, in-streaming sunshine. The burning blue waters of the tongue-shaped harbour, now in full view below, hemmed in by its mountains, showed a grandiose wrack of smoke and flames and sinking ships. The seamen, crowded at the windows, saw their homes of yesterday, the ore ships "Blythmore", "Massington Court", "North Cornwall", "Riverton", "Romanby", a mass of flame. Two others were totally sunk except for their funnels, one was upended almost perpendicularly with bows sticking up through the water like a great shark, others had gone without trace. The "Jan Wellem", that sinister whaling-ship, had moved out from her retirement, alongside her lay two German destroyers which she was feeding with oil.

In the afternoon the prisoners, with their gear, were formed into a ragged column outside the school, where a German sergeant hectored in American-type English: "Now, you guys, if anyone tries to scram, we are forced to shoot." We moved off, and halted in the square where I had watched the triumph of the German invasion. On a corner adjoining the covered market was a cafe, the Kafe Iris, whose first-floor windows revealed

strangely-wrapped figures, waving at us. Taken there, we found
ourselves in the presence of fourteen huddling, shivering men,
wrapped in blankets without a stitch of clothing, their faces
whiteish-blue with cold.

These men, of whom only two were not very young, comprised seamen, stokers, one cook, and one chief petty officer of
a destroyer, H.M.S. "Hunter", sunk in the dawn engagement.
A German destroyer had picked them out of the icy fjord.

They told us that five British destroyers—"Hardy", "Hunter", "Hotspur", "Hostile", "Havoc"—were engaged in this
battle. In the early hours of Monday (a day before the German
assault) they had convoyed minelayers which laid the northern-
most minefield, across the Westfjord, and then cruised southward on patrol duty towards Bergen. At mid-day on Tuesday,
when they were already far south, the captains assembled the
crews and told them that Narvik had been surprised by the
Germans, that there were, however, only one German destroyer
and one submarine in the harbour, and that the town was held
by not more than a hundred German marines. They were to go
straight back and recapture it. "Hardy", "Hunter", and "Hotspur" would enter the harbour in line ahead, circle it, and sink
all shipping, British or whatever else, without exception. Then
these three would put out landing-parties, each party consisting
of four sections including a Lewis Gun section, and first-aid
man; the total numerical strength would be ninety men. "Hostile" and "Havoc" would support after having silenced the
shore-batteries.

At midnight "Action Stations" were ordered, and the destroyers entered Narvik harbour unopposed at about four o'clock.
They circled it, getting rid of their torpedos with the results that
we had seen. With their 4·7-inch guns they engaged two German
destroyers seen lurking in safety behind the merchantmen. A
German munitions ship, the only one, was sent to the bottom
by a torpedo; the shore-batteries were silenced. As the British
destroyers circled outward, the two Germans came forth from
their hiding-places to engage them. At the same moment, three

other German destroyers made straight for them from an arm
of the fjord. They were in conflict with these when a further
three approached, coming towards Narvik from the main exit of
the fjord. Alas for the "one German destroyer and one submarine"! The English ships were now five against eight and
were surrounded. The Germans, with 5·1-inch guns, were
heavier in armament. The "Hunter", which was ahead, swung
herself broadside on across the fjord to tackle the third batch of
Germans. She had already been hit once, a small hole hastily
bunged with old rags. A few seconds later she was hit vitally and
began to sink. "Hotspur" rammed her amidships in a vain
effort, it seemed, to keep her afloat. The captain was seen
"looking troubled" as he stared at the spot where the "Hotspur"
had rammed his ship. Then he saluted his colours and stood at
attention on the bridge.

Kicking off sea-boots, men jumped overboard into the
shockingly cold water, and clambered towards the floats which
a few had remembered to release. Those too much weakened by
shock to pull themselves up—none had the strength to hoist
them—clung to the sides, some eventually let go, and fell back
into their numbing death.

The survivors' story of the battle had a sobering effect.
Magnificent, but . . . Naval strength apart, Narvik was held by
three thousand German troops at the lowest estimate, and it was
perhaps as well that the British landing parties, numbering ninety
men, had not had the chance to reach land.

Near to me that night on the floor of the Kafe Iris was a
young Welshman, one of the "Hunter" survivors, wearing a
boiler-suit and muffler given by a seaman. Drunk with weariness, he fell asleep still rambling through memories of the battle.
"Action stations, see boy? Feeding the forrard starboard gun I
was. He sung out let 'em have it lads. 'Hunter' was ahead. Ay,
in the stokers' mess-deck. I unhooked the Carley float and I
kicked it overboard, see. Next thing I knew, it was crowded
with bloody stokers. Pushing away like hell they were, man.
Twice I was sucked back . . ."

On Friday, 12th April, two days later, the forage-cap lieutenant visited us for the purpose of interviewing the "Hunter" men. Suddenly aeroplanes were heard, then seen, approaching the harbour over the wall of the fjord. In a second they were over it, there were loud thumps of bombs. The prisoners, well placed to see, and better placed to be hit, misted the windows with eager breath. A bomb which fell thirty yards away, close to the railway-line, made a dark patch on the deep snow. The lieutenant, emerging from one of his interviews, said, vague and kind: "I hope they don't drop a bomb on you people."

The raiders, ten British bi-planes, were doing their best to avoid the town. Circling over harbour and ore quay, they loosed visible strings of bombs whose bursting started fires in the wooden structures. Anti-aircraft machine-guns, squirting streams of coloured tracer bullets, caught one of the bombers in a vicious cross-fire. It lurched, wobbled, came dangerously close to the granite edges of the mountains. With breath-taking zig-zags, a ballet of aeronautics, it seemed just to skim the snow off them, and then drove, as it were, up the main street of Narvik, nothing to spare between itself and the chimneys. The pilot stood up in his seat and swung an arm to left and right, warning all to scatter. Then he and his machine vanished over the brow of the hill.

While bombs were dropping, one of the "Hunter" men had been engaged in a battle of wits with the forage-cap lieutenant, about whom was something odd and likeable. The lieutenant advanced vicious points with masochistic daring, and seemed to snarl with delight as he waited for vicious retorts.

"Hardly very heroic torpedoing your own ships, was it?" he sneered.

"We had to get at your destroyers which were hiding be-hind!"

"Oh yes," said the lieutenant, "they were inside." Then: "You in England are so much under the influence of Jewish capital. You have got rid of all your good men."

"Didn't you have a good man once called Niemöller?"

"Ah, Niemöller, yes . . ."

"God knows how I managed to think of that bastard," said the sailor afterwards.

During the raid the "Jan Wellem" had been hit, she was sinking slowly, and her supplies were being hurried ashore. In consequence, the prisoners, ravenous after three unfed days, received their first issue of food, a hefty soup made from pea-powder blocks called "Erbsen". Loaded with food as well as oil, the whaling-ship had been an important part of the invasion plan, and we just then felt pleased with the Germans for their thoroughness.

Towards the middle of the following morning our attuned ears intercepted throbs, muffled but thrilling, of far-away guns. For more than two hours this distant thunder increased gradually like an approaching storm. Norwegians gathered in the square in crowds, grinning upwards with shared excitement at the prisoners' staring eyes and window-pressed noses, throwing hostile looks at German officers who walked swiftly past with anxious, resolute faces. Dispatch-riders in side-cars hurtled past. At last the thunder cracked over our heads, Narvik shook, the whistle of shells could be heard, Norwegians began to run for cover. When the pandemonium reached a height, which seemed the highest that it could reach, a German destroyer, that had lain all the while behind an unsunk merchantman, slipped out, and moved obliquely up the fjord, spitting flame from her starboard guns. The destroyer, there could be no doubt, was moving out to her death.

In twos and threes, German soldiers sprinted up from the harbour. Their heads were camouflaged with white handkerchiefs or towels, some had white linen jackets, some were in full-length white shrouds like the ghost-soldiers of the Finnish Army. A few were on skis. Junior officers marshalled them into parties which then were speeded off to points on the snow-mantled hills. Red Cross flags were lain across flat roofs in such numbers that the whole town looked like a hospital.

While this landward commotion developed, a prisoner whose
eyes were still seaward shouted suddenly, in ringing tones,
"Here they come, lads!" As a thread through a needle the bows
of a destroyer passed between the walls of the fjord. Slowly the
complete, graceful length came into view and glided towards
the harbour. Might she be German? No, said the "Hunter"
men, and even as they said it a machine-gun salvo met the in-
truder. Her guns answered it twice; the machine-gun fell silent.
A German truck, packed with boxes of ammunition, approached
the railway-bridge from the square. The destroyer put a shell
behind it. Accelerating for his life, the man at the wheel leapt
the bridge like a kangaroo, skidded, and stuck fast askew in
snow-slush. The destroyer circled, fired no more shots. Then
she went out astern.

In the Kafe Iris the strains of "Tipperary", "Long, long
Trail", and the "Marseillaise", bellowed in tuneless triumph to
a tuneless piano, had given way to roars of "Pack up, boys!"
soon followed by enthusiastic packing-up. Correspondingly, the
spirits of the guards plunged zero-ward. "Deutschland—starke
Luftwaffe. England—starke Kriegsmarine!" They gathered
around us. "Good treatment here, yes? In England how is the
treatment of prisoners—also good?" Through me as interpreter
Captain David Nicholas, master of the "Blythmore", assured
them that, since they had treated us straightforwardly, they
themselves would receive similar treatment. Those men were
glad to hear it. They gulped. The air was charged with nobility
and *Kameradschaft*.

But hope, now so vital, so strong, was still a prisoner. Hope, in
the next twelve days, was put to the torture. It resisted fiercely,
fought, got weak, passed from agony to apathy, and died. Outside, nothing more happened. The great naval battle, which left
the Germans in Narvik without a single ship, almost munition-
less and almost foodless, and without communications except by
air, had after all been, from our point of view, only an incident.
Hundreds of German sailors straggled ashore, exhausted, black
uniforms clinging soaked, gold buttons hanging loose. Gradu-

ally chaos became discipline. Fitted out with odds and ends, ranged into companies, the wrecked sailors took over the town, while the invasion troops—specially picked, mainly Austrian *Gebirgsjäger*—went into the hills. The shifting of wounded was carried through, and funeral processions, escorting painted polygonal wooden coffins, crawled black through the white town. The German "Biscuit Bomber", a large monoplane that dropped supply-laden cylindrical cases on white parachutes, paid daily calls. Damaged ships settled down gradually, irrevocably, beneath the blue water. One day the Germans set dynamite to the iron-ore quay and destroyed most of it. A desperate measure—perhaps again they were expecting to be turned out? Perhaps. Hope had grown too weak to make much of that.

The Kafe was a long room, eighty feet by eighteen feet, with tremendous windows overlooking the harbour, a few tables with black glass tops, a few steel-framed, S-shaped chairs, one or two old brown armchairs. At night the chairs were taken out to an adjoining small room, where some of the captains, chief engineers, and first mates bedded down. Even so the brown linoleum floor was congested. We were one hundred and nine men. Those who found no floor-space extended themselves along the glass tops of the tables, and these soon cracked, to the bitterness of the Norwegian proprietor, who one morning rushed in, like a wild Westerner, chewing a cigar under a ten-gallon hat, railed at us, and reverently unhooked from his walls two framed pictures of Norwegian mountains.

In one corner an informal administrative centre developed. Four chairs faced each other, on the sill were essential items— tin, matches, ash-tray, cigarettes, clasp-knife, piece of soap, one stub of pencil, one toilet-roll adapted as writing-paper. Here Captain Nicholas, bony and thin in navy-blue suit, picked with long fingers at the throat-collar of his slate-grey jersey, while his low-pitched, soft-needle voice solved intricate distributive puzzles: "Let's see now. Ay. There's woon packet of papers to eighteen men, woon of tobacco to twelve men, those as don't want tobacco can take five cigarettes, and who wants pipe tobacco, now?"

Captain Nicholas was the haggard, tall man whom I had seen when he marshalled his crew before the Germans in the hall of the Royal Hotel; I did not meet him until the following day when we were all in the class-room. That day I was sick, drills were busy in my head, I suffered. Someone brought me a cup of water.

"I can see you're not used to it," he said. "I can go without my grub for a day or two without feeling any the worse."

This was the captain. He was forty-five. He had thinnish greying hair, a stoop, a fastidious manner, and a persistent sense of responsibility. To everyone, he was the good angel of the weary days in Narvik. Nobody ever questioned the authority which he never claimed. Exercised with energy and fairness, in the general interest, it banded together men torn from their moorings who were liable to jarring collision. I, belonging to the peculiar breed of journalist, stood inevitably a little outside his band. But his instinct was to enrol me in it, and I was glad to be enrolled.

The captain's foresight was unsleeping. On the foodless day when we moved to the Kafe Iris, he suggested, and the guards agreed, a visit to a ship's chandler by whom customarily the British ore-ships had been supplied. The provisions thus obtained warded off starvation, while the sacks of coffee and sugar did wonders in keeping up morale. At the height of the naval battle, when nobody else had any thought except of joyous, triumphant rescue, the captain *sotto voce* tipped off his stewards to set about kneading some pea-cakes. Not that he was less excited; elation burned in his dark eyes. But when the hush fell, when began the infinite hours of anti-climax, his foresight proved a blessing by which many were distracted out of despair.

The captain was always up earlier than anybody else—unless six Lascars, of whom it was said that they were up praying at four o'clock every morning, were earlier than he: I never could be sure of that. The windows were curtainless, the dense white light of dawn pressed in about five, by seven-thirty we had washed, swept or scrubbed the floor, and were squatting all silent in thought and hope. Under the direction of the captain, who had organized this service, two chief stewards made coffee, cut bread, scraped it if there was anything scrapeable; two galley-boys served from wooden trays, impatient as we deliberated like chess-players before lifting a slice out of the pile. "Come on! Come on! They're all the same." They were not, they could not be; they might differ by as much as a mouthful.

The Kafe had a fine, up-to-date kitchen with white-glaze cupboards, still well-stocked, and an electric range. The Norwegian family cooked first; then the Austrian guards; all day we smelt delicious culinary smells which had no relation to what we ourselves were about to receive. The guards ate next door and our eyes ached at their spread table, rich by comparison only, in fact.

The guards, wiry, tough, resilient Austrians, brimful of confidence, had been shaken by the battle of the destroyers, but soon perked up with their slogan: "In war, speed is everything!" According to them it had taken the eight German destroyers, each carrying between six and seven hundred troops, two days to reach Narvik from Bremen. But uppermost still in their minds was the rapidity of the victory in Poland; that had intoxicated them. Some who had fought in Poland told stories of the bravery and cruelty of the Poles. Polish women, they said, allowed themselves to be seduced by German soldiers, and afterwards murdered them as they slept. "Das war kein Kampf!" they said reproachfully. Experts in *Realpolitik*, they thought the Hitler–Stalin Pact a clever stroke and inquired: "Why didn't England make a treaty with Russia? England too slow!" Facts and figures were their gospel, they invoked no moral argument: "Raw materials are more important than ideology!" and rhapsodically ascribed all credit for their country's successes to Hitler.

"Unser alter Führer! Aber nicht alt! Junger Führer! England
—alte Staatsmänner! Junger Führer ist gut! Und nicht ver-
heiratet! Auch gut! Eine Frau spielt eine zu grosse Rolle!"[1]

The exhausted "Hunter" survivors slept day and night; their
most prodigious sleeper the young Welshman of the muffler and
boiler-suit, whose original burst of eloquence, with the crushing
memory of the swarm of stokers that had got aboard his float,
seemed to have taken everything out of him. His muffler twirled
recklessly round his neck, he reeled from chair to chair, falling
instantly asleep wherever he happened to alight. His facility was
envied. Though cards were played, songs sung, tales told, all
activities wilted in the presence of hunger; the only book available was one by D. N. Pritt called *Must the War Spread?*—a
subject too significant in the circumstances.

"Guns," the "Blythmore"'s gunner, a naval veteran, square
and sturdy, had a wallet bulging with photographs, and could
spend hours peering, through forests of black beard, at the faces
which peered back at him. Besides years of family and holiday
snaps he had many photographs of his house in a housing-estate
of Brighton Corporation, for which he worked, and of his allot-
ment-garden to which he confessed himself a slave. Sated at last
with these, "Guns" would take from the wallet a tiny silver
horseshoe "handcast in a Sussex forge", the gift to him of an unknown lady "deeply interested" in men of the sea, who had
asked her clergyman to put her in touch with a sailor.

The entourage of Captain Nicholas included also the "Blythmore"'s second mate, freckled, ginger-haired, fierce-chinned,
whom no lack of calories deterred from arguments, in which by
inclination, principle, or habit he always took a "contrary"
view—with frantic agility if several people were arguing.
"Second" carried proudly a reference from a skipper who wrote
in it that he had "argued his way from Percy Main to Mombassa
via the Cape" and finished: "I am now leaving him behind in this

---

[1] "Our old Führer! But not old! Young Führer! England—old
statesmen! Young Führer is good! And not married! Also good! A wife
plays too big a role!"

ship so that he may argue the toss with somebody else. He is too hot for me."

For imperturbability, no prisoner equalled an enormous Cockney from Woolwich, who wore a buttoned waistcoat over a flannel shirt held at the neck by a stud, while his face glistened perpetually with what looked like, and no doubt was, honest sweat. Every morning, stroking the sides of his waistcoat complacently over his chest, and towering over me, he said, "Well, 'ow d'yer feel today?" Our circumstances did not trouble him because he had known worse. "Me and my mate tramped through Wiltshire during the depression. Putting the 'ard word around. All you could see was hundreds of —— men in the casual wards." His good-humour was invincible; and though he came to me for information I almost always found that I was learning from him. He also had unromantic views about his job. "Been a seaman since 1914. There's nothing in it. Remember when GBS went on a three months' cruise? When 'e got back 'e said all seamen were arf —— lunatics. 'E's a cheeky old bastard. That's 'ow 'e gets by."

One morning I was told to pack and go up to the Royal Hotel. The forage-cap lieutenant, now nicknamed "Whatdoyouwant", was waiting below, and he led the way. In the lounge he left me with a guard of two soldiers. Eventually he returned, sat down near by, and said, "Well, Mr Romilly, how do you feel now?"

"Fairly well, thank you."

"What will your uncle say, Mr Romilly, when he hears what has happened to you?"

"I don't suppose it will affect his policies," I answered.

"You have an uncle who is a high personality in English politics, haven't you?"

"Yes, Mr Churchill."

"Oh, is it so?" Whatdoyouwant looked vague, and sucked a cigarette, pushing his long head forward like a baby bird reaching for food.

He left. The hall-clock had stopped, nothing signalized the passage of time except the changing of the guards every two hours. Germans, clattering downstairs on nailed boots, stopped to look at duplicated sheets, pinned on a wall, and headed "Northern Edition Front Newspaper in Narvik Fjord". I read them and learned that the Norwegians were fighting in many places, and that "the enemy" had landed troops on the island of Hinnoy, thirty-five miles north-west of Narvik. This was exciting news. But the day wore on, the sun began to leave the cold snow on the mountains, and I gave way to speculations which deviated all to easily into fluttering hopes. Why had I been told to bring my suitcase? I let my mind dwell on the possibility of freedom. An airman stumped in with crash helmet, goggles pushed up on his forehead. Could it be that . . .? No, he was collecting post.

At last Whatdoyouwant appeared. "All right, Mr Romilly. You can go home tonight to sleep." Back I trudged, and was greeted with a derisive cheer. My hopes had died; but the news of the landing and land-fighting was alive, and it heartened everybody.

Time passed. Then one night, when the prisoners were all asleep, I was woken and told to dress and pack. A car was waiting, and by it was the harbour-captain, wearing heavy leather gloves, stamping to warm his feet. There was the usual whirr of snow hurried about by a freezing wind. A fair-haired German in the back of the car made room for me silently, the harbour-captain got in by the driver, and the car lurched forward. Having passed the harbour, it turned sharp left along a narrow road ledge running parallel with, and fifty feet above, an inland finger of the fjord. The end of this road, as I knew, was a tiny village beyond which were nothing but headlong mountains.

The car halted above a wooden landing-stage. Sentries in white gowns, white handkerchiefs on their heads, moved in the trees. There was the chug of a motor-boat. We got out and slithered down a steep slope. On the flurried waters of the fjord a large grey seaplane was taxying. The motor-boat cruised near. The seaplane went far away down the fjord out of sight.

When this had gone on for a long time the harbour-captain, who had been grumbling piratically, turned to me, sheltering vainly behind a tree-trunk from the stinging wind, and said:

"For which department of the government do you work?"

"For none," I said. "I'm a journalist."

"Journalist! Ha, ha! We know very well what that means."

"I don't know what it means in Germany, but in England it means journalist and nothing more."

"Well! Don't tell me stories. You're a spy, aren't you?"

"No, I happen not to be one."

"Everyone here is convinced that you are a spy. But of course you would deny it until you are shown proof."

"And I can't ever be shown proof."

"You will have to tell that to other people. You will find it more difficult then. It is not safe to be a journalist in war-time."

This conversation certainly started the day pleasantly.

The seaplane could not go; one of its three engines was in trouble. The motor-boat took me back at speed up the fjord and across the harbour, now a wide scene of momentous, terrifying desolation. Twenty-nine ships, warships and merchantmen, lay, with many drowned sailors, under those cold blue waters.

After angry telephoning for mechanics—"Aber sofort!"—the harbour-captain returned me to the Kafe Iris. Soon afterwards a short, fat officer came in beaming, and proclaimed:

"All de men from de steamah will today go free. We do not want civil prisoner in Narvik. You must be ready to leave in two parties, one at 12.30, de other 1.30. You will be escorted along de Erzbahn to de Swedish frontier. A nice walk—maybe two days—take your *Lebensmittel*. If one try to leave de party, he will be shoot. First give away all your knives to de guards."

A wild shout of pleasure and joy.

Beaming, the German called my name. "You must stay."

I said goodbyes, shook hands with everybody. Then I was taken out.

In the afternoon the seaplane again failed. The harbour-captain took me to a tiny summer-hut, one of several on the snow-bedded slopes between road-ledge and mountain-wall, where the ten sentries of the landing-stage were living. Their leader, a young man who looked as hard as diamond, leaped to attention, and asked in a respectful voice if one of his men might return with the car to Narvik to fetch food, as they had received none that day. The harbour-captain replied that this was not necessary, he would see to it himself at once, and bring it out.

The grey, choppy water, the grey cliff, the dripping masses of snow, and the falling snow, made a scene whose dreariness was only deepened by the bright curtains and gay mats inside the hut, and the panels of yellowy wood, on which in summer the sun would dance prettily. The sentries, surly and low-spirited, came back from their cold watches with aching appetites. No car came, no harbour-captain. Darkness began to pour in. A soldier put a mouth-organ to his lips and played a sad song, "Heimatland". They hummed and sang softly. "Schönes Lied, 'Heimatland'", one sighed.

Curtains were drawn, a match put to an oil-lamp. Along one wall was a divan with a green bolster. There were stripy deck-chairs and a few hard chairs. The leader of the watch gathered a blanket round him like a cloak, threw himself into a deck-chair, and fell instantly asleep. I dozed upright. Hours later he woke me, motioned me towards the divan, and threw me a blanket. "Sie sind unser Gast," he said.

It was dead of night when a commotion broke through my sleep; then the unmistakeable voice of the harbour-captain, sounding to be giving some very weird instructions. Fire was to be made in three big cans? "It's the only way!" I heard. Did they intend to steal out and burn the hut with me in it? Activity and talk, then, "Quietly!" the harbour-captain roared. "He speaks German." "He's asleep," said a soldier. "That is, yes"— again the harbour-captain—"the nephew of Winston Churchill, who is sent everywhere—to Iceland, Finland, Narvik. Now we send him to Germany, and . . ." His voice dropped, no words carried; through half-closed eyes I saw the soldiers craning. Gradually the voice rose again, as to a finale, and the last phrase came over clear. "They are always blindfolded."

"Das ist aber nicht schön!" said one of the soldiers. There was a general sigh and pause, and the party broke up.

At dawn, after another long wait by the landing-stage, I entered the seaplane's pipe-like and icy belly. Narvik was whirled away in a drenching roar.

All at once we were so low that blue-grey, calm water ran beneath like a broad road. There was the coast, barren and grand. A big, blurry, rimless sun made wondrous arches and gateways.

Trondjheim appeared, tumbled splendidly across hills, a boulevard-like fjord on which seaplanes rested in crowds. We stopped, then flew four hundred miles overland to Oslo, spread out as on a tray, brick-red, gilded by sun. A lake of wonderfully calm blue sea, bathed in sunset, where the wake of a tiny steamer lay for miles like a fan, brought us to the olive-green coast of Denmark, to pastel fields and crooked toy jetties. The sun sank. Black night had long fallen when the sea-plane spiralled, and I saw far below a welter of blue, dancing lights, guide-lights. Travemunde. Germany.

Chapter Two

Night Walk in the Desert

Michael Alexander

IN August 1942 the pearl city of the Eastern Mediterranean, prize port of the British Navy, social safety valve of the desert soldier, Alexandria, from being a roystering city of naval and military activity, suddenly contained fewer British troops than at any time since the defeat of Arabi Pasha. The navy had sailed out to the safer shores of Syria and Suez, the army, almost to a man, had been recalled from leave to defend the Alamein line twenty-five miles to the west. An hour's drive out of the town along the coast road Rommel and the Afrika Korps, victorious from beyond Tobruk, sat gathering strength for the final pounce.

The few officers and men of the S.B.S. (Special Boat Section) were almost the only troops left in the city. As the situation became serious Axis flags were kept in readiness and rich Alexandrinian Cadillacs began to move south to Cairo or east towards Beyrouth. We stalked the almost deserted bars, wearing our pistols in deference to a current order, acting to the anxious inhabitants as military spokesmen, placating worried cotton magnates, and no doubt influencing the Bourse with a single statement relating to the Allies' ability to hold the line.

In the absence of competition, we lived well. Sometimes

we sought expiation in a nocturnal sortie behind the enemy lines.

One such outing took place unexpectedly on a Thursday evening. I was sitting beside the swimming-pool at the Sporting Club after a game of tennis when I was called to the telephone. A voice said: "There's a party on tonight. Better hurry if you want to be in on it." Two hours later I was aboard a motor-torpedo-boat, almost sole residue of the Mediterranean fleet, roaring out towards the open sea in company with another officer and eight men of the S.B.S. Our target for that night was the rear areas of Rommel's army and in particular the ammunition dumps that had looked like matchboxes on the aerial photographs at 8th Army Headquarters.

With bows thrusting out of the water and a great stern wave building up behind, we turned towards the setting sun and sped along parallel to the coast, a possible meeting with E-boats the only immediate anxiety. It had been dark for some time when the naval lieutenant announced our imminent arrival. As we turned in towards the land the ear-splitting noise of engines was reduced to a low hum and the eager bows subsided into the sea. Through binoculars I made out the low coastline of Africa, a dim range of dunes and a long white line where sea struck sand. The boat nosed as near inshore as she dared, engines were stopped, and we unlashed the Folbot canoe and the black ex-German rubber float that were to carry us on the last lap to land. It was a fine, calm night, the phosphorescent water lapped gently against the hull; the sea, after frustrating us on so many former occasions, was at last on our side.

The plan was to paddle ashore, lay the stock of time bombs we carried on likely targets, and rejoin the waiting M.T.B. at 2.30 a.m. In the event of complications we were to walk the odd thirty miles due east to the Alamein line. We heaved the craft over the side, lowered ourselves aboard, and pushed off. The raiding fleet, cigar and circle shapes, paddled softly towards the shore on a gentle swell.

As we came nearer I seemed to make out solid objects of a

darker colour than the sand. Outlines focused into familiarity—tents—had we chosen somebody's headquarters for a landfall? The convoy conferred. Then things began to happen. There was a sudden shout, a dog barked, lights flickered, and figures could be seen moving dimly. Headlights of vehicles were turned on and shone out to sea in an ineffective effort to probe the night. We came in under the lea of a rocky bluff, dragged our craft into the dunes, and made a dash for cover.

Eight men had little chance of operating unobserved in an alerted camp. The main party decided to go back while the going was good; when the excitement died down they crept back to the beach. But we had turned back too many times, similar excursions had too often proved entirely futile; this time something would have to be done to justify those fat days in the fat city. So we lay, Corporal Gurney, Royal Marines, and I, very still in an excavation in the bank, waiting for the enemy to sleep. After a quarter of an hour all was quiet except for the alarming rattle of our equipment as we got up to move off into the night. Too many waterbottles, too many tins of food, too much First Aid; we dumped most of it and travelled light, if necessary we could live off the land. But we kept our sack of bombs, devilish balls of gelignite and magnesium with an acid pencil-fuse inserted; three hours after nipping the acid chamber the thin wire safety catch would be eaten through, the hammer would drop and the charge explode. We set off through the dim and now silent tents looking for a likely target.

A motor bicycle or two, a little car—no good. Then the outline of two vehicles, vast great things that seemed to loom up as big as buildings against the stars. Tank transporters—worth a bomb or two. We stepped over a simple trip wire with tin cans attached. Snores were coming from the high-perched cabins, but this was no time for scruples and we laid a bomb beneath the petrol tanks. Then we saw an armoured car and gave this the same treatment.

It was almost time to return to the boat, but now our blood was up. We each had an almost full bag of bombs, if we took the hard way home we might meet with some more worthy target on the way. We knew the ammunition dumps were south of the coast road but were uncertain where they lay in relation to our place of landing, which seemed to have been misjudged. We headed due south towards the open desert if only to be as far removed from the populous coastal area when daylight came. After several alarms and excursions we crossed the road and kept on south.

Suddenly, not more than fifty yards ahead , a low block-like mass took shape in the dim light of dawn. It was a large ammunition dump. It s only protection was a strand of wire around the perimeter; in the distance a dim figure paced, the only guard. Very casually we placed a dozen or so bombs in various corners of the dump, then we walked away. It was about this time that we heard the first of a series of explosions behind us, evidence, we hoped, that our bombs at least could make a bang.

The sun was now sailing up above the horizon and its rays were soon hot enough to make themselves felt. The main job now was to get back home; we sat down under the only tree and considered our situation.

It was twenty-five miles or so to our lines; a seven-hour walk on that burning day with no food and very little water in full view of ánybody who happened to be passing was not a promising prospect. We would be wise to conserve our energies by day and make our main effort at night.

As we pondered on these matters we saw a strange group approaching from a distance. We lay flat on the ground hoping we would not be seen. They were making straight for our tree— and soon materialized as a band of three Arabs leading a donkey. We greeted them enthusiastically and joined their little caravan— in such company we should be less conspicuous than if we walked alone. We asked them if we could spend the day in their village or encampment, but as they were going in an opposite direction they did not approve of this idea. With many beckonings and pointings into the distance they encouraged us on towards the south. After we had walked a long three miles their leader pointed to a small mound in the distance, topped by a heap of stones. Reaching it, the Arab rolled the largest stone aside and proudly revealed a hole, into which he crawled, beckoning us to follow.

We found ourselves in a large circular excavation with a thick central column; it was cool and a perfect place to hide. The Arabs suggested we spend the day there and promised to return in the early evening with food and water. We did not think it likely that they would return with our enemies, for they were Senussi and well-disposed towards the British, who were pledged to free them from Italian domination.

In general the Senussi showed a model impartiality in their personal relationship with both sides. On an earlier expedition, several hundred miles behind the enemy lines, I was royally entertained by a tribe who had been given to understand that I was a German. To me they made enthusiastic remarks about the Germans, nor had they fault to find with the British. Their attitude towards the Italians they indicated less favourably, a finger passed across the throat from ear to ear.

Feeling that all our problems had been resolved we said good-bye and settled in to our new home.

The cave, which was filled with sand to within about eight feet of the roof, must have at one time been used as a place of worship. The roof and walls were covered with large Moslem symbols in whitewash and letters of green pigment in an ancient and almost pictographic script. We lay down gratefully on the cool sand and prepared for sleep.

Suddenly, my ear to the ground, I heard loud clicking noises and a dry, scraping sound. I had an instant memory of a pale brown snake with a flat puffy head that I had once seen slither into a cave at Mersa Matruh. The corporal had heard something too. He leapt to his feet and shone a light. "Beetles!" he cried. "Big as racehorses!" In spite of a beetle Derby round my head I soon dropped off to sleep.

Except for occasional trips above ground for reconnaissance, we stayed below ground all day. As the sun went down we began to wait anxiously for the return of the Arabs. Darkness descended and still nobody came. If we waited much longer we ran the risk of not being able to get through in the dark and having to spend another hungry day at large.

Preferring not to rely on the Arab sense of time we decided to start. We headed due east hoping to get through the line before first light; if we walked fast we should just make it. The desert night was cold, our pace soon began to lack briskness. I had to make frequent stops on account of stomach cramps and wished that I had eaten less and exercised more in Alexandria. After several hours walking the desert still looked deserted and the front seemed far away. We began to run.

By now the crisp night sky was thickening up and we sensed the coming of day. Then suddenly the sun switched on and instead of the waste we had felt ourselves walking through, a surprising world was revealed. All around us, as far as we could see, innumerable tents and transport lay passive in the first cold light; they were no more than a hundred yards apart and it was difficult to understand how we had not walked into one on our route. To the north-east, now clearly visible against the brightening sky, was the concrete tower of the little railway station of El Alamein.

Now, apart from being disappointed, we were thirsty and hungry; our first concern was to seek refreshment. Selecting the most isolated tent in sight we walked over to it. As we approached a figure came out and began to shake his bedding. He was tall and blond and obviously a German, shirtless and in shorts he looked like a giant boy. We walked over to him and, to put him at his ease, I asked in Italian for some water. Before he had time to consider my request he was facing an unfriendly pistol, so confusing to him that he almost fell back into the tent. We dashed in after him.

Four Germans, just beginning their breakfast, stood round a table. At my cry of "Hände hoch!" they raised their hands above their heads and gaped. Rope, conveniently in a corner, gave Corporal Gurney an opportunity to exercise his naval training in knot tying. A German, frailer than his companions, while he was being tied up, went white and almost fainted. He said he felt ill and I told the corporal to treat him gently. When they were all trussed up we ate their entire ration of spaghetti bolognese and drank several cups of coffee.

Our dining-room appeared to be an ordnance workshop, spare parts of various weapons lay around, there was a bench with a lathe and other equipment. This must be a rear regimental area a mile or two behind the front line. If we tried to walk through in daylight we would almost certainly be picked up. If we stayed in the tent with our captives someone was certain to visit it during the day; the idea of tying up successive visitors until the tent was full was droll but dubious. I thought that the best course would be to try and pick up a lorry and drive down to the Quattara depression twenty miles to the south; we could probably find a way through this area of soft sand or else walk it at nightfall, there was unlikely to be more than an occasional patrol at that extremity of the line.

In those days in the desert, more especially after an advance or retreat, the standards of dress of the fighting soldier on both sides were variable, though my own outfit, consisting of a light-coloured silk shirt and a pair of buff-coloured trousers was perhaps too eccentric for the German lines. I had originally brought an Astrakhan hat as worn by the Circassian cavalry so that I could more easily be identified by my men in the dark, but this had come off in the confusion of landing—when they found it would they think that they had had a visit from the Russians? To protect my head from the sun and to make myself less liable to instant recognition I took from one of the Germans in the tent a light canvas cap such as they habitually wore in the desert, more practical than any British headgear; to support the two Luger pistols I had taken from them I put on a green regulation canvas belt with the motto "Gott mit uns" on the buckle; the corporal, in his khaki shirt and shorts, already looked sufficiently ambiguous. Thus armed and accoutred we bade *Auf Wiedersehen* to our hosts and sallied confidently out.

Already at this early hour there was activity in the area, lorries were warming up and troops were beginning the day's work. We strolled leisurely along affecting unconcern. After two hundred yards there was a sound of shouting behind us, raw and urgent, then a sort of police whistle, then the spit of a bullet somewhere above our heads. We broke into a run pathetically trying to look as if we ourselves were raising an alarm. Then there were more shots, strangely ineffective it seemed, and I began to develop an exhilarating sense of invulnerability. We ran on. But by this time people were emerging from tents everywhere and even lorries seemed to be bearing down on us from all directions. The chance of seizing a vehicle and making a dash for it had now gone. I dived into a small slit trench and, covering myself with a straw mat I found at the bottom, buried my head in the sand. Seconds later I heard vile shouting above me and I peered up to see a group of Germans pointing rifles in my direction. I surrendered.

Corporal Gurney had also been rounded up and thus the debacle was complete. Among our captors were the gentlemen we had so lately captured ourselves. Either the sick man, who had not been bound so tightly as the others, was less of an invalid than we imagined, or the Navy do not design a knot for securing men.

From the first the Germans did not seem pleased to see us. They refused us water and kept us standing for a long time in the hot sun until a Volkswagen was made available to carry us to some authority more competent to deal with visitors. We were driven to a large tent pleasantly sited near the sea and presented to a Major of Intelligence, who was in the middle of eating his lunch.

The Major, friendly, offered us a sandwich. He seemed to have heard about various acts of sabotage that had been committed two nights before but did not know how it had all happened. Our canoe could not yet have been discovered for he appeared to think that we had come by car and that we were members of

David Sterling's organization, the S.A.S., of which we were, in fact, a sort of sea subsidiary.

The Major was a man of parts; he seemed to know all about the Sterling group, and said, to my surprise, that he had recently had a fine breakfast of bacon and eggs at their desert head-quarters. He mentioned by name George Jellicoe and several other members of the unit so that it seemed there might be some truth in his claim. Apparently he and a general had been cap-tured by a long range patrol of the S.A.S. but had managed to escape on a donkey obligingly provided by a so-called "Free German" member of the unit.

"Do you know Alexandria?" he said.

"Pretty well," I replied. "Cairo, too."

"The other day I was in Alexandria," he said, with a note of pride.

"Fancy that! How on earth did you manage to get there?"

"By car," he said, "in a Mercedes."

"Did you have a successful visit?"

"I saw many of my friends. Before the war I was Consul there."

Now, I felt, it was I who was interrogating him and led him on into an exchange of local gossip in the hope that he would reveal the names of people sympathetic to the Axis cause. His conversation served to compromise in my mind several prominent citizens, at least one of whom was well known to British officers for her excellent parties.

After we had parted with the approved information relating to names and numbers the interview came to an end and we were driven away to El Daba, roughly in the area where we had arrived two nights before.

We were summarily thrust into one of those barbed wire en-closures known to desert captives as "cages". The sole conces-sion to luxury this one had to offer was an erection of packing cases forming a small kennel into which we crawled to escape the hot sun.

That evening we were visited by a small sad man with the

status of *Dolmetscher* or Interpreter, sent, no doubt, to make conversation and try to trap us into an indiscretion. He proved amiable and was soon agreeing that in spite of their current successes the Germans were unlikely to win the war. He even gave momentary consideration to my suggestion that he should return with us to the Allied lines.

When the stomach is empty enterprise also is liable to be atrophied. We received almost no food that day and were in no mood to attempt an escape, an idea that was further discouraged by a strange incident during the afternoon. We were taken from the cage and led over to a wooden hut nearby. As we reached it a Volkswagen drew up beside us, and its occupants, two field policemen, went inside with our escort, leaving us, and the car with its engine still running, unattended. An immediate reaction might have been to leap aboard and drive off, but it struck me that this might be a primitive trap to put us in a position in which we could be disposed of "while trying to escape". There seemed to be no other explanation for this interlude as we did not even enter the hut but were led straight back to the cage.

The following morning found us still lying low in our kennel. The postman called in the form of a Feldgendarme, one of those strange military policemen who carry round their necks a large silver plaque on a chain like a Lord Mayor's badge and chain of office. He handed me a paper in the manner of a bailiff serving a writ, which in fact it was—a very official looking document well covered in eagles and swastikas. The *Dolmetscher* explained that it was an indictment to appear before a Summary Court Martial on a charge of being (a) a franc-tireur, and (b) a murderer. I was told that I would have a defending officer and that the trial would take place next morning.

The "Counsel for the Defence" came to see me later in the morning. He was a young man who spoke perfect English and said that he had been up at Oxford in 1938.

"Why are they bringing a charge of murder against me?"

"German soldiers have been blown up by a bomb."

"I am sorry to hear that. It was not my intention. I was not interested in killing anybody."

"There are very serious instructions about how to deal with saboteurs. This is a very serious case."

He was presumably referring to Hitler's notorious order that all Commando troops should be shot. He told me that the canoe had now been found and that they had been able to follow my route. It seems we had landed right in the middle of the headquarters of the 90th Light, crack division of the Afrika Korps, and that there was much anger in that quarter. They had found our abandoned equipment near the beach and were puzzled as to why we had left so many rubber contraceptives behind. I did not tell him that we used them to keep dry such items as drugs and torch batteries. They were also interested in the large amount of morphine, the issue for the whole party, which indicated that they had not realized that we had started off in greater numbers. All things considered, my defending officer did not think I had a very good case, but he undertook to do his best on my behalf.

That afternoon the idea came to me that there might be a greater chance of survival if I could persuade the Germans that I was not just a vulgar saboteur but was related to General Alexander, who had recently arrived as G.O.C. Middle East and was a personage the Germans had come to respect. Accordingly I put out via the corporal via the Interpreter that this distinguished soldier was my uncle, intending to play on the caste snobbism that I knew was part of their military tradition. I had, in fact, considerably exaggerated the propinquity of our kinsmanship, but I reckoned on knowing enough of the family ramifications to satisfy immediate questionings. To have volunteered the information myself might have been unconvincing but as it was passed in a roundabout way I was actually confronted with the suggestion by the Germans and a half-hearted denial only served to establish the certainty in their minds. Next morning, half an hour before the appointed time of the Court Martial, I was told that proceedings had been postponed and that I would be sent to Germany for trial. After that I was treated with considerably more respect by the guards and the food improved.[1]

At that time all P.O.W.s captured in North Africa were, under some agreement or other, supposed to be the property and responsibility of the Italians, presumably to counterbalance the large numbers of their troops in our prison camps. So when we were moved to Mersa Matruh into an Italian "cage" I thought the Germans had acted according to the rules. But after a day or two under extremely unpleasant conditions we were collected again and driven away in a Volkswagen under a German escort.

We drove off in good spirit along the coast road to the west. It looked very much like old times especially as almost all the transport to be seen had been captured from the British; sixty per cent of Rommel's supplies were being delivered by courtesy of the Royal Army Service Corps. We drove on through Bardia and on to Tobruk where I had spent four months being besieged. Here we paid a call at an old stone castle garrisoned by a company of German soldiers who gave us red wine and sang sadly beautiful songs, "La Paloma", "Lili Marlene", to an accordion.

Next day we came to Derna, set in the green strip between the arid range of mountains and the sea. The narrow streets, that

[1] General Siegfried Westphal, Rommel's Chief of Staff, gave the following evidence at the Nuremberg Tribunal:

Question: Could you briefly run through the case of the Commando action in which the nephew of Field Marshal Alexander took part?

Answer: In the autumn of 1942 a close relation of General Alexander was taken prisoner behind the German lines. He was wearing an Afrika Korps hat and was armed with a German pistol. He had thus put himself outside the rules of war. Marshal Rommel gave the order that he should be treated like any other prisoner. The Marshal thought he did not realize the consequence of his conduct.

Brigadier Young in his book *Rommel* says that when somebody suggested I should be shot Rommel said: "What! Shoot General Alexander's nephew! You damned fool, do you want to make a present of another couple of divisions to the British Army!" I find it hard to believe that Marshal Rommel could seriously have thought that the demise of the G.O.C.'s nephew could have the slightest effect on the Order of Battle in the Middle East. I still think that his goodwill was dictated by his feeling for the solidarity of the military caste. In any case I am grateful.

only recently had been thronged with British soldiers, were now crowded with Germans who almost outnumbered the resident Arabs. Corporal Gurney and I were taken to the town gaol, a pretty whitewashed building on the edge of the town, and were put in separate cells.

My cell was clean and cool and mercifully free from fleas. Outside the window was a fig tree and a winding path with a cactus hedge that led invitingly up into the country beyond. I spent four days trying to remove the bars, replacing the plaster with dough from the bread ration. Escape was inviting, for in the mountains were friendly Arabs and British agents in touch by wireless with Cairo. On the fifth day, however, just as one end of one bar was out, we were moved.

We were driven to Derna aerodrome and made to board a large Savoia aeroplane that stood waiting on the grass. Standing around were our fellow passengers, several elegant Italian cavalry officers, who in peace-time probably spent their days within a hundred yards of the Via Veneto, and three very scented and powdered ladies in billowy silk presided over by a large Madame in mauve chiffon. These Italian camp followers proved a friendly lot and I thought of an occasion at the battle of Beda Fomm; an officer in the Rifle Brigade, who had just captured an Italian tank, lifted up the hatch to bring out the commander when out peered a little old lady in a black dress, whose first enquiry was concerning the fate of her girls.

We flew over the Mediterranean unmolested by the R.A.F. and landed on the heel at Lecce, surprising city of baroque buildings and quarries of red sandstone. Thence by train to the sleazy seaport of Brindisi, much the worse for the naval bombardments it had recently suffered. Here we spent an intolerable night in a barracks that crawled with lice and buzzed with mosquitos. For our next move we took a German plane, a JU52, which had no civilians on board to divert us, only a few soldiers and our escort of two elderly officers and two N.C.O.s. We followed the Italian coastline and in the early afternoon turned in over Venice that in the heat haze seemed to be sitting on a cloud, wheeled over St. Mark's, and dropped down on the airport on the mainland. One of the engines was spurting oil and they were putting in for repairs.

It was a fine modern air station. The white buildings, covered in bougainvillea, shone in the warm sun; smartly dressed businessmen with brief cases hurried to and fro, beautiful women passed us by, seeming not even to notice us standing there dirty and unshaven. Our escorting officers went inside for lunch. They sent us out a ham roll and a peach. We felt very much out of it.

From Venice we flew over the Alps and landed at Munich. Dusk was falling and this large aerodrome looked grimly unsympathetic after the elegant gaiety of Venice. It was cold and raining, ugly, lethal-looking aircraft stood around on the shiny black tarmac. I felt I was entering a new and unfriendly element and for the first time I really began to feel homesick. We spent a gloomy night in a Luftwaffe barracks and were taken early next morning to the railway station. The Germans have a habit of being mysterious about destinations, but I had an airline brochure containing a small map that I had picked off the ground at Venice; when our train passed through Nuremberg I guessed we were bound for Berlin.

It was dark when we drew in, and the great Anhalter Bahnhof was lit like a cavern in hell. Enormous engines belched steam and flame to an accompaniment of martial music on a loud speaker interrupted by announcements of sonorous destinations, Stuttgart, Breslau, Leipzig, Ulm. Banners bore the words "Räder müssen rollen für den Sieg"—wheels must roll for victory. Troops were everywhere, jackbooted soldiers in field-grey uniforms, camouflaged parachute troops, black S.S. men, and naval ratings with their long-tasselled caps and almost English uniform. At carriage windows lovers were saying what was probably a last goodbye before leaving for the dreaded *Ostfront*. We were given a cup of ersatz coffee in the waiting-room while we waited for our next conveyance. It stood under the portico, a square black van with barred windows. Was it the German equivalent of a Black Maria?

Chapter Three

Eclipse: Bavaria
Giles Romilly

A DIFFERENT aeroplane carried me from Travemünde to an airport outside Berlin, where I was lodged in a building occupied by Luftwaffe officers. This was luxury after Narvik, and the colonel of the detachment took pains to make me feel more like a guest than a prisoner. I was told that *der Feldmarschall* —Göring—wanted to see me. The attentions of the officers, whose saluting arms clicked up and down like signals in the comfortable, tasteless drawing-room where they sipped their ersatz coffee, became urgently deferential, awful, and curiously unsettling.

Then one morning a car came, a grey open roadster, by which stood two men, a monocled major of the *Oberkommando der Wehrmacht* (OKW), and a sallow civilian with a brief-case. I got in. They got in. The car moved, and soon was on an *Autobahn* going south.

The civilian, with whom I shared the back seat, began to ask questions about English life, which betrayed all too plainly the kind of information for which he hoped. He notably lacked charm, and the bald blatancy of his approach irritated a professional nerve which reminded me, unexpectedly and opportunely, that I was a journalist. Seizing a silence, he frowning towards his next question, I asked him whether he belonged to the Gestapo. The man flinched. "We do not call it that," he said.

What surprised me was that he should have admitted anything, even indirectly. Sensing advantage, I asked him about the hours of work, pay, conditions, duties of the *Geheimstaatspolizei*, (as he had corrected), and whatever else I could think of. His answers soon became irritable and scant, and at last he backed into a silence more acceptable than his conversation.

It was a most beautiful end-of-April day. The country began to be attractive. The major's monocle flashed with enthusiastic dismay whenever we passed uncultivated land, sparse wood, half-finished building. So much to construct, so much to improve —but war was being won, all had to wait. The major was drunk with the wine of victory, almost maudlin. "Keine Zeit! Keine Zeit! Keine Zeit!" he cried incessantly, like a drunk parrot.

"Now you are in Bavaria!" said the civilian, grimacing.

After Nuremberg, whose cobbled narrows inspired a frenzy of "Keine Zeit!"'s, maps were read, the car forsook main roads, and was overtaken by darkness as tortuously it went up hill and down dale. Side-lights only were used, my escorts rubbed the glass and peered impatiently into the forest of the Bavarian night, where for hours we seemed to wander more and more lost. Then the car was put into bottom gear, and slug-crawled up and up, a spiralling, steepening eternity of night-hidden height. There was a drawing-up, a groaning as of a mammoth hinge. The car's headlamps, suddenly and piercingly alight, illumined a rugged cave-like passage. I got out and stumbled, stupid with fatigue, into this vault, which seemed enormous, then across rocky open ground, to and through a slit of door, up a wooden staircase, and into a small, austere room which contained, I most thankfully noticed, a bed.

Returning day showed the rambling insides, a fircone of a tower, copper-red tiles aslope, corners scarcely sharper than a haystack's, of an old castle. Night's awe had gone; the picture was almost friendly. The small room contained, besides its bed, one table, one (hard) chair, one cupboard, one washstand, and one urn, big and heavy, painted with blue foliage, which stood in a corner. Outside, there was a landing with heavy oak seats, a heavy, round oak table, and five doors (mine making the sixth)

opening into rooms occupied by German officers. At one end
of the landing, in front of a barred wooden gate, stood a
sentry.

In this castle, which was called the Wülzburg, were hundreds
of interned civilian prisoners. They lived beyond the barred
gate. I was not to be allowed to meet them. *Einzelhaft*—
solitary confinement—was the order.

Below, there was an open space where the prisoners walked.
I could see both it and them; but could go down only when they
were inside, at mid-day, and in the evening.

My door was not locked. But if I moved about in the room,
the sentry outside soon started a suspicious patrolling; if I
stayed silent, he did the same. Eventually, in either case, the
handle would be turned with excruciating slowness, the door
part inch-wise on an unblinking, wordless face. I used at first to
go out on to the landing just for a change; but the instant,
heavy step and morose stare soon put me off. I did have to go
out in order to reach a lavatory. The sentries came too and waited
outside. One, a huge man, opened the door, and planted himself
half-inside, and stood there stock-still while we continued our
respective duties in a grotesque silence. When I emerged he
said sepulchrally (I had not thought he could speak), "Über-
wachen hat man nicht gern"—"Being overlooked does one not
like." He was right. I began to dread the unavoidable visits, and
to smile at the sentry in a confiding way, as if to assure him that
he need not follow, I being the sort of reliable person who would
really be going to a lavatory, if he appeared to be doing so.

These were mere pinpricks; if they maddened me, it was because they pierced through the numbed surface which had grown,
like an extra skin, in the first days of this backwater solitude.
Here, I had seen, was the beginning of real imprisonment. But
I did not wish to see it. I did not wish to recognize the fact,
which blatantly claimed recognition, that every feature of active,
youthful life had been whisked away at one swoop. Narvik, the
battles there, the rushing journeys, the Berlin days unpleasantly
glittering: that had all still been something. This was nothing.

I did not wish to look at nothing, still less to meet it, to get to know it; I blacked it out.

Gradually this failed. The weather was bad. On the far side of the castle's grounds were lime-trees and horse-chestnut trees. Walking over there, I looked through the trees, driven by wind and rain, towards dilapidated battlements patched with clumps of turf and green fern. The wind, always the same boring wind, got up rapidly, the circle of sky filled with blobs of cloud like cotton-wool, till it seemed as small as a medicine-cupboard. All I heard was the sound of rain, the sound of wind moaning through trees. All I saw were grey sullen walls and overhead, seemingly not far overhead, the blacker greyness of clouds running before the wind. Then I remembered that there was only the room to go back to, and when I got there, nobody.

Escape! Could I? I looked at the walls, they looked back, daunting. Even if I could get out on to them (a thin if) there was the moat, eighty feet deep, I would have to have a rope. While I brooded, a glider swooped above. I watched, envying its happy freedom, and suddenly my thought seemed to be liberated. The glider was flown, as I knew, by a nineteen-year-old Bavarian boy who did odd jobs inside the castle. He used to bring me my food. He was friendly and simple, a few chats convinced me that I could trust him, and after some very moving arguments turning on the justifiable desire of prisoners to escape, whatever their nationality, I revealed my plan, which was to walk out by the main gate, quite openly, in borrowed German clothes, and to find a bicycle waiting on the hillside. He would bring the clothes and place the bicycle; I, when free, would do my best to repay him. He seemed agreeable, and we had got well forward with practical details when one day he called to tell me that he had just received call-up papers for training for the Luftwaffe. He would be gone next morning. That was that.

This fiasco, instead of depressing, freshened up my spirits. The chatting and planning, by feeding the escape urge, had made it less hungry. It stopped nagging; and the spirit it had enlivened turned readily elsewhere. There were the table, the chair. There was time. I thought about time—which I had never thought about—and concluded that it was both terrible and precious; a terrible asset. Suppose, when it had gone by, I looked back, and looked back on waste? Now, time seemed to have stopped; but it would go by, and what went by would not come back. I had no books. But I could think, work, write. I began; and as I went on the sensation of imprisonment lessened, and a sensation of freedom arose, curiously innocent, independent of circumstance, different from anything that I had known.

Soon I was working in the still night hours (which I liked best), and my late light was being disputed by the sentries, with much headshaking, and recoil from its unthinkability. "Das geht nicht!" They turned the light out. I turned it on. They threatened. I put the table against the door. They sent for the *Wachkommandant*, who came to command, and stayed to argue: in whispers, for fear of waking the *Oberzahlmeister*, a fat short-tempered German, whose room was next to mine. Eventually, tacitly, the sentries gave way. The light burned unmolested. In the dead of night the sentries themselves became quiet as hens on a perch; and the only disturbance—it *was* disturbing but could be counted on to cease before midnight—came from the room of the *Oberzahlmeister*, as he regularly made sport with a succession of women, confusing their cries by turning up the volume of his radio.

Diet was meagre. The potatoes (three a day, and two slices of dark bread) were full of warts and black bits. At first I cut both out, leaving a slender, ridiculous chip; soon I was eating the black bits, soon afterwards the warts too. I preferred them cold (if there was salt) and would peel and prepare with ceremony, in the late evening, a cold boiled bad potato. The shortage of food, though tiresome, was offset by one great blessing. The Wülzburg prisoners sent tea to me. I had no way of making it, and this was undertaken by a prisoner called Jock Brown, a seaman. To prevent us from meeting, a strict procedure was organized. I put a spoonful of tea in a tin, and placed the tin, and empty teapot, on the oak table outside, a few feet from the sentry. That was early afternoon. By about four—I had opened the door several times to look, I could not resist to—tin and pot had mysteriously vanished. Jock had fetched them. I went back to work in a tingle of anticipation. Twenty minutes later the vanished objects were back in their place. The tin was empty, the teapot full; I entered an interlude of perfect pleasure, and blessed Jock every day for his invisible kindness.

The sun began to come out. Lime and chestnut in full leaf dappled the bright ground with spots of warm shadow. I lay absorbing heat and watching the wagtails pompously walking and conferring. Gradually they and other small birds got used to me, they hopped close in a wary, alert fashion, and once, as I lay still, one landed on my back, a very great honour.

One afternoon my door was thrown open and in stamped a *Gauleiter* with several satellites, all in repulsive chocolate uniforms with big black swastikas on red armbands. Escorting them, but keeping well back, was the Commandant of the Wülzburg, a Bavarian *Oberleutnant*.

"Heil Hitler!" cried *Gauleiter* and satellites, all together— and all together raised arms shoulder high in a solemn movement that seemed simultaneously to bless and admonish. Then all together planted their feet apart and stared.

"Der schreibt!" said one.

"Zu spät!" shouted another.

"Na, freilich war er zu spät!"

"That's what he ought to call the whole story he's writing— 'Too Late'! 'Zu spät'! Ha! Ha!"

"Ha! Ha! Ha!"

All laughed hoarsely, heads thrown back all together as in gargling. Then all stamped out.

A few minutes later the *Oberleutnant* put his head round the door, and his one gold tooth winked as, waving a conniving cigar-stump, he muttered: "Eine Viehaufstellung!" [1]

I had met the *Oberleutnant* when visiting a shop in the grounds, managed by an elderly peasant woman, Frau Scharre, in order

---

[1] "A cattle show!"

to buy a bottle of beer, one a day being allowed. This time, however, Frau Scharre shook her head. "Verboten!"

It happened that the *Oberleutnant* was passing. He stopped, heard, and explained that beer had been forbidden to the English prisoners because two of them had got drunk. I stood puzzled, my German being sketchy, and the *Oberleutnant* was driven to illustrate his explanation by draining off imaginary tumblers—which brought a grim smile to the stony features of Frau Scharre.

The *Oberleutnant* was a comfortably fat man, with milk-blue eyes like the Bavarian sky, a crisp-toast moustache, and a bare, bumpy crown on which a few hairs stood up and curled like anxious question-marks. He had won the highest Bavarian medal for bravery during the First World War, when he commanded a battery of artillery. He sometimes joined me on walks, and we talked about business (he owned aluminium factories), politics, the war, impersonal topics. He was amiable and gentlemanlike and never pried.

I had a closer but less comfortable acquaintance with a German called Hofstetter, a slight, half-bald man of about forty, with soft brown eyes and a soft, passive mouth. Hofstetter was a *Sonderführer*—(untranslateable) German non-commissioned rank, a sort of sergeant without portfolio, available for special duties. He had been a schoolmaster in German South West Africa, and wore his uniform like a civilian, the belt hanging lopsided. His voice was soft and educated.

Hofstetter's intelligence, especially on its literary side, made his company, when offered, attractive and even tempting. He lent me his "Faust", rice-paper in limp vellum, a "very personal" copy carried everywhere, he said. He brought "Der Zauberberg", a forbidden work, and adjured me to hide it under the bedclothes. He also had a sense of humour.

When Hofstetter called, he always took his military hat off and scratched at his sparse head. Often he left the hat behind, or else it might be the prisoners' mail that he forgot. I never quite believed in this absent-mindedness, nor in the hush-hush about forbidden books, nor in the refined softness of personality, which seemed to have maggots in it somewhere.

All the same, I was glad of his company, encouraged him with cups of tea, accepted his German cigarettes. Like the *Oberleutnant*, but far more often, Hofstetter joined me in the roundabout walks. This was the time of conquering German war, of the *Stuka* lunges of aerial fury terrorizing Europe.

"Und England ist nicht mehr Insel. Der Führer hat es gesagt."[1]

I heard, but could scarcely believe, that it was Hofstetter whom I had heard. The one thing about him that I had never doubted was his intelligence; how then could he adduce something that Hitler had said as proof of any proposition, not to mention one so nonsensical?

Hofstetter stuck to it. "Der Führer hat es gesagt."

So he believed in the infallibility of the Führer? And in what else? In racial superiority, persecution of Jews, concentration camps? He, an intelligent man, believed in nonsense, perhaps actually called himself a National Socialist—was that possible?

Hofstetter, softly, obstinately silent, suddenly seemed upset, and he answered: "You could not have lived in Germany and stayed outside the Movement."

Intelligence, obviously, was not the point. It was the *emotion* of Nazism that had betrayed him; and, in his answer, it was to emotion in me that he appealed: an appeal for forgiveness. There were the maggots, crawling.

On the day of the fall of France even the *Oberleutnant*, no Nazi, succumbed to Hitler. He got drunk. Then he visited me and just kept muttering "Der hat etwas, der Kerl!"[2] in a thick voice, with incredulous chuckles.

A few days later the *Oberleutnant* called again—to say goodbye. He was posted elsewhere; a major was coming to command on the Wülzburg.

I missed the gold tooth, the toast-moustache with one tiny

[1] "And England is no longer an island. The Führer has said so."
[2] "He's got something, the fellow!"

sprig of pure white in the middle, and the two chins, the lower
an immense roll of fat in which the upper rested like a head
pillowed in a cushion. They seemed, when gone, to have en-
sured more than their owner's equable well-being. With Hofstetter I could not be as before; his visits dwindled, and I had to
realize how much they had brightened the solitude of which now
once more I felt the weight. My routine of work broke down,
sleep seemed to desert me, I believed that I was ill. Probably
because of the meagre, mainly ersatz diet, my teeth had truly
gone black. Yet I was scared of requesting a visit to the dentist
in Weissenburg, the village at the foot of the hill. Once, as I
walked, Hofstetter had been standing with an unknown
German whose eyes followed me unswervingly with such fierce,
rabid gaze that afterwards I mentioned it to Hofstetter, who
said that this man had wanted to "trample me into the ground".
I imagined that, like this would-be trampler, the Weissenburg
dentist would know of my connection with Hitler's chief
enemy, and would joyfully inflict torture.

Suspicions shot up. New feelings about people, disagreeable
feelings, flourished. I seemed to detect nothing, in the Germans
who crossed my path, except pettiness, intrigue, meanness,
sometimes under a mask of goodwill or friendship: that was
worse. If I, at any previous time, had been the target of these
common failings, I had not noticed it. Now it appeared to me
that they were the prevalent things, that the greater part of
human nature was contained in them. I paced the room cursing
—Hofstetter especially was cursed—and nothing answered
my curses except the solitude, which echoed them more loudly.

The Wülzburg seemed a stage on which failure only was to
perform; a shabby down-at-heel old castle set for shabby down-
at-heel people who had been turned into it by their subordinate
fates. For I recognized, while it was me they were stinging, that
the meaner traits of the German underlings were, at root, aspects
of failure. There was the sentry who ordered me to walk only
on the further side of the grounds (beyond a square stone platform enclosing a well and pump) on the pretext that I might

make contact with other prisoners. He would lurk in wait to rush out, seize me by the shoulder, rasp angry words. A pink-necked man, with sour, angry eyes, he was loaded with cross-grained energy which he unloaded on me. It was not much for an energetic man of forty to be a guard in an internment camp; I could understand, though I hated him, his harryings.

There was Beler, the *Feldwebel*, a tall, loose-looking man with large, empty, vulgar eyes. His trade was that of *Ausbesserer*, "improver" (of pictures), one who makes old pictures look new, and Hofstetter had said, ''I think sometimes he makes new pictures look old." He had specialized in grandiose paintings of scenes from Wagner which he would take, after freshening up the swirls and generally "ausbessering", to the Bayreuth Festival, where they commanded, he said, large prices. He was always on the look-out for "early Hitlers".

Beler, like Hofstetter, was a National Socialist, but for him there was no question of emotional urge; he was in it for what he could get out of it. His keen nose scented possible advantage, wherever it might lurk, in whatever guise, and the scent brought him several times to my room, where he sketched out for me his version of National Socialism, which went like this:

"There is very much in common between National Socialism and Communism. But in Russia the workers have not the paradise they hoped. Those workers, you know, only think: how much do I earn, and what life can I have? They don't care who rules, if they are looked after. I was travelling in Turkey, Greece, Canada, Australia—nowhere are the workers so looked after as in Germany since National Socialism. Who is the most enthusiastic supporter of Hitler? The working-man! Those Trade Unions, you know—the workers were only paying something every week to keep a few men comfortable. It was not worth the expense. For every one who is saying to the workers 'Do this' and 'Do that' from the heart, there are nine who are making their own careers. Of course the man who first thought of the idea was an idealist."

Finding me profitless, Beler ceased his visits, and soon he was in alliance with a black-moustached, English-speaking prisoner, tall and smooth like himself; they chatted on the oak seats in the window-bay of the landing outside my room. Beler, unabashed by his own surprisingly youthful appearance, told stories of bayonet wounds received in the First World War; dramatic stories, of a tallness exceeding his own. In exchange, he heard about the glories of "haring up to Scotland in the Lincoln" and of parties with "a crowd of artists who had come into town". Or, as I passed, the black-moustached man might be saying, "It was dreadful in Vienna—Herr Direktor this—Herr Baron that!"

Beler was, despite his air, one of the many types of failure on the Wülzburg: the man who pursues success of the cheapest sort. What he said was guided, never by truth, always by a standard, a very vulgar standard, of personal advantage. Everything that he touched or talked about turned to vulgarity. He had a passion for whatever, in the shoddiest sense, was above him, a contempt of the same quality for whatever was beneath. He was not noticeably mean or vindictive; yet had any superior suggested to him that I, for instance, ought to be done away with, then Beler, I was sure, would have done away with me, without malice, even perhaps with a sort of likeable absurdity, in the normal furtherance of his career.

The major called. I had been told of his arrival by Beler: "A very charming gentleman, I know him personally." The charming major was fussing, when he called, about an imminently expected visit of an *Oberstabsarzt*. His eye, darting about, was met by spots on the glass over the wash-stand and he wished that I should remove them. He was a thin, tall, small-headed man, in toto something suggestive of a safety-pin.

When the dreaded inspectoral moment came, when the major ushered in the *Oberstabsarzt*, I was writing, paper lay all around. The *Oberstabsarzt* looked. It was a gentle, smiling look.

The major was nervous. "You see, he has central heating," he said, striding to the (never-heated) radiator. "I don't think that there are many prisoners-of-war who have that."

The *Oberstabsarzt*, silent, still looked at my papers. The

major fretted. Suddenly he found his cue, he was inspired. "*He has his writing!*" he cried, triumphant, as if this, far from having anything to do with me, was a further privilege, like central heating, conferred by magnanimous Germans.

The major was in fact a nervous, weak man, who acted from worry and had developed to ingenious lengths, in the service of superiors before whom he grovelled, a talent for circumlocution and misrepresentation. He was not a bad man; he was a man through whom bad things could be done.

The news was grim; the Germans who wrote about it used their powerful language powerfully. Nevertheless, it was the reading of these reports, the only source I had, which brought my shaken morale back to health. There were, for instance, many accounts, from German correspondents in Berne and Stockholm, about the "changed life in England". These were intended to illustrate the decline of English morale; in fact they illustrated, if you had known anything of English life, the opposite. A clergyman had been given a year's imprisonment for ringing his church bells? The Germans were shocked, saddened. Dancing in the London streets? The frivolous fade-out, they said, of a once-great nation. Air raids accompanied by the B.B.C. with running commentaries like the Boat Race or Cup Final? Yes, the correspondents were ashamed to have to tell it, they were goaded to disgusted, incredulous eloquence. "The inhabitants of the coast towns," wrote one who seemed to feel that he had to speak up for them, "would be very grateful if such commentaries could be dispensed with."

The sense of a falseness of interpretation pervading every fact removed also the queasy effects of doses of Nazi propaganda, the only other reading I had, in illustrated magazines. "We have set up work as an ideal and stripped it of all its former purely materialistic attributes." "The German face of today is perhaps most beautiful when men and women are standing before their Führer." *Frauen schaffen für Deutschland*: new 'protection of mothers' laws: new simplicity, new friendliness, new sense of community: wood-sculpture: "Mütterlichkeit"—it was all false. And ridiculous? No. False.

It would be interesting, I decided, to collect cuttings from German newspapers. I did collect one cutting, from the *Frankfurter Zeitung*, by far the least offensive of the newspapers; I had been able to order it direct, and had received from its editor a markedly polite, old-fashioned letter with the customary ceremonious "sehr geehrter . . ." "Hochachtungsvoll." My cutting was taken out of one of the *Frankfurter*'s cream-paper Sunday supplements. A reproduction of a drawing by a "forgotten German painter" of the eighteenth century, it showed a naked woman reclined in a swoon of passion across the knees of a naked man, whose left hand was round her left breast, whose right hand gripped her left thigh. I did not collect any other cuttings.

My only books were tattered Tauchnitzes scavenged in the grounds, usually Hugh Walpole—"there was a smile of real tenderness on the Duchess's face as she stepped forward to embrace the newcomer"—an emotional diet corresponding too closely to the daily thin soups.

One day in the midst of this mental famine the castle was visited by the First Secretary of the American Embassy in Berlin, exercising the duty of its Government, then neutral, as Protecting Power on behalf of British war-prisoners.

Hooked to his smart Embassy car was a trailer, packed with forgotten luxuries—wines, liqueurs, chocolate, cigars, cigarettes, tinned foods of the more delicate sort. The visitor himself was an apparition of elegance. Rumour of the trailer's riches ran before him, and Wülzburg Germans declared, with approving respect, that he always carried it with him when travelling in Germany.

My turn came. The First Secretary looked round. He seemed, despite contrary gambits by me, to be taking a connoisseur's rather than a reformer's interest.

"You're quite like the Count of Monte Cristo here!" he noted in a pleased way.

Three fingers of his right hand were held, as if habitually, pointed and close together against the right side of his lower lip. Putting his head outside the door to complete his literary impressions he was at once besieged by a crowd of uncouth Dutchmen clamouring for money. The three fingers moved from lower lip to breast of dove-grey suit: involuntarily, it seemed, protecting his wallet. There, as he stood beset, it was plain that the First Secretary, "spending a year or two in Embassies", had not anticipated duties of this type.

But he proved a benefactor. His trailer scattered gifts. He sent me books, the first real books I had, for instance the "Letters of D. H. Lawrence". He sent Shakespeare. I read, and the pettinesses of the petty, which had loomed so threatening-seeming, ceased to matter. I read and the Wülzburg was forgotten. I read and did not feel alone.

Now though I liked to watch the prisoners I lost all wish for nearer contact with them. Reading absorbed me. A Dutchman came by from the pump, spoke, and pushed something under my nose. I motioned him away. As he walked on I saw that what he had offered was a bowl of ripe cherries. I felt sad, both for the cherries, and because he might have felt insulted.

I watched some English prisoners who were helping to build new offices outside the wire fence that separated the prisoners' enclosure from the *Kommandantur* area. Perching close to this fence, on the prisoners' side, I watched and listened as they patted bricks, tidied cement, pushed wheelbarrows, leaned on spades, and wisecracked.

"I can't say you're earning one and sixpence a —— 'our."

"Ah'm no *gatin*' one and sixpence a —— hour."

The German foreman, a passionately active little monkey in blue dungarees, whose childlike smile seemed to deprecate his over-indulgence in work, had learned the English words "square", "triangle", "straight-edge", and delighted in shouting them fiercely.

"Some new barracks for the officers," said Beler, going

actively by—more active than usual that day because a glossy French colonel, in top-boots, breeches, and silk khaki-shirt, had appeared meteorically among the prisoners. French, German, or Hottentot, a colonel was a colonel for Beler.

I watched the queuing Dutchmen when the American Embassy paid its second visit.

This time the visitor was the Third Secretary. Tall, convex, terribly thin, lacking the aplomb of the First Secretary, shying and backing at the slightest upset like a nervous horse, the Third Secretary nevertheless proved nobly disputatious and fought the major hard on fundamental matters such as accommodation, rations, and drainage.

Pressed, the slippery major was obliged to dive deep into his talent for ingenious misrepresentation.

The Dutchmen, admiring the pertinacity of the Third Secretary, wishing to back it up heartily, had moved in close, where they now stood patient, solid, unwontedly silent. Unfortunately it was just this that gave the major his break. He scanned the Dutchmen, called out the most enormous one from among them, and placed him side by side with the Third Secretary.

"See!" the major cried. "He's much fatter than you are. He lives well here!"

"Brot und Speck!" happily nodded the Hollander, whom the point of the demonstration escaped.

"You see?"

Going back into my room, despondently conceding that the enemy had been too smart, I suddenly heard a many-throated bellow. It was the Dutch. The point had hit them. Half-an-hour later I looked out. The struggle was in full course and I thought the major was looking tired.

These Dutch had all been factory-workers in Germany. They were horny-handed, rough men, and they looked what they were. There was one Dutchman, however, among the Wülzburg prisoners, who did not look like that; a young man of refined features with a stamp of education and of easy back-

ground. It was not only these differences that drew my eye to
him. What I noticed was that he always walked by himself. His
face too was pale and the expression on it was strained. He would
pace, stop, frown, look hard at the walls, then pace again. He
was always out there and always alone.

It was obvious that some struggle was going on inside him.
Young, pale, preoccupied, unhappy, romantic, he struck the
Byronic chord in every visible particular except one: a pepper-
and-salt-knickerbocker suit which was not in key.

I grew so curious that finally I questioned Hofstetter, breaking the reserve between us. I thus learned that the young
Dutchman, a short while before he was taken prisoner, had
become engaged in Holland to a girl of whom his family did not
approve. His family was rich and influential; hers was not. His
family had discovered that they could procure his release by
approaching important friends of theirs in Germany. Having
discovered that, they had held a family conference at which
it had been decided that they would not use their influence
unless the prisoner first agreed to give up his girl. The break-
ing-off of his engagement was to be the condition of his
release.

No wonder that the young man paced and frowned and
wrestled with his problem. For several days he continued to
wrestle with it. Then one day he looked much worse. He actually sat on the ground, which he had never done, and his head
hung down between his shoulders.

A great-aunt, titular head of the family, had visited him. In
harsh words, without a trace of sympathy, she had repeated the
terms of the bargain. Then she had left.

Next day—where was the young man? Alas! he too had left.
Pepper-and-salt knickerbockers had proved victorious.

One September morning I was visited by the Wülzburg
Security Officer, Hauptmann Sichel. "An order from the OKW.
You are to live with the others. You must move your things by
two this afternoon."

Einzelhaft had lasted for five months. I had not on

balance enjoyed it. But I felt more nervous than pleased at the
impending change.

The eleven hundred interned civilians on the Wülzburg,
English, Dutch, French, Egyptian, were fantastically over-
crowded. In the room I went to seventy-five men slept, ate, and
lived. Jammed with triple-tier bunks, tables, chairs, clothes,
personal possessions, people, refuse, and noise, it seemed to
combine immutably the characteristics of a slum and a madhouse.

On the other hand their comparative immunity from German
interference left to these prisoners, who had no physical space,
a bit of mental space; so that there was an easy-going individualism rising at times to an unharassed *Gemütlichkeit*, even gaiety.
This was the chief compensation for the squalor. But it had a
dubious side. Socially the prisoners were disintegrated. There
was no issue on which they stood together, whether against the
Germans, or among themselves.

The Dutch, clogs clattering down stone stairs, went out to
work in a nearby factory making buckles and metal badges.
They were courted by fellow-prisoners chiefly on account of
trading with the Dutch Red Cross Parcel, considered a very
good one.

The French, underfed and miserably shabby, regarded with
disfavour by their government on the grounds that they need
not have stayed in Germany and got captured, had no parcels
(unless private ones). Lack of tradeable food set them apart:
that, and political passion. They did, as Höfstetter had said,
"*politisieren*" all the time.

Egypt was not at war, but her government had arrested a few
Nazi officials, among them a friend of Hess, who had retaliated
by interning Egyptians on the loose in Germany. The haul had
fetched in a number of students working for German degrees,
and one millionaire, owner of seventeen cinemas in German
towns, who now had a private room on the Wülzburg, where
selected prisoners were invited to sip tea with him.

A large minority of the British prisoners (the largest group) were merchant seamen, including the entire crew, officers and men, of the 20,000-ton Orient liner "Orama", sunk off the Norwegian coast. There were also business men, teachers, missionary and religious people (Buchmanite, Jesuit, Toc H, nonconformist, evangelical), and a sprinkling of musicians. The business men comprised one solid group of forty known as "The Danes" because they had all been picked up in Denmark, and a good many who had been in business in Germany, or as hotel-managers or agents of organizations such as Cunard White Star and British American Tobacco. Some of these, and some of the teachers, had been settled for years in Germany with their families. Their wives, if English, were interned in a camp for women on the Bodensee. Among the men of Germanized background were a few who had come over with the Army of Occupation of 1918, had stayed, and now spoke a horrible dialect, German and English words mixed in the same sentence, which was known as the *beide Sprache*.

There were a few hapless individuals who had got captured for utterly grotesque reasons. One was a Negro called Johnny who had been on his way to Europe to do a bicycle-tour. On the day that war was declared he happened to be on board a German ship which made straight for the nearest German port, carrying him and his bicycle too. Johnny however (his bicycle was in the Wülzburg censors' office) had a blunt way of dealing with Germans who heavily twitted him about the tiresome consequences to him of "der britische Imperialismus". There was a bearded Canadian who had been travelling to Poland with some buffalo which he was donating to a park; another Canadian, arrested in 1936 in Vienna for alleged offences connected with diamond-dealing, had been under arrest ever since, had had five trials, and had been awaiting a sixth, when the outbreak of war imposed on him the yet more indefinite sentence of internment. There was an English student who, on his way out of Germany on the last day of peace, had stopped most unwisely to take a snapshot of the Cologne bridge.

The six rooms opening off one corridor, where all these

British were massed, differed greatly in atmosphere. Some
tinkled quietly like lounges of secluded hotels; others were perpetually rowdy with cards, darts, and bad language. Only one
room, populated chiefly by north-country seamen from merchant
ships captured in Norwegian ports and from a few trawlers sunk
by U-boats in the earliest days of the war, had any sort of
corporate feeling. These seamen, lively, friendly men, fond of
fun, stories, and song, had happily assimilated some "Czechoslovaks" (Englishmen who had been living and working in
Czechoslovakia) and a party from the British Consulate in
Boulogne. One of the "Czechoslovaks", a gentle lecturer from
Brno who was the Camp Captain, worked at a new "Grammar
of Basic Moravian" and in winter evenings recited ghost stories
after Karel Capek.

These men, the Old Guard of the Wülzburg, told of times
when, fabulously rich in food-parcels, they had developed an
extensive trade with Germans for eggs and cognac and wine.
Urged on by a Yorkshire "Czechoslovak", a physically big business man whose speech reflected both places, they had hoarded
used tea-leaves, dried them, put them back in the packets, and
sold them as new. They had waited anxiously the first time this
was done. Then a German who had bought some of the first
packets approached and said in a puzzled way:

"This tea was rather weak. I always thought English tea was
strong. But," he added, "my wife likes it weak."

This delighted the seamen. "Said 'is broo was weak. Ah'd
'ud *mah* broo out of it."

My room was a noisy one and the noisiest people in it were
the oilers, wipers, and greasers of the "Orama". My neighbour
on a top bunk immediately alongside was a forty-nine year old
vegetarian theosophist whose unlucky passion for fast motor-
cycles had caused him to break a leg while scorching across
Denmark on his way, as he said, to a theosophical conference in
Bombay. In fact, he maintained that he was still on the way to it,
the present hold-up being a temporary and unwarranted nuisance.
Eccentricities such as these, lucidly and untiringly uttered, made

him an object of brutal teasing by the oilers who nevertheless, when they discovered that he could drive stern bargains in trading his sardines for their tomato purees, began to regard him with a sneaking respect and affection.

In this crowded squalid existence, not to me a change for the better, more definitely unpleasant things began soon to happen.

The Commandant ordered the institution of a segregated room—in fact, a ghetto—for the Jewish internees. Between twenty and thirty declared Jews, after they had first done all the scrubbing and cleaning, were moved summarily into it. But then there were six so-called doubtful cases. These were ordered to parade in front of the German Camp Doctor who was to determine by physical inspection whether they were circumcized or uncircumcized. If circumcized, they would be reckoned as Jews.

This contemptible proceeding induced me to write a letter of protest which I addressed to the German Foreign Office and handed to the Commandant.

The Commandant was the compliant, ever-slippery Major. He feigned surprise, this sort of thing was "normal bei uns".

When I asked why he should subject British internees to Nazi racial practices he cried: "But your own people want it! I have letters," and flourished a paper off his desk.

It was already believed that the Jewish order had been provoked by a handful of prisoners of German sympathies, collectively nicknamed "P.G.s" (Pro-Germans); angrier suspicion attaching to one, a youthful, spotty, ex-Mosleyite, who had never hidden the fact that he, an Aryan, objected to living with Jews in the same room.

Suddenly the thing took a new turn.

Of the six "borderline" prisoners one, pronounced "guilty" by the circumcision verdict, insisted that he was, nevertheless, an Englishman and a Christian and that he would not go to the ghetto. This courage made him at once the centre of a Resistance composed of prisoners who had been longing to express their disgust. The numerical strength of the active Resisters was small. There was a croupier, Ronnie Rose, a trainee hotel-

manager, Brian Taylor. There were two business men, Goode
and Peters, inseparably bracketed as "The Repatriation Committee" because of their persistent and preposterous efforts to
achieve repatriation for all the prisoners. There was a young,
pink, burly, pious-looking man with rugger shoulders and a new-
springing moustache whom I had thought of as "The Prefect"
ever since, from my solitary sill, I had watched him energetically
organizing, heartily ordering: "Would you send two men down
for post duty, please?"—"I want three volunteers for grub
right away, please." His name was Felix Palmer, and he was a
major in mufti.

The Resistance was opposed actively by others, including
some friends of the disobeying prisoner who said to him:
"Come along, old chap. Shall I help you to get your things
down there? There's no sense in making a fuss and getting other
people into trouble. The Germans will only make it worse for
the rest of us and that's not what you want. And it won't be so
bad you know. You'll have your meals with us just the same."

It was opposed passively by the anarchic mass. Some mur-
mured that Jews liked being together; some that they were only
"bloody Jews"; some, as if the point was self-evident, that the
German order could not be withstood. In the quiet rooms heads
burrowed into books. In the noisy rooms missionary work was
continued among the loud-mouthed oilers, always its favourite
target.

The Major sent a corporal to inform the prisoner that he had
to be in the ghetto with all his things by six p.m.; if he dis-
obeyed he would be put into the castle cell. The prisoner was
naturally high-coloured and youthfully buoyant; now his colour
and his buoyancy had begun to drain away. The Resistance felt
that he should go to the castle cell if necessary; so did he. But
he was harassed by contrary advice and upset by the argument
that he might cause trouble for others.

At six the corporal arrived. "Wo ist der—?" "I am not
going." The corporal went out and returned in a few minutes to
tell the prisoner that he had till seven o'clock.

The cell, deep in the foundations of the castle, was known to be unpleasantly cold. Thick socks, sweaters, coats, blankets were fetched, which the prisoner drew over him one by one till only his perspiring, unhappy face emerged out of a cocoon of wrappings. Neronically recumbent, he gave audience again to the advocates of non-resistance who plied him with heavier warnings. But even if he had wanted to agree with them he now could scarcely have done so, for he was practically suffocating, and only gasped, and nodded his head, or shook it.

At seven the corporal returned. The same thing happened. "You have till eight." At eight: "You have till nine. It is your last chance." There was astonishment. The most optimistic had not believed that defiance could succeed so far. Now the whole castle was sympathetically excited.

Nine o'clock! But this time the corporal did not come. Nobody came that night, nor the next day, nor the next one, nor ever afterwards, nor was the subject ever again mentioned by the Major or any of his subordinates. Blankets, coats, sweaters, socks, were hauled off, and the unmuffled prisoner, yawning mightily and almost tearfully happy, clambered down from his bunk into a congratulating throng.

The victory was too small unfortunately to dissipate the gloom cast by the Jewish episode as a whole. The ghetto, repugnant to English feeling, was there. Its existence, a few steps away, punished self-respect. All the Jews had friends among the other prisoners. One, a physicist and chess-master, was unreservedly admired; an expression of freezing dignity on this clever man's sad face when he was taking up his new quarters stayed afterwards graven there, a formidable warning to anyone who would lightly intrude, or dissemble, or commiserate.

The "P.G.'s" became the first scapegoats of a new unhappy spirit which soon spread beyond them and irrupted into an epidemic of quarrelling, bullying, and fights. Contrarily, nothing good was in sight. News was stagnant or bad, food short. Long dark reaches of German winter lay unglimmering. Trees held naked their crooked arms and fingers. Snow swelled out, diseasing

the air. There were cold days, colder nights. Visions of an
ordeal of patience rising interminably towards an invisible future
took on a monotony like shutting-in walls: imprisonment within imprisonment.

Fights were shrugged at, watched, cheered, jeered, even encouraged: they "let off steam", "cleared the air". But once, in
my noisy room, when an enormous grizzled deckhand, grandson
of a cave-dweller, hurled a beer-bottle at an oiler, an aghast
silence did fall—even though he had missed.

The oilers had extraordinary poise. I did not realize that at
first. But gradually their voices seemed to me more real than
other voices. They flung words out with surprising speed,
balance, and control. Certainly the words were often "bad".
But the "bad" words were timed and placed to point a quick
answer or to clinch a joke. Their jokes were witty and original.
Cockney was their idiom, Tilbury and Gravesend their home-
ground.

They were happy: never by effort, never with calculation. In
the winter the value of this constitutional happiness seemed to
stand out. My vegetarian theosophist neighbour, whom they
called "Vittle", had grown fond of them and tittered when
teased. Vittle believed in reincarnation. The oilers, glad of any
topic, were happy to discuss reincarnation.

"Wot'll you be, Vittle," asked one called Smith ("Smithy"),
"when you come back?"

"My dear man, that's a question which nobody can answer."

"E'll be a rabbit, Vittle will." This was George Chase
("Chasey"). "'E won't 'arf —— them —— dandelions
about."

The oilers did not appreciate a habit Vittle had of immateri-
alizing whenever the floor was to be washed; they quickly
grasped and pointedly expressed the inconsistency of this with
his ever-iterated philosophy of unity and brotherhood. "Where's
Vittle?"—as the hot buckets swooshed across the filthy floor.
"Re'carnated 'is —— self. E's 'ere somewhere buchyer can't
—— see 'im."

They were fearless and outspoken, often clever and just, in appraisal or criticism. They could not be taken in by affectations of manner or by bluff of any sort. When missionaries called, the oilers gratefully accepted and later critically inspected presents of "gear" and other hand-outs. Conversion was never near. A young ginger-haired Scottish Evangelist from Budapest, dashingly gay and brilliant at football, was at first more successful, but one day he rashly announced, in their midst, that he had "seen the light". "Light" then was his name; and little faults that he might have—excessive appetite perhaps or a suggestion of a tendency to meanness in trading—were mercilessly judged with reference to the standards expected from one who had "seen the light". Even his football, ace of his missionary hand, collapsed under this test. Whenever he shot wild, Chasey, waistcoated, nautically rolling, cried, "I wish 'e could see the Light between them —— goalposts!"

Self-contained and extremely independent the oilers achieved their best flights among themselves, especially at night, after the lights were out. A subject had to be started, any subject. Women. "Woman's only a rib off 'er —— man". "Yers"—Chasey's gay voice—"I'm 'er —— rib short!" At that moment Chasey, having finished rolling a cigarette from papers and loose tobacco stored in the flap-pockets of a waistcoat which was never taken off by night or by day, struck a match. "For heavens' sake!" a serious voice called. "That light can be seen five miles!"

Chasey's speed kept him always ahead. Forty, he was the best darts player and his joyful "Copped!" seemed to smack out a split instant before the dart itself smacked into the double-twenty. He had extraordinarily long sight. When he read he sat five feet from a propped-up book and only the punctual forward move to turn a page made it credible that he was reading. Most of the day the big tiled stove was thronged by people boiling water for tea in converted tins held in the red fire with long, home-made handles. If I was in this scrum, Chasey, coming into the room, at once spotted me, and would sing out "Did you corl me, Charlie?"—which meant that he hoped for a cup of tea. I never minded, his gay voice cheered me up.

Smithy was a heavy, funny second, especially good with set pieces (such as the fable of "The Donkey and the 'Orse" or "'Ow a Donkey worked 'is Loaf") which he only could tell. Strong feeds were given by "Tich", a tiny oiler who earlier had been a "fiddler": painting sparrows yellow to sell as canaries had been one of his lines. Tich's code did not quite march with the rest. He was ambitious. When the "Orama" crew were rescued he had somehow persuaded the naval Germans present that he spoke German; they had put him in charge of prisoner food distribution, and for a space of days Tich had had the three-hundred strong "Orama" crew, captain to cabin-boy, at his mercy. Here too on the Wülzburg he had somehow got control of all the German rations for his room. He was unkindly hard on his chief friend, a house-painter's assistant tinier than himself. When laying out their afternoon tea Tich varied the size of his friend's helpings according to the way he happened to be feeling towards him, and it was cruel to see the sick-skinned, shrimp-size friend bite his lip when the helpings were below norm. Days even came when no second place at all was laid.

Their care-for-nobody spirit did not prevent the oilers from having friendships. For Smithy I always had a warm feeling which he seemed to return because one day when the oilers and all seamen were about to be moved from the Wülzburg he put his hand on my shoulder and, slow with the words, said: "I 'ope, Charlie, that you get 'ome before I do."

After they had gone the Wülzburg seemed more dismal. Winter was past. In the spring I had got ill and while in the *Revier* I saw a fellow-prisoner die. He was forty-eight, had been known to be ill, and three months earlier his repatriation had been conceded. The Major had clung on, waiting for impregnable sanction.

I now loathed the Wülzburg and began to dream of escape.

Escape I must! But not talk about it. "P.G.s" apart—I did not really worry about them—the merest hint of escape talk was pounced on by appeasing voices (as in the ghetto business) that said: "It's selfish. The Germans will cut down the privileges of the rest of us."

The germ of a plan survived from the time, more than a year earlier, of my abortive conversation with the called-up Bavarian. Now I knew, as then I had not, that Wülzburg prisoners whose homes were in Germany were allowed to be visited by their families; that visits took place every Thursday; that visitors came in through the main gate and went out through it; that consequently there was, almost every Thursday, a dribbling in-and-out traffic of pedestrian civilians.

The very great majority of them were women. That might not matter. The Wülzburg amateur theatricals were well-established, and I had played a saucy servant in "Twelfth Night" and an American girl in an adaptation of a novel by P. G. Wode-house. Moreover, Wülzburgians, owing to the links that some had with outside German life, had been able to send for stocks of actual clothes, and the *Kommandantur* had allowed these to be brought in. There were high-heeled shoes, silk stockings, handbags, dresses in styles commonly used, sets of ordinary make-up.

I thought. I had a friend, John Ford. He had volunteered to fight for Finland, had reached that country when the war with Russia was over, and while retracing his steps had entered Oslo in time to be picked up by the Germans as they entered it. He (with four others in identical plight) had then been posted to the Wülzburg. He was a person of versatile talent and also of character. If I had to trust anybody I would trust him; I had to trust somebody.

John was a star of the Wülzburg football field whose nets had been woven by seamen from the string of Red Cross parcels. I, an inglorious spectator, hung about, while enthusiasts stamped on the touchline. Whistle blew. "Out to your wing, man!" "Pay attention to that wing, Frankie!" The Prefect, alongside two TocHers, strained vociferous. I nursed my scheme.

The match over, I told John my plan which hinged on the

fact that Frau Scharre's canteen-shop was bisected by a ground-level corridor of which one entrance was in the prisoners' enclosure, the other in the outer *Kommandantur* area. Departing visitors emerged into this outer area through a guarded gate in a continuous fence. All things being helpful, the same effect could be achieved by someone who came out through Frau Scharre's corridor.

With John I noted habits of the guards and office-soldiers of the outer area and of visitors as they walked away. Often a departing visitor turned her head to wave to a high window.

It was early September. In the hot weather theatrical varieties were given in the grounds; a goal canopied with blankets made a backcloth, in its shade a tiny piano, drum and percussion-set. The producer, a slight, nervy, brow-mopping man, invariably compered turns with apologetic references to "very trying conditions" and "exceedingly difficult circumstances". The French contributed a trick-cyclist, the Egyptians a team of acrobats and a Strong Man with a prodigious stomach whom the compere always introduced by regretting that "exceedingly trying conditions" made it impossible for him to perform his principal act, which consisted of allowing a car to run over him, any horse-power. There was a West Indian, Jeff Luis, who sang the Wülzburg signature-tune "The Castle could hardly be called a Hotel". Jeff also had charge of all costume and make-up and the time had come to broach my plan to him.

Jeff, who was enthusiastic, concluded after many things had been tried on that the disguise ought to suggest the character of a young, respectable married woman. That meant that I could not wear a richly-curled barmaid-blonde wig, pride of the wardrobe, and so would need to hide my hair, especially at the back of the neck, with a converted scarf. There were no coats. Jeff said he would make one. But out of what? I had a camel-hair blanket, teddy-bear colour, a present from home. With this Jeff made in less than a week a superb coat with a belt and large, disc-shaped woolly buttons.

The business of dressing-up had next to be co-ordinated with that of getting from the prisoners' quarters into Frau Scharre's door. I could not trip downstairs and cross the grounds in full costume, nor could the whole change be done in the exposed doorway. The main change—stockings, frock, basic make-up— could be made upstairs in the empty theatre provided that there was a screening escort from there to the shop. John chose three people besides himself and Jeff. In the doorway finishing touches —shoes, coat, lipstick, cowled scarf—would need less than half a minute and would be screened.

A date was fixed. Intervening days went like dreams. There was an outdoor concert party. Everyone was merry, everything seemed funny. The producer-compere, dripping with success, mounted a shaky stool to announce that the party would close with English community-singing "if our Dutch, French, and Egyptian friends will bear with us for just a very few minutes". "Roll out the Barrel", "Nellie Dean", "If You Were the Only . . ." The singing was thin. The little man, perilously asway, made inhibited, frantic conducting movements crying "Come on, now, sing it as though you meant it!" with the result, truly English, that the singing died altogether.

What was extraordinary was that everything worked as hoped. The din of Dutch clogs roared round on the stone stairs as I descended semi-transformed, huddling, unseeing. At the shop-door hands flashed. In the passage a little white dog, not reckoned with, yapped. Feeling suddenly the sun-white gravel of the *Kommandantur* area I turned my head right and up and did not cease agitating a tiny handkerchief until cool shade intimated that I was in the vaulted tunnel leading to the main gate. I faced a vast blank door in whose wall-like front there was a small wicket-door. I turned a handle. The wicket opened outward and revealed a sentry. I hesitated. The sentry sprang forward, opened the wicket wide and stood back, holding it open.

I was on the drawbridge. The morning was golden. The air was heavenly. The warm stone parapet wanted to be leaned on. The basking moat begged for a lingering look.

The track-like road whorled down. In the rough, pine-needles glinted like pins. Now I stepped confidently. Another bend. Whistles! My heart seemed to stop. Ahead, almost blocking the track, stood uniformed men. I drew level, they stood watching, waiting, unmistakably waiting to detain me. I was in the thick of them, as in among a herd of cattle when they, just like cattle, barged reluctantly outwards. Growls of voices, then aimed whistles hit my moving back. Suddenly, suddenly I understood. Those whistles—they were wolf-whistles! Those uniformed men—loutish *Luftwaffe* youths looking for a pick-up and very likely knowing that on Thursdays women had to walk down this hill. *Women!* In the joy of freedom I had utterly forgotten my revised exterior. Young respectable married woman—what a test!—what a triumph! Not the kind that she would care for, she would be feeling indignant now, at least looking it. I looked indignant.

Indignant I tripped through Weissenburg, rich hub of a rich plain. I was looking for a bicycle. I meant to bicycle north to a Baltic port and get aboard a Swedish ship. I had no German money, the speed of cycling might just cover my small stock of food; I had no papers and guessed that a cyclist was less likely to be stopped than a pedestrian. I approached a bicycle, untended against a wall, and was about to grasp the handle-bars when a woman no doubt its owner appeared out of a door, mounted, looked back at me severely, and pedalled away.

I was out of Weissenburg. The bicycle incident had made me timorous. They were few now and far between and those I saw seemed always too close to harvesting parties in fields. This was a big road to Nuremberg, glistening with tarry heat, thundered on by heavy lorries: never a pedestrian. I trudged stupid, increasingly planless, feeling the heat, trying not to limp on blisters made by the pinching shoes.

A man on the road, 190 yards further, was scanning the country with field-glasses. He turned them towards me. Then he seemed to go away. I knew somehow that he had not gone away. All the same I was startled when a voice at point-blank range shouted: "Heil Hitler!"

There he was, jacked out from behind a trunk, a uniformed Teuton with blue aggressive eyes.

"Heil—Hitler!" I answered. The "Heil" was a young married woman, the "Hitler" unfortunately was not; it was a basso croak.

I walked past.

"Wo gehen Sie hin?"

My unanswering silence and my demure though now torturing steps were meant to suggest unapproachable dignity.

I heard him pounding up, as I had known that I would, and there again he stood. "Papiere!" I said that they were in the bottom of my bag.

Blue eyes bored.

"Sie sind keine Frau!"

"Doch!" I protested.

With a spring he ripped back the cowl, reducing me to a hybrid state. I felt defeated. A moment later I was in a lorry covering the twenty-two kilometres back to Weissenburg with no feeling except that it was nice to sit down.

The police chief to whom my captor took me happened to be a man who liked a joke. He bellowed with laughter at my appearance, now not even "respectable", and when he had wiped tears of laughter out of his fat eyes he telephoned the castle and said that the Weissenburg police department desired that a certain prisoner, "Herr Rommillee", should be fetched to speak on the telephone. He had grasped the point that the Wülzburg *Kommandantur* might not yet realize that I had gone, and he intended to elaborate his fun. At the other end there was a long, long pause followed suddenly by faint quackings into which the policeman, beside himself with mirth, roared "No, of course you can't find him. He's sitting here with me. He left your castle at eleven o'clock this morning by the front gate."

I enjoyed this too but back in the castle I experienced the disadvantages of the policeman's humour. A frog-shaped, cavalry-moustached German, swollen with fury, set on and pommelled me. Then came the castle cell, every bit as cold as it was rumoured to be, warmer clothes refused, shivering days and nights in the caked sweat of my hot excursion; after which, a sentence of eighteen days' *Zellenarrest* was formally pronounced, and a closed car carried me thirty-three kilometres to a place called Eichstätt, where it seemed that there were some approved cells.

The first day there, which was my birthday, I saw silly hat-clutching German women running crying "Sondermeldung! Sondermeldung!" The barred window looked on a sweep of forecourt to a drive-in and a road faced by a house whose radio carried audibly. The *Sondermeldung*[1] was the capture of Kiev with six hundred thousand prisoners. I learned that I was to live on bread and water. Those eighteen days were certainly in no hurry, and I welcomed occasional calls paid by Hauptmann Sichel, the Wülzburg security officer, though his face suggested security as a rat-trap suggests it, and he called mainly to inquire, others attending, why I had been walking inland instead of towards a frontier. The suspicious implication being clear, even on bread and water, I explained my plan. The captain was not a man who took a point readily. Who had helped me to escape? Nobody. It was suggested, with humiliating accuracy, that I would have been incapable of making the camel-hair coat; which rebutted, the captain kindly offered to bring scissors, wool, and sewing-kit so that I could spend the long hours making a new coat. No, thank you, I did not need a new coat just now.

I knew to a minute at what time of which day the sentence ought to end; and the eighteen days seemed less long than the eight hours of overtime during which no tread came. Forgotten, I was sure. But later that night I was in Nuremberg station with a corporal and a guard. Entrained, trundling overnight to good-ness knew where, I looked at a small photograph which showed the cavalry-moustache lieutenant puffing angrily over against me in camel-hair coat. The corporal had taken it as ordered, then the officer ordered him to destroy the negative and all copies because he did not like the result. The corporal could not let me keep the

1 Special communique—of the OKW—to announce some big success or victory.

picture in case of search but he said that he would send it to me after the war. We detrained next day into dreadful-looking flatlands cut by an un-Bavarian wind and plodded in cortège towards a dreary mass of purple brick like a school or mental hospital. I was taken over from the unobnoxious corporal whom wearily I had begun to like and shown into an empty cell where the stone floor was inches deep in water. As usual night seemed to be falling. It fell. Unlockings occurred; there stood a guarded English prisoner with a pot of tea which he had most thoughtfully brought. The almost black tea made me ecstatically drunk. The watery bed was a luxury, I could not imagine anything more delightful.

This place was called Tost, "bei Breslau", in Silesia. The first thing I saw was a cage with John Ford in it, looking through bars sad, devoted, suffering on behalf of another, who perhaps had forgotten . . .? I felt very guilty and still did after John had explained that on the Wülzburg the Germans had threatened to punish the whole castle if those who had helped me did not confess. Ensuing squawks about "selfishness" and "the privileges of the rest of us" (it never was quite clear what these "privileges" were) had made John decide to admit his part and claim that he had been the only helper. This had worked. Soon he came out of the cage. Intermediately ladlefuls of the Wülzburg population seemed to have got to this place. Known faces surfaced in the motley stew of the Tost pot. I thought I saw "P.G.s" busily shedding old selves and laughing in the midst of new friends. I looked at a grey-gleaming sick-room which proud old Tostians said you simply had to look at. An elderly man sitting up in bed was shouting at a German doctor. Must listen to that. Listening proved painful. The man had locomotor ataxia and he did not believe, as was being explained, that an illness of fifteen years earlier could have erupted into this horrible state; he was sure that it was something that the Germans had done to him. I left. There seemed to be a lot of elderly prisoners and some bedridden ones. The tone of the Germans was very light and Tost had caught their tone. I got a feeling as if every prisoner thought that he was wearing very smart gloves. The whole place seemed chaotically over-organized and ghastly. I was tired, the cell must have been lowering, and when after two weeks a car came for me I scarcely cared, only the buoyant suavity of a young Tost adjutant, pretending to be offering this event as some rare treat, irked my numb nerves. How in squalid Tost had they managed to swing that line?

Squeezed by fat Germans I had not the slightest idea where the car was going, though it would be going still at night, I would swear, no matter what time it started. There were clanks, a voice said—"Wir haben hier ein ganzes Turistenhotel"—and I saw a sprucely-booted officer-figure greenish under artificial light with a charlatan face. It certainly was night and cobbles were being walked up. The officer fiddled a key, went before into a cell, switched on a charlatan smile: "Hauptmann Priem!" Had he bowed?

In daylight more cobbles were walked up, a door in a door opened, and I was in a close space that might almost have been a disused lift-shaft, lift dismantled, roof taken out, between sheer walls far more high and tyrannical than anything I had ever seen. A Babel of noise clattered mad and absorbed across a narrow, cobbled base.

It was November 1941. This was the Tower.

Chapter Four

Eclipse: Berlin

Michael Alexander

THROUGH the barred rear window of the Black Maria ribboned a liquorice boulevard, trees, heavy houses set back; an enormous arch receded, black and menacing—the Brandenburger Tor? Then a section badly bombed—I was ordered to keep my eyes to the front. We drove on a long way, over cobbles, perhaps to some outer suburb. We stopped, shouts, a gate creaked. We were hustled out and passed into a long dark corridor. Bells rang, a door opened, and we entered a bright light. Corporal Gurney said, "What's this now? Sing Sing?" I said to myself: "This is a gaol. Think that you are about to acquire interesting information on this subject. Don't think that you might be worried and afraid."

I had never before been in a professional gaol. It was functional, a machine to exist in, a high, five-tiered structure built round an enormous T. Each tier was a railed gangway backed by innumerable and identical doors. Across the great central T well was stretched a net of wire to prevent suicidal prisoners jumping over the rail to their deaths. Everything was clinically clean, warders sat at intervals at little desks, bells rang from time to time in a seemingly meaningless way. It was like a battleship below decks with mad signals being telegraphed down from the bridge.

Corporal Gurney was taken off in another direction. I immediately forgot the advice I had given myself on entering and a period of great loneliness began. My cell was on the third deck. It contained an iron bed with a straw mattress and a blanket, a table and a chair. I was told to undress and go to bed; my clothes were taken away. There was a peephole in the door but I was too tired to care if Hitler himself was eyeing me and dropped off to sleep almost at once. Early next morning I was awakened by those infernal little bells and my clothes were thrust in the door with cries of "'RAUS!"—"Get out!"

Up to my arrival in this place I had been treated more or less as a human being, now it was impressed on me that as a person I no longer existed: I was the number on my door. I was made to empty the slops and sweep the floor of my cell. If I sat down on the bed during the day I was spotted by a spying eye and made to stand up. In the afternoon I was led off down those metallic gangways for a medical inspection. I was subjected to a delousing process, my hair was almost all cut off and I was given a pyjama-like prison suit that was at least an improvement on my tattered uniform. An elderly doctor prodded me with a primitive stetho-scope that looked like a wooden mushroom and insisted on giving me an injection which I only hoped was not lethal.

It seemed that I was in some sort of military prison, possibly many of the inmates were deserters. Others were in a different category, for one of them whispered to me, with an expression of infinite sadness and resignation, that he was Dutch and had been condemned to death as a spy. After a day or two in these depress-ing surroundings I asked to see the Commandant. My request was refused so I demanded writing materials which to my sur-prise were brought. I wrote a powerful letter saying that I was disgusted with the treatment I was receiving and that unless I was moved immediately to quarters more appropriate to my status as a British officer I would represent the matter in the strongest possible terms to the Red Cross. Two days later, for one reason or another, I was moved.

My new quarters were also in a prison, but an older and some-how less formidable one. I was placed in a special section re-served for German officers. As I was led to my cell I noticed

Giles Romilly wearing the cardigan given to him by the SS sergeant's wife

Michael Alexander, painted in Colditz by Earl Haig

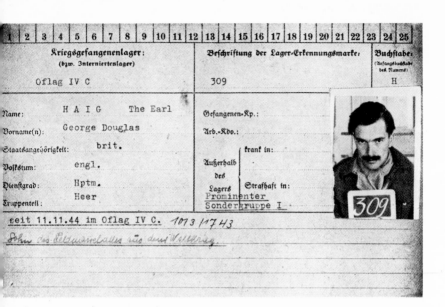

1	2	3	4	5	6	7	8	9	10	11	12	13	14	15	16	17	18	19	20	21	22	23	24	25

Kriegsgefangenenlager:
(bzw. Interniertenlager)

Oflag IV C

Beschriftung der Lager-Erkennungsmarke:

309

Buchstabe:
(Anfangsbuchstabe des Namens)

H

Name: H A I G   The Earl

Vorname(n):   George Douglas

Staatsangehörigkeit: brit.

Volkstum: engl.

Dienstgrad: Hptm.

Truppenteil: Heer

Gefangenen-Kp.:

Arb.-Kdo.:

krank in:

Außerhalb des Lagers / Strafhaft in:

Prominenter
Sondergruppe I

seit 11.11.44 im Oflag IV C. *1073 /17 43*

Sohn des Feldmarschalls aus dem Weltkrieg

Earl Haig's prisoner of war identity card, with hand-written
note that he is the son of the Field-Marshal of the First World War

The Earl of Harewood (then Viscount Lascelles)

ABOVE Max de Hamel

RIGHT The Marquess of
Linlithgow (then Earl of
Hopetoun)

ABOVE The Master of Elphinstone
on arrival at Innsbruck, May 1945

RIGHT Earl Haig

John Winant, drawn in
Colditz by John Watton

General Bor-Komorowski

that the other doors in the passage had name plates on them bearing not full names but tantalizing initials. Exactly opposite my cell it appeared there lived an Oberst Prz. z. W. I never had the opportunity of meeting this princely colonel as it was a rule that no prisoner should be allowed so much as a glimpse of another. No doubt he too speculated on the identity of Hauptmann ALE that came to be written on my door, superior at least to a mere number. At least I was a person again.

In this place the guards were all old soldiers who had not developed so strongly that rigorous and petty meanness that seems to afflict the professional gaoler. They would even make polite conversation which, though my German was limited, was a relief after the time I had been virtually incommunicado. Nobody would admit to knowing why I was there or how long I was likely to remain. I found this state of uncertainty depressing as I was still expecting some sort of trial and could not understand why everything should be taking so long; as I ticked off week after week on my home-made calendar I felt that my existence must have been forgotten. I contemplated another rousing letter but decided it would be wiser not to draw further attention to myself.

I lived in a void. There was nothing to read, nothing to do. My main diversion was in the lavatory where, acting as toilet paper, were pages of magazines and newspapers each neatly torn into four-inch squares. I disposed of considerable quantities every visit hoping that a further instalment of their War Office communique would be available next time. The news at that period was critical, Stalingrad was being besieged and it was clear that this was one of the important battles of the war. Every day I would say to a guard: "Ist Stalingrad schon gefallen?"[1] and every day the answer would come, "Immer noch nicht!"[2] A certain amount of news came from an orderly who brought my meals. He was about nineteen years old and had been given two years' imprisonment for deserting. He had lived with his Dutch mother in Rotterdam but as he had a German father he had been

---

[1] "Has Stalingrad fallen yet?" [2] "Still not yet!"

called up. After his mother had been killed in the devastating
bombing of Rotterdam he had deserted in France and made his
way to Marseilles where he had been unlucky enough to be
caught by the Vichy police. He was a jazz enthusiast and told me
that he had once played in Nat Gonella's band. This amiable
person would bring me extra rations, presumably at the expense
of the Princely Colonel and his friends. He spoke English well;
in the end he was reported for talking to me and I never saw him
again.

That winter was grey and damp rather than cold. In that sad
suburb of Charlottenburg, where the prison stood, gloom hung
like a pall. From my cell I could hear the mournful hoots of the
boats and barges on the river Spree. Every day I would be taken
out alone, made even to stand with my face to the wall as other
prisoners passed in the passages, into the dismal courtyard surrounded by a high wall of brick and for the regulation hour would
shamble round in extreme depression, loathing everything and in
particular a dirty grey hen with a bald patch on its head that
returned my angry looks with a mean and snaky eye.

On wet days I would walk up and down in a glass-covered
alleyway between two buildings. Through a window on the
first floor I had a glimpse of what seemed to be a small court-
room. Above the rostrum was a large oil painting of Göring
in full Air Force regalia. Sometimes I could see black robed
figures indicating that a trial was in progress. Once a French
prisoner was hustled through while I was exercising. He shouted
to me in great good humour that he was on his way to be
tried for having made love to a German girl while working on a
farm. I began to wish urgently for my own trial, for interroga-
tion, for torture even. Anything to end the intolerable ennui.

Somewhere nearby was a parade ground where every morning I could hear the sound of troops drilling. Twice a week
there would be songs as they marched and I came to look forward to this as my ear was literally suffering from musical starvation. It seemed that definite periods of instruction were allocated
to singing. Was it that the wonderful harmonized marching songs

that had rung through the streets of all the capitals of Europe were a part of their military training?

Routine gives bearings to time. Mealtimes were the key to my day, not so much the food that was brought, but the bringing of it, the regular break, surprisingly soon upon me. Sleep was my only refuge, dreams my only solace. I was allowed to sleep when I liked and I slept as long as sleep would stay. I courted sleep, studied its habits, often, like an over-attentive lover, lost it. When sleep went I lay on the bed with my eyes tight shut, suspended in a semi-sleep that I learned to protract for hours. Open the eyes and prison crowded in. Usually I went to bed at six, after the day's last snack. The trouble was the more I slept the less sleep wanted me. The eye trick only worked as a pro-longation, it was the attainment that was difficult. In general I was too depressed to think let alone to philosophize. I felt I had no inner reserve to fall back on as had all the best prisoners of tradition. I regretted I was not like Richard II in the dungeons of Pomfret Castle, able to "beget a generation of still breeding thoughts".

Another strange aspect of the disintegration of personality that solitary confinement can bring about is the acceptance of one's own guilt and of the moral right of an aggressor to detain one. My minor experience of this type of captivity enabled me to understand how, in a state of desperation, resistance to ideas and principles might also be broken down. Should powerful captors wish to make a certain argument accepted I was led to think that an averagely weak character could be made to believe anything and indeed would seek, without compulsion, to adopt the views of the dominant influence. Only strong men and saints and possibly old lags can be sure of themselves. I was glad not to be put to the test.

One day in December I was told I was to go on a journey. We travelled by train and after a long, hard-seated journey arrived at Eichstätt, a small Bavarian town about fifty miles north-west of Munich, and made a weary procession through the pretty streets to the outskirts. We passed between two striped sentry boxes and made towards a long white building with the word CASERNE painted in large gothic lettering on the facade. To the left, through another guarded gate, was a confusion of wooden huts and other miscellaneous buildings surrounded by high barbed wire. At intervals were wooden platforms mounting searchlights and men with machine guns.

There was no reception committee at the barracks and without further ado I was shown into a small cell, impeccably clean, with whitewashed walls and a bed with a blue and white checked counterpane. The door was locked behind me and I was once again alone with my thoughts. It seemed that this move had been meaningless and instead of a change for the better I was again doomed to the constriction of walls. After about six hours of waiting for something to happen I decided to amuse myself as best I might. I had a stub of pencil in my pocket, all around me was a painting surface worthy of a Michelangelo: I would try my hand at a mural. My first picture was of a beautiful girl with long hair, she really was beautiful, like a Madonna. Then, as I was feeling hungry, I composed on the wall one of those fantasy menus prisoners often indulge in. There were seven courses, a different wine with each, and a noticeable excess of carbohydrates in its composition. Fortified by my imaginary meal I became bolder. I drew a picture of a German officer. I had meant only to draw the head, in particular the cap, a subject I was rather good at, but after I had finished the square monocled face I was so pleased with the result that I continued with the body and then with the boots. The right arm inevitably extended itself in the Hitler salute. It was then that I thought of the story I had heard of the well-known German comedian who had stood for several minutes on the stage of a Munich theatre with his arm thus held. He said nothing until his audience had become thoroughly uncomfortable and were wondering what was expected of them. Then he said in a casual conversational sort of way: "Letzes Jahr lag der Schnee so hoch in Garmisch-Partenkirchen!"[1] He

1 "The snow was this deep in Garmisch-Partenkirchen last year!"

had been arrested and sent to prison. His phrase made an appropriate filling to the balloon I made billow from my officer's mouth. When the guard came in with the evening meal he almost dropped the soup in surprise. He shouted hysterically and called out for help. Two other guards came running down the passage. They stood gaping in amazement at the walls. Then an officer arrived, took one look, and told a guard to fetch the Commandant. As the Commandant arrived everyone stood rigid to attention. This was my first introduction: he was a short man with a red face and a square head, an eyeglass was screwed into his right eye. The reason for the excitement suddenly became clear. The Commandant was not amused by my impromptu portrait. He called me a lot of names which I did not understand but which were onomatopoeically expressive enough. I was told I should be made to scrub the walls myself; these cells, he said were for German soldiers, as though it was a privilege that I had been allowed to use them.

The next day I was transferred to a long low building like a stable. There was a single passage with about eight doors leading off. As I entered I was assailed by a wild discordant orgy of sound that made me certain that they thought me mad and that I had, for my work upon the walls, been moved to the madhouse. I was thrust into a vacant cell and as the appalling noises subsided I realized I was among friends. It was a happy moment. The other cells contained British officers from the camp beyond the wire serving small sentences for attempted escapes. In adjoining cells there were Lance Pope, a member of Lloyds, who before the war had married the daughter of Frick, the German Minister of the Interior; Tony Rolt, the racing motorist; George Kane, who had been with me in the 5th (Ski) Battalion of the Scots Guards; and Terence Prittie of the Rifle Brigade. After so long a silence my tongue could now uncurl and we indulged in an orgy of chatter at the top of our voices in order to be heard through the walls. I learned that this was Oflag VIIb and that behind the wire were over a thousand other prisoners of war, many of whom had been captured in France as long ago as 1940. I was there for several

days, enjoying books, conversation, and the food provided by the
Red Cross. I spent a few days in the hospital with dysentery and
then back to the cells. I wondered how long it would be before I
was allowed to become a proper prisoner of war, which was then
the height of my desire.

Suddenly I was moved again.

Back to Berlin. Back du côté de chez Oberst Pr. z.W. I
gathered some mistake had been made and I should not have been
sent to Eichstätt at all. I thought that sort of thing only happened
in the British army.

Days passed. Christmas came. This was a success: Eichstätt
had apparently been forwarding Red Cross parcels to me and
one miraculous day four were suddenly delivered to my cell
together. The unwrapping of these fantastic treasures brought
me great joy and soon I had arrayed on the table a stock of
groceries that would not have disgraced Fortnum & Mason.
From then on I was in a position of power; it was now Herr
Hauptmann this and Herr Hauptmann that, guards from the
other side of the building would come over and see my display.
It cost me twenty cigarettes to get a tin opener, but to particularly friendly faces I would dispense a small gift. I sent a bar
of chocolate over to Oberst Pr. z.W. About this time books,
too, began to arrive. Some intelligent selector had chosen great
fat sagas for me to lose myself in, *North-West Passage*, *Gone
With the Wind*, *The Crowthers of Bankdam*. From now on my
days were not long enough: I had, in a manner of speaking,
escaped.

A week or two after Christmas I was told to get ready for another move. As usual nobody seemed to know where I was going,
neither was I able to form much of an idea from the route. I felt
ill and the long train journey passed in a daze. There were endless coniferous forests, snow lay thick upon the ground. Then
an arrival, a meeting on the platform by a group of soldiers and
an officer, a walk through the snow-packed streets of a small
town, and the sudden sight of a great castle perched high above.

One of the escort, on account of my dragging steps, had obligingly shouldered my baggage. When the officer saw this he shouted an order; the soldier hastily dropped everything in the snow. To me he said angrily: "Do you think my men are coolies?" So, shuffling along, in no great style, over the bridge, up the hill and through the gates I entered the castle.

I was led straight off into a cell in the outer courtyard but by this time I was feeling too ill to care and lay thankfully down on the little bed. I had no idea where I had come to and began to envisage another long period of solitary confinement. Then I heard a voice say: "Who are you?" I told him. The voice introduced itself as Dominic Bruce, the place was the punishment cells of Colditz. Next morning I was led out through a great gate and passed to an inner courtyard. The sensation of enclosure was overpowering. A grey sky pressed on to tall walls like a roof. The whole yard was like a cell. A motley collection of people were shuffling round the cobbles like the figures in Van Gogh's asylum drawing. I was marched across the yard and shown into a small room. I was pleased to note that the door was not locked. By the barred window was a short, square figure, with a mop of greying hair. He was wearing an old brown dressing-gown and was trying to swat a fly. The German guard said: "Herr Romilly, we have company for you."

PART TWO

THE TOWER

Chapter Five

The Society of the Tower

THE Tower, which at various times had housed Saxon Kings, fallen women, Communists, lunatics, and dissident Czechs, was in the winter of 1941-2 the seat of six hundred prisoners-of-war who had been sent to it from milder places either on account of escaping or because they had otherwise by act or word incurred German displeasure. It was called *Sonderlager* ("Special Camp") and sometimes *Straflager* ("Punishment Camp"). A beetling spot, overlooking the small town of Colditz in the very middle of Germany, it was intended to be a firm and final immurement for these prisoners whose isolation was also, in the German view, a quarantine measure.

The offences which qualified prisoners for Colditz were many and varied and they were not all of equal gravity. For instance, there were two Belgian officers, Commandant Flébus and Lieutenant Marlière, who had eaten a cat. The skin had refused to go down the lavatory, when they flushed, and it had been traced to them. The German commandant at Eichstätt, where this happened, drafted his punishment order as follows:

"I punish with 10 days room-arrest the prisoner-of-war Commandant Flébus, No. 1161, because he on 2.3.1941 a to him not belonging German cat captured and on 4.3.1941 in the unnatural consumption of the cat took part.

(2) "... the prisoner Lieutenant Louis Marlière, No. 2984, with 14 days room-arrest because he a to him not belonging

German cat in beast-tormenting fashion killed, the same cooked, and together with Commandant Flébus in unnatural manner consumed, although the to the prisoners-of-war measured-out rations excellently prepared and amply sufficient are."[1]

These sentences served, the offenders were sent to Colditz, where Commandant Flébus, an unretiring and outsize figure conspicuous in beret and huge spectacles, lived in notorious esteem on the memory of the cat—"Delicious! Just like rabbit!"—and derided all "Boches" with contemptuous militancy. A poster by a fellow-prisoner showed him charging on a horse, about to throw a lance at a flying cat.

Escaping and harrying of Germans were the principal occupations in the Tower. There dangled from a high window in an outer wall a rope made of linen bed-covers which had been used by a Pole, Lieutenant Micky Surmanowicz, in the most spectacular break ever made from it. He and one other Pole, both being under arrest, had forced open their cells, climbed a ninety-foot perpendicular inside wall, and reached an outside window through a passage and a loft. Surmanowicz was already down on the far side when his companion, over-excited in descending, struck the wall with a ski-boot and alerted the guards, who caught both two hours later in a quarry. Surmanowicz, small, wiry, and pale, a man whom no lock could baffle, was afterwards removed from Colditz to a military prison, sentenced to four years for having exuberantly thrown a bottle at a German sentry on the day Russia entered the war. But his rope remained,

---

[1] *Bestrafung.*
Ich bestrafe (1) den Kgf. Cdt. Flébus, Erk. Nr. 1161, mit 10 Tagen Stubenarrest, weil er am 2.3.41 eine ihm nicht gehörende deutsche Katze eingefangen und sich am 4.3.41 an dem unnatürlichen Verzehr der Katze beteiligt hat.
(2) den Kgf. Ltn. Louis Marlière, Erk. Nr. 2984, mit 14 Tagen Stubenarrest, weil er eine ihm nicht gehörende deutsche Katze in tierquälerischer Weise getötet, dieselbe gekocht und zusammen mit Cdt. Flébus unnatürlicherweise verzehrt hat, obwohl die den Kgf. gereichte Kost ausgezeichnet zubereitet und reichlich bemessen ist.

hanging over river and town, a visible warning and wonder to passers-by. The Germans in the Tower could not add it to their continuously augmented museum of escape properties, because they could not reach it.

The escapers' laurel wreath was awarded without dissent to a young French cavalryman, Lieutenant Mairesse, who broke away suddenly, during a period of exercise under arrest, got over a ten-foot wall before the escorting sentry had time to fire his first shot, and reached and safely crossed the German-Swiss frontier, though he took neither food, money, maps, nor papers, and was wearing only a vest and shorts and tennis shoes.

The unluckiest effort was that of a French prisoner, Lieutenant Boulet, who successfully disengaged himself from a walking-party in the disguise of a dumpish elderly woman. After he had gone a few paces he inadvertently dropped his wrist-watch. A fellow-prisoner who knew nothing about his escape picked up the watch, shouted, and made after him. Guards helpfully intervened, till the Frenchman, supposing from the clamour that he was already discovered, abandoned his disguise.

The Germans in Colditz did not resent escapes but did find it hard to come to terms with the incessant harrying and ridicule to which they were subject. This was the long dead time when German victory arrogantly straddled Europe. The war crawled, signs of change were scant. The prisoners in the Tower, seeing no excitement outside, looked for it inside. They set out to make Germans lose their tempers, and they were at first astonished, and soon afterwards delighted, by the extent to which the Germans obliged. German officers railed, raved. Commandants jerked out special punishments and pompous edicts. "I extend to you the right hand of friendship. If that hand is rejected I shall resort to severe measures."

German rage was often painfully at odds with German correctitude. An English major, smoking with intent to offend during a parade, puffed ostentatiously at Hauptmann Priem, who struck the cigarette out of his mouth. Uproar. Hauptman Priem shouted threats. But the Commandant, after he had considered

the incident, posted up his report and decision in an English
rendering by his own interpreter as follows:

">". . . At the same moment when Hauptmann Priem caught
sight of the smoking Major MacColm, he took off his cigarette
out of his mouth and cast it away. This unrestrained be-
haviour over against an officer in a higher rank was not correct.
Hauptmann Priem has been accordingly informed by me that
it would have been more correct to report Major MacColm
for punishment.

I shall not punish Major MacColm subsequently because
he is only staying for a short time in Oflag IVC and has not
been informed by the British Senior Officer, according to his
statement, about the disciplinary instructions which are a
matter of course in the German Army."

German officers and their subordinates, slow to acclimatize
themselves, to dodge the traps set for them, did learn eventually
the value of reticence and became (outwardly) almost British
in their phlegm and humour. They cultivated elegance, sport-
manship, and repartee. They gave joke for joke, sneer for sneer.
Yet often the veneer of this adaptation would wear thin and the
plethoric Teuton would show through, fulminating—"Sind Sie
Offiziere oder Kinder?"[1]—to a hostile parade.

The society of the Tower, with its poky confines and small
compact population, was exceptionally homogeneous and from
the start was furnished with active purpose by its status as a
"special" society. To be there, the prisoners felt, was a privilege,
a mark of merit, and a challenge. Thus they exorcized the spirit
of senseless tedium, supported by convictions of failure and in-
feriority, that in many places lay heavily on prisoners-of-war.
In Colditz a cheerful aggressiveness was fostered. Something had
to be going on all the time. The best thing that could go on was
escaping. The cult of escape held moral sway and had its priest-
hood in the Escape Committees with their acolytes of selected
assistants. The cult was genuine, since the idea of escape had

1 "Are you officers or children?"

power to excite all prisoners irrespective of individual aptitudes. But it also was exceptional in Colditz in the extent to which it hypnotized the many who elsewhere might have stayed aloof, such as the elderly and senior and the studious or the artistic, who at heart believed that time was better spent at a desk than digging tunnels or "stooging" for others who dug. There were older men—a Polish admiral, a Dutch colonel of Intelligence, a few English majors—who with gravity adjusted themselves to outlast their indefinite sentence. But in 1942, out of a hundred British prisoners-of-war in Colditz, there was only one who made bold to say publicly and generally that he thought "that too much escaping was absurd". This was Captain the Reverend Richard Heard, army chaplain and don, who till the war was Dean of Peterhouse College in Cambridge. Many, he held, would be better employed in improving their minds to prepare themselves for the eventual responsibilities of freedom. "Knowledge is power," he reminded. But this mild dogma seemed in Colditz a startling and almost treacherous heresy. It had no hold even among the studious who, though unlikely themselves to be escaping or making trouble, felt obliged to contribute to these doings: drawing escapers in action, for instance, or translating into German the *Anträge* ("Protests") which bombarded the *Kommandantur* without respite.

Heard's position was lonely; it acquired a niche. By Colditz standards (and not by them only) his knowledge was large (it was mentioned with awe that he read more than a thousand books a year) and "Let's ask Dickie!" became the customary recourse for settling disputed points. Dickie, bland in face with skin of baby-like pink, brown hair sparse on top, blue cogitating eyes, had a physique of protuberant dimensions which earned him the occasional nickname "Yak". An affectionate, formidably accurate, emotionally self-contained man, he did not ardently look for disciples.

There was in Colditz a powerful and unrelieved tension which had little to do with the Germans. In part it rose from the atmosphere generated by the secret, undiscussed preparation of escapes; in part from the aggressive extravert spirit as it beat outward, found no space, beat inward again. The castle fitted like a tight glove with a palm (courtyard) and long vertical fingers (towers with spiral stone stairs mounting to the prisoners' quarters). You could go up, down, and round. At times the tension was so powerful that it seemed as if it must crack the walls of the castle, releasing the prisoners into the dismal country beyond. The French prisoners regarded it as dangerous and sought deliberately to disperse it, among themselves at least. If any man in their group was seen to be unhappy and brooding they did not, as the British way tended to be, leave him alone but pestered him until he admitted what was wrong. They obliged him if he had had a bad letter from home to read it aloud; or they read it themselves. Often at night in the French quarters, when all was silent and dark, a prisoner suddenly would start to howl. Another would take up the howl, then another, till the night shrieked. After these outbursts, the French said, they all felt much better.

The mingling of nationalities was the brightest feature of the Tower. The Germans too seemed to feel a shy pride in this speciality which fluttered flag-like above the sterile landscape of the captor-captive situation.

English, French, Poles, Dutch, and Belgians, though they had separate quarters and spent most of their time within their own groups, were all very much aware of each other. Membership of Colditz, however earned, seemed to vouch for a prisoner and thus enjoined a fellowship that slipped past national prejudice. Over and above that, the experience by which national groups different from your own in every obvious way were sharing an identical fate exerted a restraining, if not necessarily civilizing, influence. No nation, under those circumstances, ran amok in its specialized field of lunacy. Take sport. The British, instigators of a roughish game called "Stoolball", invited the slovenly, anaemic-looking French to play against them—and were beaten. The Poles, for whom all sport entailed a life-or-death defence of Polish honour, controlled, if they did not abandon, their most blatant grimness about defeat. The Dutch, though their rigid discipline and precision restrained them from playing much, cultivated an admiration for the English, associating themselves especially with their light sporty ways, and seemed in this to be making a deliberate effort, prompted by some new awareness, to lengthen the distance that separated them from their national neighbours, the humourless wooden Germans.

The Belgians, who did not play at all, were the most intractably, individualistically unmilitary group. The French, worried about their own centrifugal tendencies, were genuinely scared when they contemplated the Belgians, seeing mirrored in them the extreme perils of civilianization. This fear was indirectly corroborated by Commandant Flébus the cat-eater, who said often that his own soldierly character had never been properly appreciated until he came to Colditz. The Belgian army had been very unpopular, he said, in pre-war Belgium. Girls would not dance with men in uniform, on pavements they were expected to give way to everybody, and sometimes things were thrown at them. The Belgians of Colditz, unshaven, shapeless, striking no attitude and just as placid about large matters as about small, did look like an unappreciated squad that had got captured by some mistake. Yet they were perkily, serenely alive; and their mere presence set quizzical limits to the exorbitances of their neighbours.

There were hundreds of dreary days in Colditz. The drive to escape and the campaign to harry the Germans could never be wholly successful at the point where they expressed, not their obvious purposes, but rather the resolve of the prisoners to keep themselves active and to resist succumbing to lethargy. From that point of view there was always too much against them. There were periods when the old looked old, the young did not look fit, and the ardours of defiance, never an unforced growth, failed to leap out. The Germans would find that they had quiet parades and would patter secure along the files, almost like nannies.

In such lethargic periods each nation slipped into its special groove. Dutch, Poles, and Belgians seemed to hibernate, while the larger nations, the English and French, fought the malaise in larger and dissimilar ways.

In that fight the French were the better equipped. They had a knack of domesticating themselves. The British prisoner's corner was his castle only if he could get out of it. The *summum bonum* of the British cuisine was the bread pudding, impatiently kneaded and left to bake as best it might; a French prisoner could spend a happy day contriving a *baba au rhum*. In the general field of manual ingenuity there was not much to choose between them but the French often made things for their own sake whereas the English always made them for a purpose—usually escape. The French made mouse-tanks. The tanks were toy-sized, built of small pieces of wood, and driven from inside by a mouse revolving on a ferris-wheel. The mouse visibly enjoyed this job. There was also a "Big Wheel" for the recreation of several families of mice. Mice lay about on a beach of sand while those who were feeling more active kept the wheel spinning by getting aboard the spokes. It was the particular sport of the bigger mice to leap suddenly from sand to spoke so that their weight set the wheel flying and tipped off all the little mice. Wondrous as these mouse-machines were, the spirit of Colditz was against them, and they were readily forgotten.

The French, who had no fear of convenience, considered that *les anglais* wittingly or unwittingly believed in subjecting themselves to inconvenience. Their own way of dealing with strain was to "exteriorize" and relax; whereas the British tended to produce more and more of it and press it down inside themselves harder and harder until they were at last exhausted and could fall virtuously asleep. British prisoners rejoiced, or said that they did, at being moved as often as possible from camp to camp, castle to castle, on the principle that moving was good for you—kept you fit and so on. It was looked at askance if anyone tried to make the corner in which he lived and slept more comfortable, personal, or home-like; such contrivances being dubbed disparagingly "life-boats", as constituting a mode of private self-salvage. Their search for inconvenience drove the British out-side to the cobbles of the Colditz yard to spitting frenzies of shadow-boxing or to a hundred press-ups before breakfast. One, who on principle and on the coldest nights would never sleep under more than a single blanket, was not imitated; yet a wiry pride was taken in his unflinching austerity.

The French, in periods when escaping slackened off, fretted little. They never were so communally single-minded about escape as the English were. They rarely counted the world—even Colditz—well lost for it. There was a case where a French prisoner-of-war, offered a method which involved bribery of a German and some purchases through German channels, totted up the cost and decided that it was too high. French escapes were the outcome of individuality and daring rather than of collective patience and organization; a temperamental difference not obscured, though it *was* exaggerated, by obvious differences of situation, military and political, that made the rewards of escape less alluring for the French.

The interplay of national differences contributed a resilence and élan that often cushioned what otherwise was only noisy and hard. Anglo-French relations, more tortuously developed than others, provided a continual diversion due chiefly to the inevit-able clashing impact of French curiosity on British sluggish phlegm. The French, passionately curious about changing events and "movements of opinion", found it incomprehensible even after months of enforced and intimate contact that their British opposites could get through the day without being bothered by events and without once changing their opinions on any subject.

There was a general pairing-off between the two groups, originally for exchanges of language-lessons, later widening into friendly acquaintances and friendships, and Anglo-French pairs would meet daily in the yard or in each others' quarters. "*Bon-jour*" would lead straight to either "*Quoi de neuf*"? or "*Eh bien, qu'est-ce-que vous racontez?*" from the French side, whereupon the following dialogue (subject to variations) would develop:

"*Bonjour! Quoi de neuf?*"

"Oh, nothing particularly. Still here I suppose."

"Yes I think so. Have you some interesting letters lately?"

"No—o, nothing very interesting. Rather dull really."

"But I think the situation is rather interesting at present?"

Pause. On English side, lighting and filling of pipe.

"The Germans admit today that they are retreating in Africa."

"About time they did admit it."

"Yes I think so. It is better now than when you were at El Alamein. I think you were very anxious then, yes?"

"Oh not really."

"No?"

"Well I mean we were a bit anxious I suppose. But we never thought it would really come to anything."

"We were very anxious. Personally I thought the Germans should take Alexandria."

"Well, they didn't."

"No, of course not."

"Have a cigarette?"

"Thank you. And what about the danger from U-boats now? I think it is very serious. From the speech of your Mr Alexander one has the impression that . . ."

The British side would brace itself reluctantly, it certainly would not have read the speech. Yet all that was stimulating rather than irritating. The different groups in Colditz swallowed many a prejudice for the sake of this enlivening solidarity. Sometimes they did more. Once for instance an English prisoner suffering from jaundice coughed up some blackish ersatz German jam which he mistook for blood. He was visited by a German doctor and also by a Polish prisoner-doctor. The German was sceptical about the blood. But the Pole was enthusiastic about it; urging a muscular injection to prevent internal bleeding he marshalled phial, needle, and syringe, and said, with a contemptuous gesture at the German:

"He doesn't think this necessary. I do. You can choose."

Seeing the sufferer inclined to refuse he became offended. The German *Arzt* smiled.

Refusal, it was plain, would precipitate Anglo-Polish discord. Poles were allies, German enemies. Polish nationalism was sensitive. The British officer endured the injection.

The first British contingent in the Tower consisted entirely of escapers and their assistants (such as engineers) with the exception of a Methodist padre whose suitcase had contained a piece of metal adjudged by the Germans to be a jemmy, an Indian Army doctor in whose bed somebody else's map had been found, and Richard Heard who claimed to be the only British "innocent". Among the escapers was a colourful dash of Canadian and Australian aviators who could count on deafening applause whenever the Germans in Colditz, following the line of their press, gibed that they were "fighting all England's battles".

The French, three hundred strong, were either escapers or individuals of, as the Germans saw it, *"mauvais esprit"*. The first to reach Colditz were six officers whom the Germans held responsible for having torn down, from the walls of other French prisoner-of-war centres, Nazi propaganda posters on which had been depicted for the prisoners' edification a drowning French sailor holding aloft the flag of France and crying with his last breath: "Remember Mers-el-Kebir!" Then came a number of "anti-collaborationist" colonels who had been Senior French Officers in other camps; and General le Bleu who, for having admonished a German soldier who failed to salute him, had been held guilty of "insulte à l'armée allemande".

Among the *touristes*[1] and men of *mauvais esprit* were a group of twenty French officers known as "Les Innocents" because, although they had racked their brains, they could not imagine by what they had qualified for Colditz. It was suspected that ill-conditioned prisoners elsewhere had denounced them, either from personal spite, or in hope of release. There were also eighty-five French Jewish officers, among them several famous names—Blum, Dreyfus, Hirsch, Rothschild—and the most distinguished talents intellectually of all the Tower inmates. Lieutenant Hirsch, bald Paris banker, was a pioneer of the French

[1] Escapers.

Society of Astronautics; before the war he had awarded the prize of his Society to a German scientist who then had been moved to insert, in the second edition of his work, an eloquently grateful preface about the splendid way in which the fellowship of science transcended national animosities.

Le Capitaine Blum, captain of artillery, was a classical pianist. Musicians were the most imperturbable of captives; Blum with his sensitive features and slight professorial beard shared their remote, unirked look. Yet his situation in Colditz was unique, ironic, and not exactly pleasant. He was hemmed in by adherents of that Marshal Pétain who held his father, Léon Blum, the former Socialist leader and Prime Minister, under strict arrest in the Pyrenees. Wherever he moved in the French quarters giant portraits of the Marshal confronted him. Messages from his father reached him rarely, months after they had been written and bearing the stamps of many interested censors. The accounts that he received from his wife, though more regular, could not be much more cheerful since she, albeit technically free, was living almost as cramped a life as he himself, in the Hôtel des Voyageurs in Urdos below the Fort de Pourtalet. Three only of this hotel's rooms had occupants and the other two were Mme Gamelin, wife of General Gamelin, and Mme Bretty, a star of the Comédie Française and close friend of the imprisoned Minister Mandel. Every afternoon this forlorn trio wended its way by foot up steep paths to the lonely fort, five thousand feet above sea level, where Blum, Gamelin, and Mandel languished under Pétain's hand.

In Colditz Captain Blum's compatriots were for a long time blindly, even rabidly, loyal to Pétain. It was Pétain, they swore, who did everything for them, who even personally sent them their ping-pong sets. Yet from the start they were at pains to square their Pétainism with an anti-collaborationist outlook. The unusual character of Colditz was on their side in this effort. Controversy with allied groups—with the British for instance about the British attacks on the French Fleet—were never allowed to interfere with personal regard based on anti-German solidarity. The French too were proud of the labels of "tourism" and "bad spirit" and this fostered among them a sense of unity which in its turn promoted hope. They had no wish to return to previous camps. The confinement in Colditz was stricter but the moral atmosphere was more bracing; and this especially affected the French, who had wilted in the defeatist air of other mass-camps, where for months after the collapse of France they had seen no ray of hope and had almost resigned themselves to a popular despair.

Eventually in twos and threes Gaullist officer-prisoners, captured in North Africa, were introduced into Colditz. It was not easy for the Pétain French to accept these men who so brashly embodied all that they themselves had denied. They still looked for a way forward *through* their Pétainism. Even after the escape and political break-away of General Giraud, which thrilled all and was approved by most, they maintained a frigid view of the Gaullists as military renegades.

One day in the spring of 1943 Colditz was visited by the blind veteran and Great War hero Scapini, Vichy-appointed representative, who came with a special mission to bolster the now-flagging faith of these French.

"I know that you criticize the French Government a great deal, and even Marshal Pétain himself," Scapini told them.

The assembled French prisoners, after they had listened to his set speech, put questions to "M. l'Ambassadeur" through a chosen spokesman, a captain who was a lawyer at the Paris Bar.

"We prisoners think that Marshal Pétain is not at heart hostile to General Giraud?"

Scapini dissented. Giraud's action had done France great harm, he said. It had removed the French Government's sole means of putting pressure on Germany, namely, the existence of her fleet, and the undivided loyalty of her citizens.

The captain pointed out the pain caused to Frenchmen by the servile French press and radio. Scapini sighed and said that these did not represent the viewpoint of the Marshal.

It was gradually elucidated that the Marshal even at that date hoped for a compromise that would unite France, England, and Germany; failing that, for an allied victory by arms—but that would "take a very long time" and also would advance, as Scapini put it, the "danger of submergence by Bolshevism".

Scapini's visit, a considerable event to the French prisoners, among whom discussions swarmed afterwards for days, was also a turning-point. Argument had always been more real than other things to these typical Frenchmen for whom, as one put it, nothing was ever self-evident; in argument Scapini had failed to convince them. They, who had lived in closest contact with "les anglais" and had incessantly probed British morale, knew that there would be no compromise. The political "danger of Bolshevism" could not distract them from awareness of the increasing signs of military victory. The whole Vichy outlook had exposed itself to them as "unrealistic", heaviest fault in a French scale. Now the ping-pong sets ceased to be mentioned, the portraits began to come down from the walls. Pétainism atrophied. Only a sort of fossil bit of it survived in the fixed attitude to the Gaullists which did not change.

For the Dutch also, though in a different way, Colditz became a rallying-point where threads of individual action were drawn into a single, emblematic pattern. In July 1940, after the defeat of their country, officers of the Dutch Home and Colonial Armies had been offered by the German authority an unmolested life at home provided that they agreed to sign a Declaration, as follows:

"I hereby declare on my word of honour that I in this war, so long as the Netherlands continues in a state of war with the German Reich, will on no front directly or indirectly take part in battle against Germany, and will do nothing either by commission or omission, which could in any way whatever harm the German Reich."[1]

[1] "Ich erkläre hierdurch ehrenwörtlich, dass ich in diesem Kriege, solange sich die Niederlande im Kriegszustand mit dem deutschen Reich befinden, an keiner Front mittelbar oder unmittelbar mich am Kampfe gegen Deutschland beteiligen und keine Handlung oder Unterlassung begehen werde, die dem deutschen Reich in irgendwelcher Art schaden könnte."

Many Dutch officers demurred especially at the "commission or omission" phrase and asked for insertion of the German word *absichtlich* (deliberate). This however, the Germans said, was unnecessary. The Declaration was eventually signed by all officers of the Dutch Home Army except six generals, an admiral, and three other officers. The generals and the admiral, among whom were the commander-in-chief of the Army (General Winckelmann), of the Air Force (General Best), and of the Navy (Admiral von Laer), were imprisoned in the Castle of Konigstein on the Elbe (the place from which General Giraud escaped); the other three—Captain van der Hoog, Captain Hagerland, and Lieutenant Baron von Lynden—in Colditz.

They were impressive and picturesque figures. Van der Hoog, tall and erect, walked the cobbled yard alone with military step. His noble features and habit of wearing a black cloak gathered up on his shoulder like a toga earned him the name "Julius Caesar". The Baron von Lynden, a tall youth whose courtly back seemed permanently inclined in a suggestion of a bow, had been an aide-de-camp to Queen Wilhelmina and had become during the war an adjutant of the commander-in-chief. Two other adjutants, Captain Romswinckel and Lieutenant von Doorninck, asked permission to join General Winckelmann in captivity. This was granted. Later however the Germans decided that the captive general could not have adjutants, and they transferred the two volunteers to Colditz.

Three who signed but qualified themselves for Colditz by other action were Lieutenant-Colonel Rooseboom, chief of Dutch Home Intelligence, whose orders for the detention before the war of certain Dutch Nazis were afterwards betrayed by the Dutch Nazi Party: Captain Schepperrs, a military lawyer, who remained free until the Germans discovered that he had been responsible for shipping to England eight hundred German prisoners-of-war—parachutists, aviation personnel, and advance shock troops—a bare few hours before the oncoming *Wehrmacht* could rescue them; and Lieutenant Eeras, a reservist, for the same reason.

The Dutch Colonial officers, influenced partly by the fact that elsewhere they still had intact troops to command, had reacted much more fiercely to the Declaration. Decision about signing having been left to individual judgment, a few did sign and were left temporarily free. Sixty, who did not, came to Colditz. Their senior officer, swarthy and smart Major Englis, was Chief of Colonial Instructors at the Dutch Academy and most of the rest were pupils, cadets, or instructors of the Academy (Breda) or Staff College (The Hague), besides a few who had simply been on leave in Holland.

The Colonial Dutch, many of whom had East Indian blood, mustered a Hawaian guitar quartet whose delivery of a favourite song, "Goodbye Hawaii", was poignantly escapist, not less so because of its unfortunate naval associations. The playing of this quartet was justly admired. Its leader, Captain Pereira, who estimated that he had practised four hours every day for ten years, had first been taught to play a guitar in Singapore by Hulahula girls, a clever and artistic company who were said to have taught him many things.

In their early, scattered state the Dutch prisoners had had at first no idea of escaping. In fact they had doubted whether escaping accorded with their military honour—imprisonment itself having represented the point of honour for them. But a few individualists had broken out of earlier places, among them two who had got into the sisters' quarters of a convent at Juliusburg and then had reached Switzerland. When they all got to Colditz the Dutch, characteristically, held a conference to consider these questions. "The position was reviewed by the community." As a result they threw themselves into escaping with massive discipline and achieved substantial successes under the leadership of Captain van den Heuvel, a man remarkable both in organizing genius and personality.

In matters of action, especially escaping, they co-operated closely with the British in Colditz. Thus ties of sympathy were developed more quickly and firmly than might have happened if these had depended solely on personal contacts. For the Dutch

did not ever loosen their rigid discipline. They were by an
enormous distance the smartest, shiniest contingent and their
stout resisting of the Germans never erupted into raucousness on
parades nor into any noisy demonstration simply for its own
sake. It was rare for a Dutch officer to be given *Zellenarrest*[1] by
the Germans for any disciplinary offence. In fact senior Dutch
officers meted out their own disciplinary punishments which
were observed though they could not be enforced; and it was
not uncommon to discover that a lieutenant, seemingly unac-
countably missing, had been confined to his quarters. In the
same way Dutch escaping, more than that of others, was
governed by formal direction and military orders unquestioningly
carried out.

The tight discipline in which the Dutch fastened themselves
had some curious effects. Lively and thrustful in their escaping,
they were pleased to have struck these sparks out of a dull
captivity. Collectively there was a developing spirit of warmth
and enjoyment about them. Individually however this seemed
to lag. In the Tower theatre, when some elementary skit was
raising laughs even among those who could not understand its
language, Dutch officers beautifully turned out would sit expressionless. The younger especially seemed often to subside
into a kind of wooden boredom. The seniors watched out for
this state which they considered bad; their cure was to clap
three days' confinement to quarters on the offender. There
appeared to be puzzled attempts to carry over the feeling of
collective enterprise into a more individual expression; the
Dutch would accuse themselves of interesting vices—hypocrisy,
for instance—as if striving to break free from that picture of
admirable if severely disciplined qualities that they in fact presented. Their attempts in Colditz to individualize these values
seemed to come up against something which possibly could not
be surmounted in that setting.

The thirty-odd Belgian group, making no such efforts, basked
in the sun of Colditz approval, yet warily, as if it was strange to

[1] German solitary cell punishment.

them and might go in at any minute. Bursts of unpremeditated self-assertion, breaking the surface of their indifference, had brought them to the Tower. One, Lieutenant Scheere, was an Olympic pentathlon; he had beaten up a *mouton*[1] for having betrayed an escape elsewhere of two Belgian officers and then had been posted to Colditz where he was pointed out to newcomers with admiration as *l'assassin belge*. Another, Lieutenant le Cocq, had one day impulsively written to his wife in Belgium that he hoped that she would soon be rid of the *vermine grise*. Conscientious German censors translated this as *graue Pest*. When they grasped that what appeared to be an allusion to a garden insect was an insulting description of themselves they reported the lieutenant, who was awarded two months' imprisonment, Colditz to follow. "Inflammatory sermons" had qualified the Aumônier Schickratt, a Jesuit priest; and ten had come from mild Eichstätt, adjudged of *mauvais esprit*. The Belgians' Senior Officer, Colonel Desnet, had been put on a train in France (after the capitulation) in order, as had been promised, to be repatriated to Belgium. The train made a detour in the night however and next morning Colonel Desnet woke up in Germany a prisoner. The Germans suavely explained that the train had entered Belgium *after* the 23rd August which they had appointed as the final date for free repatriation. Irritated by this duplicity, Colonel Desnet made a tart speech which brought him inevitably to Colditz. His aide, l'officier Adjutant de Roi, had lived freely at home until December (1940) when he was suddenly arrested and sent to join the colonel on the strength of a police card stamped *très dangereux*. In Colditz all these things were titles to esteem.

The Poles brought stranger and more sombre titles. They brought their bleak heroism and their extraordinary past. In their dark shabby clothes they seemed to be wrapped in the loneliness of partitioned memories. The Polish quarters were always darkly forbidding, cupboards blocked the light from the barred windows, and the hundred and forty prisoners who moved in them appeared to have, more than anyone else, an authentic

[1] Informer.

right to be inmates of a sullen castle. Shuffling, clogging, stooping, an amorphous and indistinguishable host of drab khaki made more remote by the barrier of Slav speech, the Poles lent to Colditz Castle a dignity which, despite its hundred-foot walls, clouds of barbed wire, and giant reflectors, it did not inherently have.

There were Poles who had fought against each other in the First World War under French, Italian, German, Austrian, and Russian command—bitter mercenaries nursing the secret patriotism that Pilsudski inflamed and organized. Some had been in the Pilsudski Legion in Austria. Austrian subjects fighting as Austrian troops, they had fought to gain experience and to harden themselves for the struggle to recreate Polish sovereignty. Clashes with their masters had soon developed. There were even in Colditz a few who had been with the fabulous General Haller when he one foggy morning in 1916, after clashing with Austrian troops, broke through into Russia with his Brigade and fought detaining Russians and travelled via China to France in time to organize a new force to aid the first allied victories of 1918 and to enter ready into the service of the emergent Polish State. These and others were the type of the Polish soldiers who, having become colonels at twenty-five and generals at thirty and having accepted the rigorous caste discipline and dedicated service imposed by Pilsudski, twenty years later saw their new Poland, fruit of so much blood and sacrifice, dashed to pieces by Hitler and Stalin. Reunited only in captivity they embraced this fate with the same dark, unwavering readiness.

Their highest officers in Colditz, Admiral Unrug and General Piskor, were both rugged men who had played large and characteristically tangled parts in Polish affairs.

The Admiral, a silver-haired man of sixty, impressively hard in form and feature, had been in 1914 a German U-boat commander, sinking British ships in the North Sea; then he had charge of a German naval training school. When after the Armistice the Kaiser released his officers from their oath, Kapitän zur See Unrug had offered his services to the new

Polish Government. "Sorry," they said. "You are a sailor. Nothing for you." But several years later he attended in Warsaw a
conference of fifteen Polish-born ex-naval officers of the defeated
German, Austrian, and Russian navies. They were the only naval
men in Poland. They put him in charge of the new Polish coast
on the Baltic. He was Admiral, but he had no ship, and he decided to buy one. He bought one in Danzig privately under his
own name and with his own money. A coastal ship of 250 tons,
the "Pomojañen", she was the first ship ever to fly the Polish
naval ensign. Admiral Unrug shared his "Admiralty" with a
midwife and a postman. He watched the birth and growth of the
Port of Gdynia. He came to England, one of three, to represent
Poland at the Coronation of King George VI. He trained personnel, collected more ships. When Hitler's war started he was
in complete command of the coast and he maintained the defence
of the Peninsula of Hell for more than a week after Warsaw and
the whole Polish mainland had crumbled. At last, receiving no
word from the capital, Admiral Unrug ordered his destroyers to
go immediately to England. Then he surrendered to a German
flag-ship whose captain proved to be one of his former pupils of
the (First World War) Naval School.

General Piskor, a very close associate and friend of Pilsudski,
was in 1914 a youthful captain commanding a battalion of the
Legion in Austria; he fought on the Russian front and later
joined Pilsudski's personal staff. When the Legion, after being
withdrawn from the front, was forcibly disbanded, Pilsudski was
imprisoned in Magdeburg, Piskor in a forest fortress near
Warsaw. After the Armistice he emerged, entered the new
Poland, and became Chief of General Staff of the Polish Army.
Pilsudski later published his Memoirs and gave away four copies
in each of which he wrote two pages of personal dedication.
General Piskor, prisoner-of-war in Colditz, was one of only two
recipients who were still living.[1]

[1] The other was General Wienjawa-Dtugoszewski, a pre-war Polish
Ambassador in Rome—he afterwards escaped to America and was living
there during the later part of the Second World War.

Their hard struggles had stamped these Poles. Though hospitable, playful, and capable of gaiety, they were at heart serious, they endured and they expected to endure. To them the Tower was simply a phase in the endless struggle of which Polish national honour was the jealously guarded symbol. Their spirit was epitomized in the gnarled hobbies and creations of one veteran Polish sergeant who at sixty-two was the oldest inhabitant of the Tower. In a dingy, ill-lit corner this Pole made Chinese puzzle boxes which he decorated with tiny panes of variously coloured paper and sent to his children in Lodz. He also made an album, intricately figured, that he embossed with buttons of every obtainable sort of allied uniform. Inside, together with hundreds of inscribed names and addresses of fellow-prisoners, were the flags, painted in miniature, of all the allied nations.

The album, a strange work of patience, skill, and time, was perpetually growing. One day a British prisoner noticed in it among the allied flags the star and crescent moon of Turkey. He looked and his look was a question.

"She will be our ally soon" explained the militant old Pole, stroking his long beard as he stared out through a barred window.

Chapter Six

The Prominente (1)

IN Colditz the German word *Prominent*—a grotesque word meaning more or less what its sound suggests—was first applied to Giles Romilly and Michael Alexander. It conveyed, as a distinction, not that we were considered individually especially dangerous (in that one was a "franc tireur and murderer" awaiting court martial, the other a possible spy who had also escaped), but that we were "prominent" on account of personal connections. Respect, rather than retribution, appeared to be its bias. But it entailed also a more stringent supervision. We were held segregated in a small room instead of living in the communal quarters, were locked in every night with a private guard patrolling outside a door fitted with a spy-hole, and were restricted to the narrow interior yard for exercise. Respectful or otherwise these precautions from the start seemed ominous to their beneficiaries.

In this middle period of the war, however, the exceptional regime governing two of its inmates was scarcely even a sideshow in the busy life of the Tower. The idea that among six hundred special prisoners-of-war two should be singled out as "specially special" cut across the prevalent spirit. It was a cat-and-mouse scuffle carried on in a far corner between the Prominente themselves and the Germans who alone had conferred this dubious privilege. It loomed larger only very slowly as the war developed and the picked cast of Prominente was increased by gradual ones and twos to its small total; it did not sound full blast until the last twilight of the Reich.

Giles, chronologically the first Prominent, had been shifted, a few days after reaching Colditz, into a cell approached by a recess at the end of a stone passage at ground level. The cell had a barred window whose frame on the outside was outlined thickly with new white paint to make it conspicuous to sentries. It also had a table, a chair, a bedstead, a stove, and a spy-hole.

The inside sentries, posted from evening to morning in the recess, and changed every two hours, were raw and keen (the Prominente regime being new to them too) and often affixed their eyes to the spy-hole for minutes at a time. The motionless, glistening object filming this small globe made Giles fidgety; he took a sock and blocked the hole. The ensuing stillness, oppressive with heavy breathing, cumbrous thinking, and outrage, presaged inevitable explosion. Steps clopped up the passage, iron fussed on iron, and the puce Hauptmann Priem, whose charlatan bonhomie masked a nasty temper not improved by addiction to the bottle, screamed, as he flung the sock out, that he himself would shoot through the hole if it was blocked.

The *Wachkommandants* who took Priem's orders took his tone too; three or four times a night they entered the cell, pulled back the blankets, felt the object on the bed, stamped, clanked, chatted with the guard loudly. Giles, thus provoked, could either retaliate or stay quiet. Retaliation was not entirely unsatisfying; it was sometimes possible to shame or upset, and almost always possible to enrage, the overweening intruders.

One night a *Feldwebel*, finding that the bed had been dragged out of range of his sentry's eye, cried, in the tone of put-upon pathos into which German voices readily modulate: "Sie haben mich belästigt. Der Posten ist Zeuge dafür. Keine Frechheit! Sie sind erkannt dafür. Ich werde es melden."[1]

Eventually Giles realized that these nightly fracas took more out of him than out of his visitors. The mobile bed was clamped opposite the door and the pertinacious quietness of its occupant seemed to take the edge off the German aggressiveness.

[1] "You have hindered me. The sentry is witness to that. No impertinence! You are known for that. I shall report it."

Fifteen months later, in January 1943, Giles was moved out
of the end-cell into a larger one half-way along the same passage, opening off one side of it, and containing two beds. In-
ured now to his one-man routine he felt wary and almost
grudgingly unwelcoming towards the tall figure, haggard in face
and elongated in form, that shambled in, heralded by Priem
with underlings, and sat down on the second palliasse, on to
which it sloughed off dejectedly a sausage-like sack.

But the change was for the better. Comfort improved. It was
laid down that Giles and Michael, the new Prominent, were to
be counted in their beds at the early morning *Appels*. The
general count, prolonged sometimes for hours by escapes or
uproarious demonstrations, went ahead outside while we stayed
at peace hearing, but not sharing, the multitudinous coughings
and great-coated stampings in the icy yard. A *Gefreiter*, looking
in and finding us present, would shout for the reassurance of
the German officer taking the parade, ". . . und zwei Prominente!" Then after a staccato "Danke!" the desperately up-
raised voice of the officer would cry: "Ich bitte die Herren—
zurückzutreten!"[1]—and the parading prisoners would clatter
off.

The dual cell had its spy-hole, eyes were affixed, nailed boots
tramped the flagstones night-long as before. But now this
German watch settled down less aggressively. The situation of
one man on his own had seemed to elude and fret their minds,
whereas two together constituted a regularized group, something that they could understand. When we talked late, moved
about, played the gramophone, and burned light till the early
hours, they did not fearfully break in as if just in time to forestall
a sudden flit.

Michael, coming straight from lonely spells in German gaols,
confessed on the first evening that he was sick of his own company. His first moody remark—"Keep your eye on the ball!"—
had disarmed Giles, incompetently fly-swatting, who then on his
side acknowledged that he had had enough of unshared German

[1] "Gentlemen, I request you—dismiss!"

intervention at night. Thus introduced, the two Prominente soon discovered that they had more things in common than an arbitrary German bond. Their tongues wagged, their pencils (since both were fond of writing) scratched. Their stand-by, when tongues and pencils flagged, was music. They had one of a number of portable gramophones, that had reached Colditz from England, in more or less undisputed use. The Colditz library of records, occasionally increased, included the Haffner Symphony of Mozart which night after night, its slow movement especially, floated through the barred window into the silent, fitfully lit yard. The huge shadow of the yard sentry, thrown across the room, would then lie motionless, shifting only reluctantly when finally the unwillingness of either Michael or Giles to rewind the machine put a stop to Mozart.

This arcadian interlude of two Prominente continued into the summer of 1943 and was at first left unaffected by an influx of sixty-five British officers, who reached Colditz all together one day in June, after having been recaptured in the country about Eichstätt, from which they had all escaped by the same tunnel.

In this party, however, was Captain the Earl of Hopetoun, M.C., elder son of the Marquess of Linlithgow, Viceroy of India since 1936. He, before he had been a fortnight in Colditz, was shifted into the cell at the end of the passage which Giles had occupied, was classified as *Prominent*, and was submitted to the same regime—the eyes, the boots, the keys. At the early parade the *Gefreiter* now would shout sepulchrally, triumphantly: ". . . und *drei* Prominente!"

This development, more than might have seemed likely, broke the seclusion of the Prominente system. Giles being a peculiar civilian, Michael a bogus partisan due for court-martial, it had been supposed that these irregularities had something to do with the peculiar regime, which therefore in their case had been tacitly accepted. In the case of Charlie Hopetoun there was no such excuse. The reason for it, though the Germans stubbornly denied, could only be the fact that he was his father's son. The basis of the Prominente system was betrayed beyond doubt; the more so, in that the other noble member of the incoming group, Captain the Lord Arundell of Wardour, was not made a Prominent. He, though of ancient lineage, lacked the qualifying connection with the founts of power.

There was a surge of uproar and protest. The Senior British Officer hammered the *Kommandantur*. For days the castle was in a turmoil. Charlie Hopetoun threw himself into this battle. A fiercely reluctant Prominent, he let no nocturnal disturbance, not so much as a rattling of keys, pass unprotested. More combative than Giles and Michael, he was also more long-sighted; he saw the Prominente regime as a personal threat beyond the ordinary threat of captivity, a sort of "double cage" by force of which the end of the war might not be the end of our troubles.

We responded sluggishly to these quick alarms. But Charlie Hopetoun was a remarkable entertainer. He could dramatize anything that had happened to him and could spin so much fun into it that we listened with mere pleasure, discounting the crosses in the high, clever forehead and the monitory flash of gold spectacles that signalled the dangerous element (whose import touched us no less) in his stories.

It was in Eichstätt, Charlie said, that the moment came when he had "first suspected the Prominente racket".

One summer day he, the Master of Elphinstone, and the Earl of Ellesmere had been called out of their prisoner-of-war barrack "required" by a certain *Sonderführer*. Charlie was wanted first and on entering the *Kommandantur* office he noticed, standing beside the *Sonderführer*, a "sinister-looking gent in mackintosh, soft hat, and field-boots", also a man with a camera wearing a non-army uniform, the same uniform as Charlie had seen in 1940 being worn by a man in charge of a party of Jews going, it had been whispered, to a concentration-camp.

The *Sonderführer* informed Charlie that they wanted to take a photograph of him. "Why?" he asked and was told that that was not his business.

"But this is a civilian thing!" Charlie said. "This is not army at all."

There was argument. Charlie said that he had the "strongest objections" to orders from civilians, that he was a prisoner-of-war of the *Wehrmacht* and did not propose to comply.

"It's extraordinary that you should have picked out a relation of the Royal Family and a couple of lords!" he said.

Anger and yelling followed this shaft and Charlie "knew" that he had struck home.

Dismissed furiously by the *Sonderführer*, Charlie warned the two waiting outside, who then took the same stand. Asked if they would comply if "mackintosh" left the room, all said: "Under no circumstances."

Mackintosh did leave, and the argument was referred to the Commandant, Colonel Blätterbauer, that same close-cropped and paunchy officer whom Michael's involuntary portrait had enraged.

The Senior British Officer, Colonel Jack Higginson, supported the refusal, and the three objectors were told that they would go to the cells. That however did not actually happen. Instead they were sent for to the Commandant, near whom stood sentry-like the Eichstätt Security Officer. Blätterbauer started very "sweet, reasonable, and quiet". It was "silly" to refuse, surely, since pictures of them could easily be taken off their prisoner-of-war record cards. Actually, the new pictures were wanted "for the benefit of your parents".

"In the last war," Blätterbauer explained, "after the Russian collapse and the murders of the Tsar and his family a lady called Anastasia turned up, claiming that she was the Tsar's grandchild, the only one of his family to have escaped—but she never was able to prove who she was. We don't want that to happen with you."

At this from Blätterbauer the prisoners roared with laughter and Blätterbauer went "sky-high".

Uneasy days followed. Retribution more drastic than the cells seemed inevitable. Mackintosh was seen prowling. Eventually the *Abwehr* (Security) Officer said that he himself wanted the photographs "for our prisoner-of-war records". This being a *Wehrmacht* request, Charlie and the others felt that they had to comply, and thus the Germans got round their obstruction.

Charlie's supicions were thenceforth permanently alerted. He remembered that his letters always came in packets, letters of various dates all together after long delay. His father, mother, and wife were in India, vice-regally resident, and most of his letters came from there. A friendly censor, ferreted out by Charlie, admitted that the letters always went first to Berlin.

Instantaneously combative reactions, as in the "Anastasia" incident, had marked the whole of Charlie's war and captivity.

"Rommell came up behind—we met him on our way back— he bumped us." That was in 1940 near St. Valery after the blitz had blown up. Surrender beginning to loom, Charlie with a number of men made off, but was caught next evening by a German battery on the coast. Two days later he escaped with one other officer, John du Pree of the Argyll and Sutherland Highlanders, and one sergeant-major. Walking by night, lying up by day, several times trying to get a boat, they finally were picked up at Le Tréport in the inner harbour, a Frenchman having said that there was a boat. It was the middle of the night; a German guard company heard noise.

Charlie, who could not bear anything slow, had been doomed then to a torture of slowness as he was jogged with swarms of French wounded in a caravan of lorries, through Rouen and Tours, to a cheese-barge at the head of the Rhine. The holds of the barge were crammed tight, French generals and troops and black troops, no food, everybody had dysentery, vomiting over the sides, and Charlie made a fierce row, the first of many, refusing to stay in the "stinking holds"; and he and his two companions, the only English aboard, were then allowed to sit on a sort of roof-deck. These three, after a week in a "bloody barracks", were sent to Laufen in Bavaria, a barrack-like castle, where the 51st Division, having been marched right across France, all were. Laufen was "absolutely appalling", hideously crowded, and the near-starvation rations consisted mainly of rotting potatoes whose stench pervaded the whole place—men with gas-masks had to be called in to remove them. The German guards were at their absolute worst. An English prisoner was shot dead quite unnecessarily while drawing pictures looking out of a window.

Impulsively uttered indignation drew down on Charlie the designation *deutschfeindlich*, whose meaning "hostile to German ways" conveyed something more in sorrow than in anger, sorrow tinged with threat however and officialized by a coloured tab on the prisoner-of-war record card. As penalty, Charlie was moved with a few others similarly tabbed to near-by Tittmoning, which actually by a quirk was an improvement, a hilly *gemütlich* castle plentifully stocked with Red Cross parcels (objects of astonishment and grateful admiration to prisoners) and run by a straightforward, gentlemanlike commandant who instituted football on the village ground and outside bathing parties, on the humane ground that Tittmoning, once a bishop's palace, lacked space for exercise. Charlie knew that this was "too good to last".

It was. He was trundled away to a colossal hutted camp, Warburg, on the Westphalian plain, humming with nearly three thousand PoWs of every single sort of unit of every service. Grim and dreary though it was and the Germans a "bloody lot", Warburg was open with plenty of room for exercise, people felt well, they were fighting fit, the spirit was very good, there were seven or eight tunnels going all the time and a steady stream of escapes that included the "Warburg Wire Job" with improvised scaling-ladders, rated one of the war's best. Opposition to the Germans, purposeful rather than showy, was highly charged; Charlie sniffed the strong air of it, threw off the cosier Tittmoning mood, and soon again was in *deutschfeindlich* trouble with a new stigma as inmate of a hut distinguished by the Germans as the "berühmte Barcke" or "notorious barrack". The Germans felt sure that the heart of the Warburg opposition beat in the senior officer-prisoners, whom therefore they removed, following a line of thought conformable to them but less valid for others. Trouble increased. In the spring of 1942 the great encampment on the plain was broken up, and the different services were split different ways, the army going to Bavarian Eichstätt.

Eichstätt seeming "peaceful", Charlie kept his whetted spirit tuned in to hopes of more stirring things. He was excited by the appearance first of American prisoners-of-war from North Africa, then of Canadians captured at Dieppe. He missed the handcuff reprisals imposed on the Canadian and other Eichstätt prisoners, however, because he was doing time in a cell for having touched off the inflammable Blätterbauer whose satirically exaggerated courtesies:—"Guten Morgen, Herr Graf!"— were never long proof against the kegs of good German rage that they thinly covered. Charlie seemed sorry that he had missed the handcuffs. But soon afterwards he found something to fasten on to in the strange case of an English officer thrown into an Eichstätt cell, kept incommunicado, and not allowed to receive food, cigaretes, books, or anything whatever from the camp stocks. This was disgraceful; protests sped out to Blätterbauer, whose "Herr Graf!"'s and mock bows expanded with joy of advantage as he taunted: "You are prisoner-of-war and must hear only what you must be told."

Nothing could be learned about the solitary prisoner except his name—Alexander. It was in fact Michael, alighted there temporarily on his zig-zag, dragon-fly course through German gaols.

The new year, 1943, opened in Eichstätt with an overcast quiet. Everything had subsided. Squibs for Blätterbauer were lacking; he strutted and bowed secure, outrageous.

A brain-child of two English officers, Frank Weldon and John Hamilton-Baillie, was about to shatter this peace. Their scheme was for a tunnel 120 feet long to run from an entrance in a lavatory under the outer wall and the road that passed outside it and to emerge through a chicken-coop in the bank of open ground beyond the road.

The tunnel was completed after weeks of work. Charlie, one

of the workmen, was No. 51 in the exit queue, his work-mate, Charlie Weld-Forester, No. 52. It was therefore almost light by the time that they wriggled out, and they lay up all the day in a huge field of standing corn. Blätterbauer having had to report the loss of sixty-five of his charges, there was a kind of local martial law, patrols and walkers looking and beating everywhere, in the woods at night as well as by day, and movement became almost impossible. On their third evening out Charlie and the other Charlie, still only eight miles from Eichstätt, were caught by the German equivalent of a Home Guard with duck-guns in pitch-dark while crossing a road by-passing the edge of a village. They were taken to a Schloss, almost a ruin, with a grass court out of which a flight of stone steps led down into a wet dungeon-like room becoming a mass-cell as other of the tunnel escapers were brought in every hour. It was ordained, following a new Nazi measure whereby escapers caught with forged papers were liable to be shot, that some of the recaptured should be held back for courts-martial, but the Germans "bogged their evidence" by making one confused pile of the escapers' clothing, and finally all were sent to Colditz.

One day, while the Colditz uproar about Charlie still raged, Hauptmann Eggers, a called-up schoolmaster with manners of the treacly kind that makes pupils wary, came gloved and elate to the Prominente passage and made known with a deal of congratulatory unction that the Prominente, since they were forbidden to exercise with fellow-prisoners in the park below the castle, were to have privileged "Prominente" walks, twice a week, over a choice of five routes.

The news fell flat.

"It is beautiful country!" Eggers richly reproached. "It is rather like your Cotswolds!"

On a fine September morning the gate of the inner yard opened; the signing of parole forms was made ceremonious by the attendance of Colonel Prawitt, the Commandant, in long white dust-coat escorted by a *Feldwebel* and four soldiers with machine-pistols. The Commandant, after wishing us a pleasant walk, remarked: "Beim geringsten Fluchtversuch wird ohne Anruf geschossen!"[1]—in the same agreeable tone.

It became clear suddenly at the first cobbled steps that Prawitt's armed escort was really ours. Charlie stopped. Parole had been given. We stopped. Colonel Prawitt strode up.

"This is not for doubt, only to protect," he said. "We have duty to protect you against our German civilian population who may be angry—there is much bombing—and against your friends if they try to rescue you forcibly from the air. Both of these possibilities would be dangerous for you."

We walked. The Saxon country was flat and neat and not at all like "your Cotswolds".

Charlie, as if his thirst for opposition had been appeased by his strong draughts of the Colditz spirit, began to turn not less energetically to less controversial pursuits such as acting and producing. He had a flair for theatre and he could mime, sing, and create sketches for the improvised revues that formed the backbone of entertainment in the castle's ornate little archducal theatre. He could act too. In "The Importance of Being Earnest" he was Ernest. This play ran for two nights, which meant success. After the first night Lord Arundell of Wardour, whose cultural scruples were clothed always in meticulous speech, asked Wing-Commander Bader (the legless air hero): "Is the wit of Oscar Wilde in this play still vivid and vital? Or is it faded tinsel?"

Bader was uproariously enthusiastic. "It was written a hell of a long time ago," he said, "but it made me laugh a hell of a lot in places."

This reaction, backed by a Czech pilot who said: "Very vitty. The biggest figures vat struck me most was the ladies"—and by Canadian and Australian aviators who had especially enjoyed the tilts at aristocracy, induced John Arundell to be present at the second night. The play did not go down quite so well with the second-night audience, many of whom had been misled by its reception into expecting something more contemporary, especially in the way of jokes, a "Palladium thing" as one said. John

---

[1] "At the slightest escape attempt will without warning be shot."

Arundell, hearing this, crisply voiced dissent. "If anyone," he remarked, "says that that play is dated, my reply to him is—so am I."

The Palladium-seekers cast about for other argument; yet all, even the bitterest, shrank from availing themselves of an iron-head declaration by Richard Heard, that the play was "immoral", and should not have been performed.

The Prominente situation seemed to have settled again. Charlie, whose earlier thought turning about its danger—"how dangerous the Germans might be when they caved in"—had strained his calmness, was in active and serene equilibrium. Twenty-seven when the war started, older than either Giles or Michael (the youngest), he had the longer memory of a steady working life before the war, including three years as a chartered accountant. He was also (as we were not) married. That had happened in July 1939, and Charlie was "thumbing through ads for London houses" when, not two months after the beginning of his married life, the war came, a smack-up. We still tended to think of the war as a youthful experience and our reading and discussing reflected that outlook. Charlie, when he widened the range of his reading, was from the start more purposeful. He had questions; he wanted answers. He had chosen his life; the idea that some twist of fate might reveal new, beckoning paths had for him no fascination.

As nineteen-forty-four (how slowly!) unwound, our confidence rose and our calm was not upset. The great event was the invasion of France on 6th June. The penetrating of *Festung Europa*, while it continually absorbed and intermittently excited, at the same time made us forget, or else wonderingly deprecate, our former private fears. Energies, freed of their weight of anxiety, began to be used more freely. This was most striking in the case of Michael who had seemed content to pass his chequered captivity in a long-legged dream eased by cards and music and braced only by short bursts of prose or verse. He began to be up earlier, to read more attentively if not more earnestly, and was able to give a series of lectures on "The 19th-Century Novel", repairing with serviceable jokes the inevitable gaps in the Colditz library and his own scholarship. "Trollope," he briefly informed, "wrote sixty novels. Fifty-nine are good and there is one that I haven't read."

The change was spotted by the Senior British Officer, Colonel Tod, a pleasant and perceptive personality, who often braced the morale of individuals in quietly effective ways which they themselves did not understand at the time.

One morning as Michael in ragged, scantily clinging dressing-gown, hair matted and face unscraped, slipper-slopped across the yard with an awkward aluminium container to fetch hot water, he was met by Colonel Tod striding out on a brisk constitutional, every polished inch a Regular colonel. Michael and bucket flattened to attention. The colonel addressed detaining words; then grinned—"Good man!" rang out—and nodded and walked on.

Giles, who had watched this scene, twittingly questioned Michael, who revealed that Colonel Tod had invited him to be Laundry Officer. Michael was snappish about it. Caught at a disadvantage as he (correctly) felt, he had answered, "Yes, sir!" before he had been able to think of a single objection. In the event, however, Michael enjoyed this job. The prisoners' laundry, sent out weekly to a German firm in Colditz, always came back in a muddle, and Michael soon evolved the simple but ingenious technique of displaying unclaimed articles on his bed, as on a bazaar stall, and inviting all who had suffered losses to call and choose any article that took their fancy. Hardest to placate were several dear old majors who were continually losing monogrammed handkerchiefs, the objects of their pride and love, for which a khaki shirt or complete set of ankle-length winter underwear seemed poor compensation.

Giles from about the same time was involved by Colonel Tod in organizing dramatized readings of Shakespeare. He chose the plays and allotted the parts and a play was done at a time, once a week, with para-military regularity. He also secreted a gramophone on the floor behind piles of books, and when somebody said, "Louder the music there!" or "Music do I hear?" music, of an intendedly appropriate mood, would be heard. This was partly in answer to grumbles by Michael that the readings were enjoyable only for their organizer and were "intolerably boring" if you had a small part. Michael's best part was the Fool in *King Lear*. He had a light, happy touch, a note of "l'Indifférent" in his voice, and could play any Fool; but there were not enough Fools in the plays to stop his complaints.

Shakespeare, however, was a far weaker stimulant than escaping; and one day Giles in a fit of emulation and restlessness persuaded Dick Howe, the amiable and able tank captain who was Escape Officer, to allow him to make an ill-prepared sortie disguised as a packing-case. He was in fact in the case, one of a number in which a group of French prisoners, leaving Colditz that day, were taking out their personal gear. Giles, nailed down with friendly and slapdash enthusiasm by Lieutenant "Scorgie" Price of the Gordon Highlanders, cowered inside as Scorgie with a sharp instrument pierced the case to make air-holes. "Is that enough?" Scorgie cried, and Giles answered yes owing to terror of having air-holes pierced in himself too. But it was not enough and the pocket-knife with which he was to cut his way out was not enough. A headache brought on by being bumped down stone stairs and thrown on a truck by Polish orderlies who did not know that they were "man-handling" was complicated by incipient suffocation and symptoms of panic as the pocket-knife bent, then snapped. Exerting total pressure Giles burst the case like a baby crocodile cracking its egg and emerged into a breatheable world on the platform of Colditz station under the expressive faces of three German soldiers. Colditz Castle after the packing-case seemed spacious as heaven; and the affability of Hauptmann Priem, who treated the affair with easy good humour, was noted by the Prominente as reassuring.

The Prominente might guess, at night as they waited for sleep the idea might arise, that this calm confidence, and the various activities fostered by it, were an illusion. They did not guess, and nothing helped them to know, that the days of the illusion, as it was, were numbered and were already running out.

It was on a morning in November 1944 that without warning a new figure, whose very gauntness seemed like a herald of unhappy things to come, stalked into the Prominente arena. This was Captain the Earl Haig, Royal Scots Greys, only son of the great Field Marshal.

By choice this new Prominent, who wore silence like a dark cloak, went into the lone cell at the end of the passage that Giles and Charlie had successively inhabited. Then for days he was scarcely seen; we wondered about his white, thin, and ill appearance and his stooped height that seemed to carry a great load of captivity. It was Michael who braved the fastness of this newcomer. He had been at Stowe at the same time, though younger. At that time in Colditz armchairs were being made out of Canadian packing-cases (of the type to which Giles had consigned himself) and were eagerly sought. Michael fixed for Dawyck Haig to have one made. Then cautiously the new Prominent would manœuvre his acquisition out of his cell, push it before him dejectedly along the passage, and steer it into the double cell of Michael and Giles. At ease, with his long, thin feet on the warm, porcelain-blue tiles of the cupboard-high German stove, a book open on his lap, he would go into a brown study. He was not in any ordinary sense looking for company, it was rather as if the neighbourhood of people provided a comfort like the heat of the stove. He had no casually fluent or anecdotal chat. His isolated sentences were usually pictures, dark and deep in tone, of some facet of his experience.

One picture was darker and deeper than the rest. Italy. An autumn night. A prisoner-of-war camp near Bologna. An atmosphere of almost uncontrollable excitement that had been mounting since the British landings in the south, mounting with tension and rumour through the late summer of 1943 till "whispers of the impending armistice spread fast" and suddenly a piece of news came that proved them true: the War Office broadcast messages to the commandants of PoW camps in Italy requesting that the prisoners be kept safe, awaiting release, inside their camps. In Bologna the Senior British Officer passed on this message; anyone who wanted to walk out, he said, could walk out, but it seemed more in line with their military duty to stay. The Italians had promised to let them know in good time if the Germans attempted to intervene. The prisoners went to bed in their clothes ready for emergency. At 2 a.m. the Italians gave the alarm. It was much too late. The Armistice had been signed hours earlier. Since then the Germans had hustled. The prisoners made "pathetic little runs" to the various openings. They were cornered. The Bologna camp had been cordoned by Germans.

There had followed an "appalling" journey up to Germany in cattle-trucks, 45–50 dispirited prisoners to a truck.

Through that gloomy journey Dawyck held on grimly to some "remnants of pictures". In Italy, where he had been prisoner for a year and more, he had started to draw seriously and then to paint in water-colours; the Italians would not let him have oil-paints because they suspected that there would be maps in the tubes. Dawyck doodled, drew, and painted all the time. A fellow-prisoner had told him about a friend of his who had been a prisoner in the First World War, had spent every day hitting a tennis-ball with a stick against a wall, and had grown so expert that afterwards he had played at Wimbledon. That impressed Dawyck. He had always had a facility for drawing and had exercised it; now for the first time he determined to develop it into something more.

This resolution had made for him a stony upward track out of the messy depression of capture and its aftermath. Depression geographical as well as moral: for in Africa at first light on the morning of 20th July, 1942, Dawyck, "acting GSO3" liaising between the 22nd Armoured Brigade and its various sub-units and reconnoitring German dispositions preparatory to a night attack by a New Zealand Infantry Brigade, had discovered, as he sat in his tank with crew and two wirelesses, that he was surrounded on all sides by German tanks which were on higher ground, shooting at him from a "very nice range" of eighty yards into a sort of saucer. "Usual thing." Dawyck's tank was set alight. He and the crew climbed out unhurt but two who tried to get away in a scout car were killed. Most of the New Zealand Brigade were surrounded too and had to surrender. Their commander, the intrepid Brigadier Clifton, took off his badges of rank, slipped away, and got to the Delta, where incidentally he reported that Dawyck had been killed.

Debacle for Dawyck had come below the Ruweisat Ridge, ten miles south from the sea, fairly close to El Alamein, and three months before the great battle there. Following the "Cauldron Battle" of May, which had involved a good deal of withdrawing by us, General Auchinleck had set about organizing against the Germans before they consolidated and throwing out smallish counter-attacks to frustrate their build-up. That was still going on. Dawyck meanwhile under duress was learning a slower tempo, marching with the rest of the German catch, marching back "miles and miles and miles" to Fuka. Some men carried bedding-rolls and overcoats. Dawyck had his torn shorts, a thin shirt, stockings, and light shoes. The prisoners went on to Matru by truck and there Dawyck was taken out back to a battalion Intelligence HQ (Italian) in Gerawala. His captors had found out who he was and they thought that he would know "all about the world situation" and other more definite matters. Dawyck refused to answer, was threatened, and was told that he had half an hour to think it over. He felt that he was "in for it".

The half-hour ultimatum expired, Dawyck was thrust into a dug-out and soon another man was thrust in after him—a shot-down British pilot who however, as was quickly obvious, was a dressed-up Italian stooge. Now the technique changed. Twice a day Dawyck was called for to drink cognac with the Italian commanders who made a show of relaxing towards him, acting out a jolly impression that he and they were really just "aristocrats anxious to get together".

Tiring of Dawyck's mask of Scottish silence, these "fellow-aristocrats" dispatched him by "dreary hops" to Barche, then to

Benghazi, where he was put in a warehouse with no space or light. By now Dawyck had dysentery, he felt done for; the one ray in his darkness was the kindness of a soldier of the 4th Hussars who shared his tinned food with Dawyck and was very good to him.

Dawyck was flown to Italy to a big port on the south-east; a period in a camp in Sulmona in the Abruzzi mountains was followed by the time in the big Bologna camp, the cruel fiasco there, and the ensuing truck-jolt to Germany, where Dawyck was taken to Hadamar near Coblenz, a Schloss in the "Scottish Baronial" style, not very shut in, fairly comfortable, housing mainly senior officer prisoners and housing Dawyck for a quietish year until one day General Fortune, who was the Senior British Officer, called him into his room and told him: "Because you are your father's son you are going to be taken to a much more comfortable place." This "much more comfortable place" turned out to be Colditz.

Well before the time of his arrival in Colditz Dawyck had stabilized his prisoner depression. It was trained like an obedient dog and was under his control. Nevertheless captivity had affected him more severely than was common, certainly more severely than it had affected the other Prominente. There were reasons. One was the superficial frailty of a constitution helpless against recurrent dysentery and gastric miseries aggravated by prisoner-food which it could never accommodate. Then too Dawyck was a child of the Border country, his home looked out over the Tweed and its wild country and he had grown up out of doors, striding with long legs over the hills and far away in any weather. The sports of the country had been his pleasures: and his time at Oxford, with the O.T.C., a History degree achieved not too arduously, and clubs and more sport, had seemed only a pleasant extension of that Border background and a palatable prelude to the soldier's life by which Dawyck intended, with no apparent shadow of doubt in himself, and certainly none in his family, to follow his famous father's example. For three years, even in the Middle East, things had continued in this light. Most of that time his regiment was still horsed. Dawyck played polo. Then came the sudden moment in which everything changed.

The effort of adjustment, the acclimatization to shackled movement, starved eye, and uncooperative constitution, had exposed in Dawyck's temperament a sombre side whose surface might otherwise long have remained hidden. But this had brought with it, as if in redress, depth of perception that was sometimes startling and always interesting—as when Dawyck distinguished in a few strokes the tone of Italian from that of German prison-camps.

As gaolers, he said, the Italians were "patchy". The prisoners' quarters were cramped and the atmosphere among them was "rather bloodier", there were "bloody frictions", bickering about the food and other pettiness. On the other hand there were unpredictable let-ups and leniencies. Black Markets proliferated. Christmas produced wagon-loads of drink—grappa —and "amazing supplies" and a 24-hour "no escaping" truce was agreed. The whole camp became a bar, there was wild gaiety; an Italian sentry was carried out roaring drunk and an Australian prisoner did his watch for him.

Dawyck, seeing smiles produced by such a point as that about the drunk sentry, would look carefully from face to face, begin guardedly to smile himself, then, as if to cut the whole thing off, throw back his head, utter a snorting "Ha!" (relic perhaps of Bullingdonian nights) which was not exactly mirthful, and lope away along the passage to resume the painting that had become more expressive for him than speech. Opposite the end cell was a square of cold stone flags leading to a lavatory that had long been monopolized by a certain Brigadier. There Dawyck, straining his eyes in the bad light, would turn out sombre self-portraits in bitumen and Prussian blue that had something of the oppressive impact of Van Gogh's Potato Eaters period. The portraits that he drew of others seemed also to stamp them with the seal of their captivity. Alternatively he would escape in his mind to the Border country around his home and would evoke it in delicate tones that caused the passing Brigadier to pause and confer approval. But Dawyck, though respectful and courteous, was so deep in his own world (possessing it with the single-mindedness of an early illuminator) that he was little use for chat and soon was skirted and ignored by the hurrying Brigadier.

When Dawyck opened his eyes in Colditz, in the outer cell where arriving prisoners almost always spent their first night, he saw that the bunk underneath, empty when he had entered, was filled by a sleeping form whose youthful, ruddy face and look of peaceful health were as different as possible from his own appearance.

Dawyck's overnight companion was Lieutenant Viscount Lascelles,[1] elder son of the Princess Royal and the Earl of Harewood. Branded as a Prominent, he nevertheless at first seemed to disappear in the general mêlée of Colditz. The increase of Prominente strength to five had raised problems of accommodation: the Brigadier was ordered to displace himself, and basic furniture was lugged into another room in the passage suite.

One afternoon, in conformity with orders received, Viscount Lascelles descended to this room with personal baggage which methodically he began to unpack. For some reason there was nobody else in the room at that time. But suddenly this peace was broken by encroaching and masterful steps and there in the door stood a German officer, Hauptmann Püpcke, to whom, after he had raised his gaze, the unpacking Prominent said "Guten Tag" and graciously bowed. Then, however, as mildly he bent once more over his bags, a furious voice cried: "Warum grüssen Sie nicht?"[2] Horribly startled, Viscount Lascelles popped upright again and spotted the Commandant, Colonel Prawitt, whom Püpcke's front had screened.

"Ach!" said George Lascelles.

It was the only thing that he could think of to say. It was meant to be exquisitely polite. But the effect of it was frightful. The German colonel stamped the floor as if he would stamp it through. Then he turned witheringly, making contempt echo in his withdrawing tread.

[1] Now Earl of Harewood.   [2] "Why do you not greet?"

George Lascelles had a flair for touching off such innocent bits of comedy, a flair that seemed to arise partly from his ebullient youthfulness (he still was only twenty-one), partly from the fact that he had been captured only four months and was a skittishly unbroken-in prisoner, and partly from an irrepressibly sanguine temperament, a sort of reliable blue sky across which anger, pleasure, and combatively disputatious interest passed successively like rapidly sailing clouds.

Even the episode of his capture, serious though it was and very nearly fatal, had continually edged into comedy. It was thus that he himself saw and described it. It was also thus that he had lived it. The same story could not have been told by anyone else; if the same things had happened, they would not have happened in quite the same way. George Lascelles had the quality, as unusual as it was engaging, of filling out his own experience at the time that it happened, so that its actual shape was altered and made to accommodate the whole bulk of his personality.

It was a summer night in Italy. Lieutenant Lascelles was taking a patrol to inspect a road to see if there were any mines. The road led into Perugia, which it was thought that the Germans had moved out of; the point of the patrol was to make sure that the road was clear for British armour to go ahead and occupy Perugia. It was a "very routine thing" with no nonsense about spreading out. George had five guardsmen (of the 3rd Battalion, Grenadier Guards) and he was escorting a sapper officer who had said: "The way to discover if there are any mines is to walk up the middle of the road." This they did, there seemed to be nobody to stop them, and when George did suddenly hear a voice call "Halt! Wer da?" in unmistakeable German he was so surprised that he called back "What?"—and this exchange of courtesies was actually repeated.

Then shooting started. There was confusion, a machine-gun was fired, and George was hit by a burst of bullets that reached him in a number of different and vulnerable places. There was a clicking of rifle bolts from the invisible Germans. Then that stopped. They seemed to have gone away. All was still. Meanwhile George gradually began to feel somewhat dim. Curiously enough all his pains were in the stomach which, however (though he did not know that then) was one of the few places in which he had not been hit. "The kind man who had been looking for the mines" stayed behind. George thought that he must have sent the guardsmen back. The sapper officer forbade George to move. He held George up.

Around dawn hazy figures of one or two loutish Germans emerged shambling out of a field, motioning with guns. George and the sapper were prisoners. George was made to walk up a bank; that was painful and he reached the top in a rage. Eventually, while they were still sitting on top of this bank, fire opened from the English side and things started landing. Of course they were sitting on the very edge of the German position. The Germans rushed away in every direction leaving George sitting on a tree-trunk. They took the sapper with them.

Then English people arrived with a stretcher. The sapper had managed to break away and had reported George's plight. A corporal stretcher-bearer barged on with George into a farmhouse. He had a carrier behind the hill but decided that his patient was too bad for that and must wait for an ambulance. George thought this idiotic, but was too groggy to do anything but think. The corporal removed his clothes and dressed his wounds and he sat clothed only in beret, boots, and bandages. After about two hours of that the Germans arrived again and they were all prisoners.

No more tree-trunks. This time it had really happened. Yet what followed was curiously quixotic, even civilized, and out of it springs of comedy continuously bubbled. George was badly wounded, his large area of wounds was bruised and painful, his heart had narrowly been missed. But the oppressive and overpoweringly dingy sense of defeated constriction, that prisoners such as Charlie had found so hard to fight in 1940— that was not his fate. Scarcely was he installed in a Perugian hospital when he was noting with unconcerned interest that the

morale of the Germans—it was just after the flying-bombs had
started in London—was very high and "extravagantly hopeful", and was cordially contesting the assurances of a German
doctor—"Ah! London is flattened!"—discounting further such
outpourings in favour of the fact that the German doctor and
his staff were very good and helpful medically.

It was hot in Perugia, with masses of flies; a move to a
marvellous, palatial hospital built by Mussolini at Forli, his
birthplace, was soon arranged. There lay badly wounded
German soldiers, some with heads shot away, some dying. They
were very good, full of romantic chivalry, making signs to
George, offering chocolate. The bed next to his was empty, but
one day the people in charge approached him and said that now
he would have company because "an English officer has come
in wounded". They meant to be kind but George thought that
this might be a bit tiresome. A sort of corpse was brought along.
It turned out to be somebody he knew called Ivor Coates. He
had been shot up in a tank and had lost his foot. He was very
worried about his foot because he could not see how much had
gone and felt sure that "they" had taken too much of his
leg off.

Gradually and more or less comfortably, as his wounds
healed, George progressed northward. He had acquired by this
time a sort of personal body-servant in the form of an English-
speaking *Sonderführer* who was really a German clock-manufacturer. This attentive figure produced for George a green
German shirt and an abbreviated pair of green German shorts,
and was useful about getting him particular types of food.

The clock-manufacturer seemed to realize that he had to work
hard to live down the bad impression that he made on George at
their first encounter.

His name was Schmidtmann, he had mentioned this, and then
had further introduced himself by saying: "It means Smith Man
in English."

This ineptitude had put George in a rage. He shunned the
clock-manufacturer and in Mantua he was able to secede into

the custody of some nuns who were heavenly; they all might have been any age from fifty to a hundred, they were funny and gay and wanted to make life pleasant. They were incessantly issuing him with different sizes of night-dresses, an important problem because he had to go by their chapel to wash and often scuttled past in something much too abbreviated, whispering "Buon giorno!" while they were at mass.

In Bologna, his next stop, George had a little room and bed alone. A diminutive Italian boy of about fifteen, who was working in the great surgical hospital, used to come in to tidy. This boy wore a militant youth hat with a feather, he was a tremendous Fascist, and daily he crowed at George: "English and Americans get no further! Mussolini now free in Germany! All come right!" That sort of thing. One day George laughed. The boy got furious, drew a knife, a sort of scout knife, and rushed at him shouting: "This is what ought to happen to all you English prisoners." George called loudly. People burst in and restrained the boy, apologising most wordily and promising that it would never happen again. Later the reluctant boy was brought in to apologise.

Meanwhile where was Smith Man? Again he had fallen from favour, this time by negligence. George partially received him back into favour and consented occasionally to a game of chess or draughts, though he suspected cheating.

Soon the clock-manufacturer was accompanying him by train from Verona across the Alps. They reached Munich by the time it was light. Munich had just been very heavily bombed. They had to get out on a distant suburban platform and cross the city in a bus. The people were not at all pleased to see an English prisoner. They had had a horrible time. They spat and shouted. Smith Man—it was his last service—was very good and firm with them.

George was taken by train to Moosburg, and there to an enormous fluid hutted prisoner-of-war transit camp. He was wired off and not allowed to see anybody. Soon German guards came tapping on the wire. "Hitler's dead!" they said. They were in a state of bovine excitement. It was the 20th July 1944, the day of the Bomb Plot. The end of the war seemed to be at hand.

A few days later George was moved. He came to what looked like a fairy castle on top of a hill. This was Spangenberg, near Kassel, a regularized prisoner-of-war residence. He was there from late July until the old Armistice Day, 11th November. He had been captured only on the 18th June. There seemed no reason to be depressed. Good news kept coming through. George felt optimistic. Spangenberg was not a disagreeable rest. There was enough to eat and the weather was heavenly.

Then Colonel Ewan Miller, Senior British Officer in Spangenberg, sent for George and said: "You're going to be moved to this Colditz place. It's a much tougher place. We're protesting. The commandant says that you have to go there."

Relations with the Commandant at Spangenberg were gentlemanlike and he had agreed to forward a protest by the English colonel in which it was demanded that George should be allowed to stay where he was. However, the commandant said that he was obliged to refuse to give any reason for the order to move. The protest was sent and it made no difference.

George, despite the warning about a "much tougher place", had been so little harassed by his previous experiences that it took him a day or two to take in just how different Colditz was. Then he noticed that he had had somewhat awry ideas about captivity. But that thought did not affect his stamina. He looked back easily over his whole experience of the war. He had been at Eton when it started and then had gone to Sandhurst but he was not a regular soldier—"not even an amateur one", he professed. When eventually he was sent out to Africa, in the summer of 1943, the Germans had already been driven from its shores, and his battalion of the Grenadier Guards was left resting at Sousse—a "fig-grove and melon-patch" life. It did not go to Sicily nor to the Salerno beaches but in February 1944 was landed at Naples and began to fight up Italy, taking part in the battle for Cassino and in cold winter advances over the ensnowed Appenines. In all those battles George had been fully engaged.

The tensed-up atmosphere of Colditz left him untouched. As well as his natural reserves and resilience, George possessed the gift that was more potent than any other in assuring the equilibrium of prisoners fortunate to have been endowed with it. He was musical. Music was his passion. He had a clarinet that he kept in a box lined with blue velvet. Sometimes he would lift it out, assemble it, play a scale or two, and then put it away. He was not really a performer and fleeting clouds of disappointment would cross his face as he thought of the disembodied purity of tone that Goossens seemed able to produce so effortlessly on gramophone records. But not for long. What he lacked in command of his instrument he made up for in command of his subject. In the field of opera especially he was almost an authority. He relished argument. In Colditz Michael and Giles had dabbled in music and had developed opinions which they were unwilling to underrate. They voiced these. George replied. They replied to his reply. Then George, having bided his time, would place on top of their opinions, politely, earnestly, and deliberately, a fact ready in the store of his knowledge that exposed their opinions as untenable. The effect was heavy and painful in the same sort of way as when a horse gently places his foot on your foot. George at those times looked perfectly happy.

Chapter Seven

The Prominente (2)

A JUNIOR OFFICER in Wellington's army, captured at Waterloo after having been wounded, was taken before Napoleon. Napoleon summoned his personal surgeon, placed the captive inside his coach, looked after him, and was in every way chivalrous. Afterwards the young man's father, who was Chairman of the East India Company, had made in Canton a beautiful unique set of chessmen in ebony and ivory decorated with "N"s and imperial crowns and sent this out to "The Emperor Napoleon" in St. Helena with a thanking letter. The package was opened by the Governor, Sir Hudson Lowe. "I have no prisoner of the name and title of the Emperor Napoleon; I have only a General Buonaparte!" Sir Hudson objected as he sent back the present (unseen by Napoleon) to its sender.

This story was told by Captain the Master of Elphinstone, nephew of the Queen Mother (at that time the Queen) and great-great-grandson of the man who had wished to thank the fallen Emperor. He knew the chess set because it had been preserved by his family; and he told the story with a succinct, dry authority curiously suitable both to him and to it. His arrival in November 1944 increased the strength of the Prominente in Colditz to seven and introduced among them a personality that was to play a resolute, decisive, and quite possibly providential part in their impending dangers.

It was a personality lacking any equivalent to the obvious and distinctive colours of the other six. Its possessor, his impeccable turn-out set off by his dark military moustache, answered to the conventional picture of a British officer of the regular and more exclusive school. He could have visited, as he leanly was, a drawing-room, a crusty club, the Brigade of Guards section of a London bank, and even an old-fashioned tailor, without causing a moment's anxiety. All the others—Giles, Michael, Charlie, Dawyck, George Lascelles, Max de Hamel[1]—would have failed on most of those tests and some would have failed on all. Appearances apart, captivity had also affected their outlook and interests. But for the Master of Elphinstone, four years and five months after he had been scooped back with the Black Watch and the 51st Division from burning, boatless St. Valéry, captivity had operated only as a kind of deep-freeze, preserving and hardening his nature as it had been. The twin antagonistic demons, escape and study, had prodded him in vain. Escapes? "Just the usual old work on the usual old schemes, none of which came off," he said. Interests? "Just the usual round of PoW time-filling."

At close quarters (as the Prominente were) the blank surface of the Master of Elphinstone looked no less blank. His speech was short, his smile friendly but inexpressive; conjunction that might have been taken to cover something effaced, limited, and even timid, but for a taut upper lip and a pair of stern eyes. They were Scottish, as was the bony physique, but they seemed also to be individual; energy held in check, authority to support it, clear-cut judgment—all these seemed to lurk in them with latent fierceness behind the flat and correct mask.

The Prominente walks had become pretty sloppy. It was not that the guards were fewer, in fact their numbers increased proportionately with ours; but they had never got over the laughter of German housewives who had found the spectacle of tense, bristlingly armed men convoying a few shuffling and outnumbered prisoners a good joke, and had hurled raucous abuse about the distribution of man-power and the needs of the Ostfront. It was not the Prominente (as Prawitt had pretended to

---

[1] Max de Hamel, introduced later, was the seventh Prominent, who arrived on the same day as John Elphinstone.

fear) who were threatened, it was their escort that was derided, and the stung soldiery soon took to slouching and trailing their arms as if they too were simply out for a walk and were not in any case doing what they obviously were doing. They had roped us into this camouflage by ingratiating relaxations of discipline. The roads were bordered at identical intervals by nationalized fruit trees; notices at identical intervals emphasized that the un-official picking of fruit was *streng verboten*. The apples and plums that in season lay thick in the grass verges were desired, not so much for food, but for the giant containers that would fizz away on warm stove-tops in the castle and turn their sugar content into alcohol. The ban on picking, at first enforced by the soldiers with scandalized reminders about an official "fruitcollecting-vehicle", soon went by default. In spring and summer there were dandelion leaves useful for salads (vinegar being made from sour Colditz wine) and wild thyme which pleasantly varied the flavour of fried bully beef (though the name that the French gave to this, *singe à thym*, seemed only ambiguously approving).

We did at times look quite picnicky as we darted about the roadsides while our soldiers, sweaty and capless, sprawled; roomy old jerseys and baggy battledress, that had been put on with a purpose, became gradually a habit. Pockets sagged with chocolate and tobacco for working parties of shrunken Russian prisoners, since the soldiers, at first furiously prohibitive, had relaxed about that too; but often there were no Russians, the pockets continued to sag, and balaclavas served as fruit baskets while buttonholes sported posies of nutritious weeds. The sights, sounds, and smells of country life, as well as giving relief from the aridity of the castle's claustrophobic yard, had also brought out the amateur naturalist in Charlie and Michael especially. But this "naturalist", reliably excitable at glimpse of pheasant, partridge, or rarer game-bird, was otherwise fairly weak, not to say ignorant. As the five routes became familiar he faded. The vacancy was usurped by chat of a more speculative kind. Theories of Eddington and Whitehead (Charlie, Giles): aesthetics of opera (George, Michael): expositions as to the way in which

Rubens, Rembrandt, Vlaminck, Cézanne, Piper, or Dawyck would have treated a certain view (Dawyck): such were our topics—and often, if they petered out, Charlie was willing to tell the wonderful stories about tiger-hunting that he had heard from the great Jim Corbett in India and that he made happily farcical (imitating all parties including the tiger) as well as alarming.

The impression made by these walks on the Master of Elphinstone provoked, to the surprise and chagrin of all, the first of his sharp interventions. He criticized the shapeless balaclavas, the stubbled faces, the buttonless battle-dress, the torn gloves and jerseys, the caked shoes; he criticized the slop, the slouch, the shamble. His criticisms were not received kindly. Vaguely it was felt that the spirit of a Scottish Sabbath had descended—and that Colditz was not the place for it. This appraisal in fact (as became clear only gradually and later) fell wide. The severities of the new Prominent were not a zealous moral flail (even though privately he did have something perhaps of a John Knox in him and it made him less tactful); nor did they represent the conventional notion that we were "ambassadors" and should behave as such. In reality they depended on an appreciation of the Prominente position which rated it as especially important that the Germans should be given no handle to allow them to think that they were "getting the Prominente down"; that, John Elphinstone believed, would make them also think that they could do what they liked with the Prominente. We ought therefore for our own sakes to look and behave with as much dignity as possible. At present that was the most that we could do. But it also was the least and the walks offered a special chance. To throw that away, to go "unshaven, dirty, and mucky" and to give grounds for an impression that the Prominente "could not be bothered to turn out", was a mistake. The Germans would feel easier in executing any evil plan. We would pay.

Though the components of this picture were far from new, there was a new completeness in the way that it applied a clear understanding of German mentality to the practical possibilities

of our case. Its exponent continued to receive for it more kicks
than half-pence. The time to test his realism had not yet come.

Retrospectively the tenor of John Elphinstone's captivity had
for long periods suffered no unusual disturbance. The photograph incident in Eichstätt had scarcely impressed him. His
letters, by previous arrangement, bore no distinguishing
addresses; his royal relations were mentioned by nicknames
known only to themselves, a boy's name being used in references
to the Queen his aunt.

One day however a strange and unpleasing experience had
begun. It was the summer of 1944 and John Elphinstone was in
Eichstätt, a regularized prisoner-of-war correctly and gratefully
inconspicuous, when suddenly without warning he was ordered
to be ready to leave in two hours. An interview with
Blätterbauer, conceded at John's insistence, produced no explanation. Alone and under heavy escort—*Feldwebel*, corporal,
two soldiers—John was taken by train to Berlin; there he and
the escort travelled by Underground to an outer residential
suburb and walked to a "sinister-looking large house" standing
in retired grounds.

The *Feldwebel*, confident in this ordained destination, rang
the bell. Nothing happened. He rang again. For twenty minutes
he rang vainly, and he was about to turn away, bereft of purpose
and miserable, when a shuffle was heard and the door opened and
disclosed a wispy-haired old charlady in carpet-slippers. She
obviously was very much surprised to see anybody. The German
"officers", she answered to the incredulous *Feldwebel*, had all
left "because of the bombing". Yes, the whole outfit had moved!
Where? She did not know. Caretaker? Yes she was the caretaker
but she knew nothing.

The *Feldwebel* was completely nonplussed. A rudderless
man, a German without an order or a duty, he drifted back with
his charges into Berlin, where John for the first time saw the
point of the old woman's "because of the bombing". It was not
so much the big new bomb sites that impressed him as the "chaos
of disorganized ignorance" in the headquarters and command

posts. They went from one to another, a *Feldwebel* in search of an order, a prisoner-of-war in search of a camp; no one knew anything. At last impatiently a secretarial lieutenant suggested—"Take him to Lichterfelde!" Then the *Feldwebel*, his stolid, *Wurst*-munching morale abruptly revived, escorted John to a different suburb and into a sort of "chicken-run" encampment filled with prisoners of all nationalities, mainly Russians and Yugoslavs. A few days later he was pushed on to Kustrin on the Oder. The place there was a teeming hutted "gefaffel" of miscellaneous nationalities including eight British officers who had been in it together for some weeks and did not seem to know why. One whom John liked was a naval officer who soon escaped. Three were fairly elderly majors. They seemed sound, even dreary, yet the general atmosphere was puzzling, the whole set-up "odd" and remote from that of a regular PoW camp. There was a British sergeant who spent his days "coffee-housing" with the Germans and who after air raids uttered sycophantically slanted remarks such as that "all the dead Germans won't bring the armies across the Channel"! But that at least was clear, bad, and criticizable. It was the feeling of being in a limbo that John had to combat. The enigma of the journey to Berlin, the wandering there, the helpless blankness of the Lichterfelde and Kustrin Commandants, and the curious inmates, all created an impression that he did not welcome. Characteristically sinister was the time when some Croat soldiers, after having guarded a party of Russians to the Kustrin camp, were at once imprisoned in it themselves. John was grateful to the naval officer for having done something so "normal" as to escape. His own "normal" course, he decided, was to beset the Commandant with unremitting requests to be allowed to return to Eichstätt.

Meanwhile the Russian prisoners in Kustrin engaged his interest. Their cheerful spirits on very low rations seemed astonishing. They gave impromptu concert parties for the British, who were fenced off from them, with vigorous singing to balalaikas. They danced, having first made a floor by lifting doors off their hinges and laying them flat on supports. In this, after a long day as orderlies, they achieved an aplomb that almost for John conjured illusions of the professional stage. "Macaroni! Macaroni!" they cried with delight when one day some bedraggled Italians, scooped up after the Badoglio Armistice, were brought in. The entrance of these unlucky men seemed momentarily to unite all nationalities, Germans included, in a common joke. A Yugoslav professor, a man of charm who spoke good French, brought to John's cell a Russian officer, the only one in the camp. The professor interpreted. Understanding was limited. But the Russian officer impressed John.

At last the verbal bombarding took effect. John left the strange, bleak camp in the bleak countryside and made his way back to Eichstätt with the same escort. The mystery remained a mystery; and the return to normal proved brief, for six weeks later he was jogging off again—to Colditz.

This lonely excursion apart, little had distinguished John's progress from that of the thousands of British officers who had fought in France in 1940 and had been captured. Like many, he had skirmished before the Maginot Line and had been whipped up to defend the Somme after "the thing started". Like many, he had known the daily retreats and nightly actions, the diggings in and leapings out, the never-more-than-one-night-one-spot, and the harsh irony of waiting "under orders for embarkation" in an empty harbour whose cliffs were held by enemy guns on either side. He had experienced, with the whole of the Regular Battalion of the Black Watch and with most of the 51st Division to which it belonged, the parade-mocking formality of surrender, the startling arrival of German tanks from all round, the milling intermixture of small parties of a disintegrated French Army, and the "ghastly march" right across the north of France, through Belgium and over the Dutch frontier, to the Scheldt. Then John had known as one of many the transport by the river-steamer which he like others had come to speak of as the "Hell Barge"—a crammed black hole where, if you stood up, the space that you had occupied "closed" on you. He had shared the mouldy black bread, the long Laufen days "down to beam-ends", the interregnum of Warburg, and the handcuff episode in Eichstätt through all its phases from scowling discomfort to the last scenes of amiable farce when a German soldier would enter a hut, bid a cheerful "Guten Morgen", put down ten pair of handcuffs on a table and go out, leaving the prisoners (who anyway by this time had keys made out of sardine-tins) to put them on themselves.

Connoisseur of castles as camps from the inside, John rated Colditz as "nicer than Laufen" and he especially appreciated its capacity to quake all over during the big raids over Leipzic and Chemnitz to which he listened with glee. For all his experience John Elphinstone was no master of the curious distinctions of atmospheres. It was elsewhere that his mind fastened and held effectively. Strong hooks were busy behind the blank facade, grappling the fragments of the Prominente puzzle. "A purely idiotic bit of German psychology"—that stood out; and some sort of sense appeared if you attached a German assumption that the Prominente would turn out to be of use. It seemed probable that that was their assumption: they *were* being polite, according to their lights, and they *were* keeping us. Unfortunately this unalarming conclusion pointed back to the "idiocy" of the German logic. "Six miserable officers and it wouldn't make one bit of difference." The Germans would discover that. Then, John thought, they would shoot the Prominente. There were plenty of bad men and bad organizations; yet was the *Wehrmacht*, whose prisoners we were, as bad? That was not yet proved. At least the *Wehrmacht* liked to be correct; and could be confirmed in that by an answering correctitude, a civilized and impassive front that asked no favour and surrendered no principle. What was vital was that we should stay with the *Wehrmacht*. Of course that was easy to say; and the worrying factor, even now, was the segregation of the Prominente.

No one else wanted to grasp these nettles. Salon-like topics prevailed; and there was a new Prominent whose specialized interest enriched their speculative fare. His name was Max de Hamel, his rank lieutenant, his battlefield a tank, his specialized interest theology. War for him had not been a break with the past, nor a new direction in any immaterial sense. The symbol of this continuity was a Bible. It had gone with him to France and had stayed with him in his tank. On the night of the 22nd May 1940, he, the Bible, the tank, and the tank's driver, had been in a wood near Arras. The tank was wrecked and Lieutenant de Hamel and the driver were concussed (an effect caused by "several large German shells"). Next morning as they lay asleep on the ground they were woken by a smiling German soldier kicking their feet and pointing a small pistol as he said : "Komm mit mir!" Thus Max's captivity had begun. But that same day, while he waited in a German front-line position, confused still by concussion and with confused despondence envisaging a nameless future, the smiling soldier reappeared. In his hand was Max's Bible which he had salvaged out of the remnants of the tank.

"Those men at the front were exceedingly kind," Max remembered.

By the time that he reached Colditz, after the journey from Eichstätt in company with John Elphinstone, Max's captivity had amplified the overtones of the incident in the Arras wood as a sermon enlarges a text. He was acquiescent about his new status as a Prominent and also reticent. He had been asked in Eichstätt : "How is your relation to Mr Churchill?" Taken aback, Max had answered that he was a sort of distant cousin—"third cousin" would be correct, he said. How had they suspected? Retired to his attic office, granted by the Germans as a tobacco store, but adapted by the prisoners as a rendezvous for secret trade with the Germans (over which Max presided), he scrutinized his old letters and came at last upon a line of homely gossip from his grandmother to the effect that his father had "met some of Mr Churchill's grandchildren who are cousins of yours". That must be it.

Curiosity satisfied, Max put the thing out of his mind; and later the regime entailed by it in Colditz meant to him, above all else, unusual facilities for study and exceptional freedom from communal service. Colditz was small, highly organized, and at sixes and sevens over the encroaching war. There was no welfare and no tradition of it; even if there had been, the most altruistic Prominent would have found his efforts seriously restricted. The struggle between a social conscience and a studious ambition, that for four years and more had raged in Max, ended suddenly and painlessly. In the score-sheet of earlier victories conscience had kept its lead. There was the time in hospital in Coblenz when Max had acted as interpreter to a staff of overworked French doctors. Conditions were dismal, he had pressed to go to an organized PoW camp, at last he was going—the French doctors begged him to stay. He stayed. There was Laufen, materially miserable, morally amorphous. Max found a makeshift sanctum and in it wrote a "short theological book" (destroyed later when wider reading had invalidated it for him). Conscience attacked. It was tea-time and Max was about to bite into a Granose biscuit spread with butter and jam when a prisoner he knew slightly stepped up and offered him £2 for it. "No really," said Max, "I really cannot sell it—but" (hungry, hard moment!)—"but if you like to give me £2 for a charity you can have it." No sooner said: a cheque made out to "China Inland Mission" lay on the plate where Max's tea had lain.

And the subsequent hunger was virtuous surely? Yet still conscience pressed. Trained before the war in evangelistic work as well as in theology, Max applied to the Germans (who jealously managed every detail of Laufen life) for permission to hold weekly a Sunday evening meeting. It was given. For a year meetings (ranged under "Educational Programme") flourished. Discipline among the prisoners themselves was sketchy; when they received wads of back pay (following a delayed agreement between the warring governments that 15 marks should represent £1), German beer and "coarse wine" flooded the barracks, and Max, who preferred to spend his marks on food though no teetotaller, found the noisy company of "semi-intoxicated comrades" most unpleasant and once watched with amazed disgust the ascent into the pulpit of a padre who twelve hours earlier had had to be carried to bed from a canteen.

Meanwhile many who at first had crowded into religious services fell out as gradually conditions eased. Red Cross parcels were coming, and Max took on daily work as interpreter in the Laufen Parcels Office. There seemed nothing more that he could do; and now when he studied, cooked, read poetry, or walked down a passage to "gaze through a window upon the river valley and look at the mountains in the evening"—the Untersberg and Salzburg with its rock and the massive Alps that were most beautiful when a moon "lit up the snow"—he was left undisturbed by his harrying Social conscience, which seemed to have retired into winter quarters.

In Warburg it sallied out. Not himself a passionate escaper, Max felt called to the duty of helping the escapes with which Warburg hummed, and he was able to answer the call when he voluntarily changed identities with a major whose part in an imminent escape with scaling-ladders (the "Warburg wire job") was threatened by a German order transferring him elsewhere. "Major" Max, although he was suspected and finally was exposed by lack of an appendicitis scar, held out long enough to allow the transfers to go ahead without the appendix-lacking major, who afterwards was overlooked and scaled his ladder as planned. Eichstätt, by contrast with Warburg, appeared to invite studious comfort, yet it was not "happy"; a large black market was operated for private gain by a "number of gentlemen" (prisoners) who bought cheap from Germans—bread, flour, eggs, wine, sugar, in exchange for cigarettes, soap, chocolate, coffee—and sold dear in the camp. A man who bought forty bottles of wine for 400 cigarettes sold the wine at 700 cigarettes a bottle; one who bought quantities of flour for 100 cigarettes retailed them for 300. Such profits caused a boggling in Max's mind. He had evolved in Laufen clear notions, offshoot of his habit of precision, of cost and profit in terms of cash and goods; but they remained only notions until in the cold, under-supplied winter of 1943–44 an Australian for whose mess he cooked said jokingly "You are the cook, you must get us more to eat." Then gradually, after a first diffident approach to a German guard from whom he had "scarcely expected a reply", Max invaded the market and later he took it over for the whole camp, casting out the speculators and profiteers and running the entire trade on a non-profit-making basis.

Nonconformist though he was, Max's appearance suggested a different aura. His forehead was high and domed, his nose distinguished, his smile full, rich and secret. Evangelist, admirer of Schweitzer with missionary aspirations? More likely, it seemed, some lesser Renaissance prelate, young Monsignore in the outer ante-rooms of the Papal Court. Fantasy apart, there certainly was something of the Jesuit, temperamentally as well as physically, and of the office Jesuit: by such a figure might a heathen emperor have been led from astrology to astronomy, from astronomy to Christianity. There were no "ancients" in Colditz, no confidential counsellors. Scope for such did not exist. Yet it was for a role of that sort that Max de Hamel seemed to be ripe. He had the air of a chamberlain who was looking for an emperor. He perched in a corner secretively smiling, allegiance unfixed. Much of what he heard, in fact, was foolhardy philosophizing; and much of what he said was restricted, either to theological grammar that he alone knew or to the standpoints of particular theologians among whom two Swiss, Barth and Brunner, predominated. Their names were new in Colditz and their notions began to accompany the Prominente walks. Charlie especially, when his conclusions had raced from the field, was often slowed by a citation from Barth—or Brunner.

Colditz Christmas approached. Max baked a Christmas Cake for his mess. On and off he had done a good deal of cooking. But this was 1944, everything was terribly short, and Max's oppressive feeling of responsibility was aggravated by his acute appreciation of the value of the ingredients that he was committing. 1,000 cigarettes were worth £150, a four-ounce bar of chocolate stood at 70 cigarettes, raisins 50 cigarettes a pound, a pound of flour equalled a 4 oz. bar of chocolate. The cake weighed five pounds; what was the value (icing uncomputed) of the cake?

The Prominente looked blank. They had no idea. They were

beaten. Barth seemed unavailable and so did Brunner. "Do
we know," said someone suddenly, "if Percy [a newly-appointed
orderly] will wash our socks?" Chatter plugged the gap of
silence while Max with pencil and paper pursued his calculations,
smiling his chamberlain-like smile in which shyness and strength
of character seemed equally matched.

On the 5th of February 1945 General Bor Komorowski, the
Commander-in-Chief of the Polish Home Army, who had
ordered and personally directed the Warsaw Rising, arrived in
Colditz accompanied by five Polish generals and six other officers
of his staff.[1] General Bor, indisputably "Prominent", was given
the cell that Giles and Michael had occupied. The British group
of seven was concentrated all together in the cell immediately
opposite.

Even at this late date, when conditions were chaotically confused and hunger had ousted every dispensable feeling except war
fever, the appearance of General Bor excited the imagination,
as it aroused the interest, of the Colditz prisoners. Generals had
come and gone as far as Colditz was concerned. Besides, the
romantic career of this general was not widely and immediately
familiar. We saw only a small, quick-moving man attended by
others equally unidentified in a sort of flexible unity. When
John Elphinstone called he found General Bor seated at a table
receiving reports from his officers; he was reading with great
concentration and "Nyet!"—"Tak!" (no—yes) were the only
expressions that came from him. John was struck not only by
this reducing of speech to an economy that evidently General
Bor's officers were accustomed to and understood, but also by a
sense of the sharp clarity and quick firmness of judgment that it
expressed. At the same time there was no self-importance,
nothing remotely consequential. The stillness of the balding head
and dark Polish uniform had an effect that was ascetic and almost

[1] Generals Kossakowski, Pelscynski, Sawicki, Skroczynski, Chruscici.
Colonels Iranck-Osmécki, Sdanowicz. Captains Rubach-Polubinski,
Jankowski. Lieutenants Hermel, Wójtowicz.

monk-like. Yet the vivacity that instantly replaced this, when General Bor rose to shake hands, was equally striking. As General Bor stood talking and listening his lively eyes all the time darted over the other person and he seemed to be summarizing (rather than judging) with a precision increased by sympathy. There emanated then from him a quality, distinct from the effect of his beautiful manners, that was felt to be a quality of leadership not less real because its outward signs were unusual.

This widespread impression of General Bor depended very little on his part in the Warsaw Rising. Four eventful months were sufficient at this stage of the war to have effaced many things, however exciting, tragic, or heroic, from minds avidly attached to the main prospect. The Rising seemed already a distant side-show. There were also dim and uncomfortable recollections of threatening politics in connection with it. The Germans had said that Russian armies had sat ten miles from Warsaw refusing to help and German propaganda had built this up as an act of inter-allied treachery and betrayal and a symptom of the crumbling political unity of the Alliance. In Colditz, whatever the political views of individuals, belief in the military solidarity and might of the allied powers took first place. Facts controverting that belief (and thereby incidentally supporting the hated German propaganda) were not best suited to advance the man who could proffer them to the status of a local hero.

Yet it was, ironically enough, the unwelcome political aspect of his story, rather than the patient heroism of Polish resistance or the tragic gallantries of Warsaw, that first substantiated the impression made by General Bor personally. In the first place his truthfulness was transparent. He dodged no questions, all his answers were straight, short, and to the point. He defined the extent of his own responsibility for the Rising and described the Russian reaction while limiting himself strictly to what he knew and refusing to guess at motive. General Bor was of course a soldier; simplicity might be expected from him. Yet Poles by definition were political creatures; their very existence, poised between the magnetic fields of "London Poles" and "Moscow Poles", quivered with problems of corridors, minorities, lines drawn by British Foreign Secretaries—and no one would have been surprised if General Bor, after his experience of the Russians, had disclosed a political hand. At the very least he might have felt a bitterness sufficient to influence and perhaps to confuse him when eventually he was left with no choice other than to surrender Warsaw. The record revealed, however, that this was a man of different calibre. There had been no politics; there had been no bitterness. Instead there had been a profound and responsible realism directed by a sense of duty and clarity of judgment that never once wavered from the military course. Thus General Bor had out-manoeuvred all the temptations and wiles that had beset him since the morning of the 4th October, 1944, when, having negotiated terms for the capitulation of Warsaw, he led 40,000 men of the Polish Home Army out of the city to lay down their arms and himself surrendered personally to General von den Bach, the commander of the besieging German forces.

Wile and temptation went to work at once. General von den Bach, a bespectacled Wolhynian who looked "more like a professor than a general", greeted General Bor as if he was his "best friend" and there and then expansively invited him to dine at his headquarters on the Orjarov estate. General Bor declined politely but said that he would willingly meet General von den Bach in his office to "discuss the situation of Warsaw's civilian population". The German later sent a car to fetch him and was "terribly nice" while for three hours he pressed General Bor to order *all* Polish Home Army forces (1) to cease fighting against Germany, (2) to fight with Germany against Russia. The unvarying refusals were taken lightly by General von den Bach, who said soothingly that anyhow Hitler and Himmler wanted to meet General Bor and no doubt all would be arranged. Invitation to the highest honours and position was, it was largely inferred, intended. General Bor was then in fact conveyed by aeroplane, accompanied by General von den Bach, to East

Prussia, to a point close to Hitler's H.Q. in an S.S. camp. There during the night he was visited by two S.S. colonels who repeated the request that he sign a surrender on behalf of the entire Polish Home Army. These emissaries used the same tactics of suavity and seduction. A "lot of mistakes" had been made in Poland, they conceded; but now Germany was "going to win" conclusively, war conditions would disappear, all would be put right. They seemed no more inclined to take General Bor's "No"s seriously (perhaps his politeness misled them) than General von den Bach had been. At last General Bor had an inspiration. "Even if you successfully pressed me into signing," he said, "nobody under my command would obey." The colonels rose; and next day, instead of the doubtful glories of the supreme Nazi presence, it was a train that encased General Bor and carried him by long stages to the small Bavarian town of Langwasser where, on alighting, he was taken to a hutted camp full of all-but-starved Russians and Yugoslavs. Then began for him and his personal staff a hard time, cold and hungry, isolated in a special wire pen and held incommunicado except for unwelcome visits from a civilian Gestapo aide of Himmler by whom General Bor's intransigence was again tested. Three months later his party was moved to Colditz.

There was a touch of gratitude in the admiration felt for General Bor's inflexibility which had persisted in putting first, "in spite of all temptation", what we put first—and in a way that was not only that of an ally but seemed also somehow to have been an almost English way. Warsaw had been a lonely battle beyond reach of help except by Russia, who had refused help. When this story was told it was we who were excited and shaken, General Bor who was dispassionate, almost *phlegmatic*. The politico-military lines of the story, as he had seen them, were cruelly simple. He had commanded an underground force of 300,000 men, the Polish Home Army, whose anti-German efforts, including much of the actual liberating of Lvov and Vilna, had been lauded by Russian propaganda which at the same time continually demanded greater efforts. He had been

instructed unequivocally by his government in London, having
himself asked for directives when the Red Army penetrated
Eastern Poland, that Russian commanders were to be accepted as
hosts, that they should be helped to the utmost, and that Polish
units were to be at their disposal. The Polish Home Army had
then fought the Germans all over Poland in support of the 1944
spring–summer offensive of the Red Army; and when the
Russians reached the River Bug, five days' march from Warsaw,
General Bor summoned to his Warsaw headquarters the leaders
of all the Polish political groups including the Communists
(who had appealed ceaselessly for a general rising) and put it
for decision, whether they should liberate the capital themselves
or wait for the Red Army. Decision was unanimous for a rising.

No elaborate preliminaries were entailed. Plans had long since
been worked out for a general rising all over Poland and it was
only necessary to excerpt the Warsaw section of the plans, in
which all knew what they had to do without special orders. On
31st July, convoyed by messenger-girls from General Bor's
H.Q. to all units in Warsaw, went the secret order: "5 p.m.
tomorrow afternoon—X". X was the code-letter for the project,
5 p.m. the hour chosen because workers would be leaving the
factories and the city would be busy with casually unsuspicious
movement.

X-evening in fact completely surprised the unexpecting
Germans. With machine-guns, machine-pistols, and hand-
grenades three-quarters of Warsaw were quickly seized. German
strong points in big buildings, occupied mainly by S.S. who had
heavily prepared them for defence against the Russians, were
approached and breached more slowly with explosives carried
through the sewers.

At the time of this auspicious opening the Russian armies
under Marshal Rokossovsky had pressed their rapid advance to
within ten miles of Warsaw, east of the Vistula. General Bor had
food and ammunition for a week; it seemed certain that that
would be enough and that the Russians would in good time
enter a city whose own people had hastened and facilitated its

liberation. But suddenly during the first day of the rising the Russian front went dead. The sky that had been full of Russian aeroplanes was vacant. The streams of exhortation from Russian radio ceased all at once. For thirteen days this silence in the east continued. On the thirteenth day it was broken. The friendly, familiar voice of Russian radio sounded once again—but the words that General Bor heard were not quite so familiar. He heard himself described as a "war criminal" and he heard the Rising stigmatized as "irresponsible". Then immediately with fatal clarity he saw that the struggle must fail, and knew equally that he "could not now stop it". The one hope, he thought, was that the importance of Warsaw might yet oblige the Red Army to intervene. But meanwhile the initially surprised Germans, who at first had reacted only defensively outside the city, had brought up two Panzer divisions, an S.S. division, and a quantity of bombers. They did not actually recapture much of what they had lost; but they did not have to. Their bombing, incessant and unhindered, brought havoc to the half-million civilian population, now foodless, and increasingly buried in collapsing cellars from which many could not be rescued. British aeroplanes from Italy dropped supplies, but so many were lost on their homeward journey that they had to desist. An American promise of 100 Fortresses was doomed by the refusal of Russia to allow her airfields for refuelling; and when finally Stalin, after several telegrams from London reminding him that such contravention of the Anglo-Russian Treaty might have "politica' consequences", professed to alter his decision, it was too late. Warsaw was in the last throes. By radio telegram General Bor informed Marshal Rokossovsky that he would have to end resistance if within 72 hours he received no support or promise of support. He received neither. He received no reply at all; and when 72 hours had passed he sent two of his officers to General von den Bach, who had many times requested a meeting, and who now suggested, pleasantly if long-windedly, that there was "nothing left to fight for" and that Warsaw might as well capitulate rather than be completely destroyed. On this report from his officers General Bor overnight drew up his "conditions" for capitulation. The battle for Warsaw, planned for a week, had lasted sixty-three days; and perhaps the most remarkable testimony to the Polish defence, to General Bor, and to the blows that the Germans had received, was the alacrity with which General von den Bach accepted the "conditions", in all their unpalatable clemency, that General Bor had laid down.[1]

The protagonist of these events appeared in some ways to diverge, though he too was a regular soldier, from the normal character of the Polish senior officer as Colditz had seen it. He had experienced, after the military collapse of his country, the life of irregular underground war with its motley civilian base. He had shared that "terribly hard" life and he had shared the hope without which it could not have continued. "All people had B.B.C.", the forbidden, chief instrument of hope, and all were "sure of German defeat". He had known the nearness of arrest, the shifts of disguise, the false and precarious documents —"business agent", his said, travelling to "buy wood for coffins". He had seen his commander-in-chief, General Revetsky, tracked down and arrested; and when General Revetsky was shot in Oranienburg in 1943 he himself had been appointed to the vacant command and had gone to Warsaw, there to dodge unrestingly from one to other of the back-street, back-room headquarters given by the civilian population, and to organize with a staff of seven, who arrived one by one for conferences at intervals of fifteen minutes and departed similarly, and whom a second's warning could transform into innocent birthday-parties, the plans that threw against the Germans a partisan army three hundred thousand strong and that culminated in the epic of the Warsaw Rising and its hard tragedy.

---

[1] Among the chief conditions agreed and signed were:

(a) All Polish Home Army to have PoW status as under Geneva Convention—a white-red armband sufficing as uniform.

(b) This equally for women as for men.

(c) All Communists to have the same combatant rights.

(d) No civilian to be charged in respect of any earlier anti-German activity.

It was by all this perhaps that General Bor's sympathies had been broadened. Yet one also felt about him that the sympathies had been there already in the bed-rock of his character, biding their inevitable time. He had intended, after Hitler's invasion of 1939 had rolled all before it, to keep intact his brigade formed out of cavalry units which had taken part in the last fighting outside Warsaw, and to take it over into Hungary. On the way he had met General Anders with his brigade and they went along together. But on the banks of the Wieprz it just happened that General Bor's force attracted all the Germans at that spot, so that only General Anders was able to cross. General Bor disengaged, retreated, and looked for a different route. The quest brought him to the edge of Krakow. It seemed that something jolted him. He stopped in his tracks. He gazed. He suddenly felt that civilian Poland was being too much deserted. Somebody ought to stay and build a resistance; and so in Krakow General Bor began to do that.

The decision seemed to carry no weight of personal ambition. General Bor's character suggested the opposite. There was nothing in him of the ambitious Polish militarist. He had kept aloof from the "Union of Active Fight" and the "Pilsudski Legion" of 1914 (though eligible as a lieutenant in the Austrian army) because the military caste system that Pilsudski inculcated—and afterwards for several years imposed on the new Poland created at Versailles—was inimical to him. Such independence however was not the spirit that set the young Polish officer on the main road of promotion. Democratic views were equally unrewarding; and Bor at the age of forty-four was coloneling it at the cavalry depot of Grudziadz, far, far away in Polish Pomerania while men scarcely more than half his age, but of unimpeachable Legionary records, were generals commanding divisions and even armies. Colonel Bor was planning to leave the army. His situation was unsatisfying. He owned land in Galicia; but his colonel's pay was less than the salary that he had to pay during his enforced absenteeism to an estate-agent. It would be less expensive, he decided, to resume his life of a countryman—

and he wanted to resume it. His mind was made up. Other and
alien minds, however, were also made up. It was September 1939
and the *Wehrmacht* was tramping into Poland.

The battles outside Warsaw a few days later were not altogether the first encounters with the Nazis that Colonel Bor (as
he then still was) had experienced. He was a great rider. In 1924
he had ridden for Poland in the Olympic Games in Paris. In 1936
the Olympic Games had been held in Berlin. There he captained
the Polish jumping team. There his team won the first prize; and
there Colonel Bor, summoned to a dais, received the prize
personally from an enflagged and beaming Hitler.

Chapter Eight

Break-Up

NOW began a period of violent oscillations: hardship and hope, excitement and anxiety. The martial hurricane was near and its gusts reached the hitherto out-of-reach castle. It seemed to the secluded prisoners that they were standing under it, holding on hard with heads down, eyes screwed shut; sometimes that they were at its airless centre. They could make out the immediate elements, such as hunger, the cold and the news, but nothing beyond.

After the invasion food stocks ceased to arrive through the Red Cross and reserves dwindled. By December the prisoners were eating half as much as in June. At the same time the hard-pressed Germans cut down the prisoner-of-war rations, particularly in bread and potatoes. An elementary orange-coloured vegetable, fibrous and tasteless, called Kohl-rabi—anglicized first as "Cold Rabbi" then in a more popular version as "Chilled Yid"—became our staple diet.

By Christmas Eve (1944) the last reserves had gone, there was only alcohol (not much, because the forbidden stills made out of bits of the castle plumbing lacked their quotas of sugar, raisins and prunes) and any food that had been hoarded. One mess had preserved all through the hungry weeks a tin of chocolate biscuits, to be the *pièce de résistance* of a Christmas tea. The round tin crowned the decorated table, waiting its moment, its colours and lettering a spur to appetite. When it was opened all the biscuits were found to be green.

It would have been considered wrong, despite the torture of

this discovery, to betray a feeling, and no feeling was betrayed. British *sang-froid* triumphed. Even neighbouring messes, that had been jealous of the tin, were silent in appalled sympathy.

The German Medical Authority took alarm at the spread of sickness and the general haggard appearance and carried out a weighing of the whole camp which revealed losses of between eight and thirty pounds in every prisoner except one, whose unaccountable gain of ten pounds made him the butt of facetious suspicion.

There were no letters; tobacco disappeared, winter clothes became scarce, it was suddenly fifteen degrees centigrade under zero, and the German allowance of coal almost ceased. These discomforts happened to coincide with a dismal patch in the news. The German counter-offensive in the Ardennes had its powerful initial successes and the Russian front lay stagnant. Excitement had mounted rapidly after the invasion, the end seeming imminent, and many had confidently declared that they would be home before Christmas. Having thus suddenly thrown away the caution of the dull middle years they could not easily recover it, and veered to a gloomy opposite extreme, that the war against Germany would continue far into the coming year. They nailed their diminished hopes to the daily spectacle of armadas of Flying Fortresses and Liberators, escorted by fighters operating from newly captured airfields in France, that crossed the German sky scarcely molested by occasional squib-like bursts of flak, and made the castle shake incessantly when their bombs thudded on Leipzig or on Chemnitz.

Colditz lived in a state of siege, physically against the winter, morally against the bad news and the breakdown of normal activity. Games and physical exercise stopped; no one could afford an appetite. In the theatre, those who rehearsed and made scenery could scarcely continue and found that every job took three times as long as before. Conversation was reduced to irritable outbursts. Many shut themselves up in silence. The atmosphere was frayed, strung-up and exasperated. But some by an effort of self-discipline adjusted their outlook and calmly balanced the current discomfort against the improving prospects. One who had done this would say more or less "At the back of my mind I know that I'm bloody cold, I'm bloody hungry, and I'm bloody bored. But I don't care."

Thoughts about the future were tinged with a strange anxiety and emptiness. The prisoners had made terms, in varying degrees of success, energy, and strain, with the grotesque and limited life of the castle. This life was not such as to breed qualities responsive to sudden change. Even the most active had had to learn to curb impatience, to inhibit initiative, to maintain an unresponding endurance, and to foster sedentary interests. They had thus achieved (painfully perhaps) a more limited equilibrium in which curiously there was a kind of freedom. Expert in their improvized burrows the prisoners knew exactly how much they could do in them, better than they had known before—better, they now wondered, than they would know afterwards? The freedom gained by this knowledge was, or might be called, the hot-house flower of internment. The flower would die once the glass of the hot-house was broken. The prisoners hoped that the glass would be broken; yet they had grown fond of the flower—proud of it almost.

It had become real. When they first were prisoners these people were as people might have been who had found themselves living in the world before God said "Let there be light". There was no light and nothing that was made real by light unless they themselves could make something. The shock absorbed, the numbness passed, the soreness of self-recrimination endured, they had set about this, looking inside and outside and fingering the broken bits of existence all about, bits that looked like nothing and that seemed to have neither grace nor use. They had at first little faith in such improvizing, they were sarcastic and derisive. Then one day however, where there had been nothing, there was something: a tunnel, a brief escape, a language mastered, a story written, a prisoner-personality matured—or one of a hundred much smaller things, that nevertheless others also acknowledged. That day the prisoner felt that he was alive again.

The hobby, whatever it was, became a passion; the passion a
need; the need opened to his nature a new window. There *was*
his light; when it went out might there be sudden darkness?

General Bor had already evoked the anxieties of the forgotten
world by his horrifying, meticulous detailing of the part played
by Soviet Russia towards Poland. Prisoners who earlier had
blithely ignored an invitation from Richard Heard to hear him
preach on the Church of God in Russia under the text "Come
over into Macedonia and help us!" and who had flinched from
his dogmatic certainty that the Katyn massacre was Russian
work, now wondered if he had been right in his consistent and
implacable anti-Russianism; and felt ill-equipped even to wonder.

Like a Martian, Colonel Florimond Duke, an American
officer captured on a breakneck mission to Hungary to prod
into action the repentant but broken Admiral Horthy, stood up
in the castle and illustrated American schedules. Flights: 10 a.m.
Washington—3 p.m. Casablanca for "personnel in a hurry—
unless you have priority you're liable to be thrown off for important freight". Construction: nine months to make one complete runway (rock, sealcoat, rock, 1½ foot foundation) "in
virgin jungle, all kinds a snakes and everythin' fallin' aff the
trees". Roads: one in 29 minutes complete, for combat-group,
including descent from 60 ft. perpendicular cliff: "took a squad
of engineers to do the same thing—I don't know how long—
because we'd left by then." Next, a fable for *les anglais*:

"This question of ahtomobiles—I had to get an English
chauffeur in Cairo—he'd go about half-a-mile in second, then
he'd change to third, and every time he came to a bend he'd
slow up and change down into second again. I said: 'Listen, this
is a Chevrolet car, it's capable of 108 m.p.h. and it's got four-
wheel brakes—you can stop it whenever you want to—but
don't keep changing all the time you'll drive me crazy!'"

Colonel Duke's drawl was agreeable, his manner modest. But
what he said and how he said it were planets away from everything that had ever before been heard in the Tower.

All the debates about the war, the economic future of Britain, the history and future of religion, the significance of psychology and philosophy, the fundamentals of art and education, all the topics that had been ransacked to supply Colditz with intellectual nourishment—were they dust at the touch of this, by us, unimagined American speed-up? It seemed that they were—and that was enough to encourage anxiety.

The Tower society of the middle years, which would have played a straight bat to all assaults on its nerves and stamina, had changed by the winter of 1944 almost out of recognition. Escaping itself, the life-blood of that prime, had died a slow death. There still were prisoners, in the second half of 1944, who were making tunnels or engaged in the many subsidiary activities of organized escaping—keeping watch, forging papers, making German uniforms. But a sense of futility clutched them. Hunger was a deterrent. On 24th September, 1944, came the last and desperate attempt by Michael Sinclair, who broke from a walk, ran for a wall, ignored shouted "*Halt!*"'s and was shot dead just outside the castle. A lieutenant of the 60th Rifles, whose red hair and bitter courage had earned him the respectful German nickname "roter Fuchs", Mike Sinclair was a silent person; his lust to escape, which had made him the dominant figure of British escaping in Colditz in 1943–4, was unclouded by a single distracting thought. He walked alone, died alone. A funeral sermon paying tribute to his character and courage was preached in the chapel of Colditz Castle by Richard Heard.[1] This tragic and isolated death of Mike Sinclair was in one way a measure of the sporadic individualism to which escaping had come. As an event it was almost eclipsed, even inside Colditz, by the rolling, advancing clouds of war; and Heard's powerful sermon, with its emphasis on the leisurely traditions of a peace-time and public-school youth, seemed also to belong to things that were moving backwards, perhaps out of sight.

At various points on the up-curved long gradient of its mid-war years, the allied groups of foreign prisoners-of-war had been moved out of Colditz; it was an Anglo-German castle when

[1] Since the war Richard Heard has himself died.

it stood at the last steep ridge, in the autumn of 1944, of its war-worn trudge. The cheerful, aggressive front of the British was growing a bit thin after they had seen out three years. The loss of the French, Dutch, Belgians and Poles drained off much of what was left of British buoyancy. The undiluted opposition of English and German mentalities was not, though fierce, interesting; and successively new batches of British prisoners-of-war had filtered into Colditz, whom the spirit of the old Colditz had proved unable to assimilate. The majority of the newcomers, especially the large Eichstätt group, had qualified, like the old Colditz hands, by escapes, and they certainly were not enemies of escaping. But they had preserved a certain urbanity and attentiveness to peace-time manners such as hitherto, in Colditz' hammer-and-tongs style, had found little place. They were not fanatics; they cultivated forms of sophisticated banter that baffled old Colditz. Rifts appeared. Many of the earlier inhabitants, who had bowed to the lusty rule of escape and uproar, sprang back like bent saplings to their natural stance. They had been overwhelmed; they had not been won over. They had made concessions; none had been made to them. The homogeneity of Colditz was disrupted; and during one short unhappy phase, the old élite, whose moral sway had formerly held on serene above all mutters, took on the character of an aggressive and noisy minority whose characteristic expressions (such as imitation air raids) were freely criticized.

The Colditz spirit, though it collapsed by its own flaws, had effected in its heyday a dispersing of vagueness, a sting and stimulus of emulation, an abolition of passivity, and an unleashing of limitless enthusiasm for inevitably limited results. In Colditz the tough and the studious were united by the notion of fitness, if by nothing else. The direction of activity shifted; but in the intellectual field, as formerly in the physical, things that were begun (such as plays and novels and pictures) were not uncommonly finished, despite the rigours of the winter conditions.

In mid-January (1945) the face of life suddenly changed as a violent Russian offensive uprooted German armies, while allied movement in the west quickened, less spectacularly at first. Depression vanished; tongues clicked, limbs were galvanized, and a dash to maps—where is it? what is it?—set up hubbubs which over-powered, though they did not silence, the cold, distinct voices of self-control experts: "not really very interested I'm afraid"—"hysteria in the camp which I ab——hor." Book-making on the victory month flourished, and February at even money was the heaviest-backed. The rash optimists of the previous autumn maintained that they were on their guard against a second attack of optimism; it was clear that they were not.

On the same day a fleet of food parcels reached the castle. The brink of hunger was pushed back and this by the inspiration of one old Colditz hand, Major Miles Reid, who ten days earlier had been sent for repatriation on medical grounds and had eloquently bespoken this delivery from a transit centre en route.

Colonel Tod, the senior British officer, said to a parade as merry as a Palladium audience that Hugh Dickie, the British medical officer, had advised him that "every mess ought for one week at least to go on the full half-parcel."

"What's the use of having a doctor if you don't take his advice?" cried Colonel Tod, bringing the house down.

But this switchback winter had tricks to play on Colditz's happy tenants. Close on the heels of the parcels came one thousand Frenchmen in the most dreadful state imaginable, exhaustedly pushing little carts with personal gear that they had pushed for eighty-five miles from the east, the Germans harrying them out of range of the forward-leaping Russians. The British were not in good shape for this ill-timed moral fix and the cobbles pattered with mutters: "damned sorry for them, but when they start scrounging they're a bloody nuisance"—"reduced to hawking frying pans and dirty postcards for bread, poor b——rs"—"Marseilles . . . exactly what one saw"—"not very spiritual types"—"did all that I could for him; gave him one of my precious cigarettes". Such seemed likely to be the sum of allied charity until Colonel Tod summoned a general British meeting. When the miseries of parcel-decimation had been vented publicly by many voices, kindness returned, and argument focussed on the question: should help be general and equal or personal and various? Extremists of the first course, who urged that private hoards should be "cleared" as well as the camp parcels and "thrown" into the pool (Heard was their champion), were confronted by brutalists of the second who said it would be enough to "chuck in an old toothbrush" as had been done with collections for Russians. Heard's lot seemed ahead until there fell, on the proposal of an over-reaching Heardite that private tobacco too should be "cleared" and pooled, a jolly but devastating call: "SIR! HE DOESN'T SMOKE."

Personal giving mess by mess having been approved, the British braved the chapel, where in half-light the French lay in shivering crowds on straw, in quest of feedable guests. Ententes soon hummed. Hasty impressions were generously reviewed, each mess acquired its favourites, and individual personalities emerged out of the indistinct chaos of the one thousand decrepit evacuees. Soon this rapidly advancing hospitality struck a novel and wholly different embarrassment. As one British officer put it: "You've no sooner said goodbye than you meet them in the lavatory."

After the crest, the trough: the food was eaten, the news subsided. After sensational news any temporary halt had the same effect as, earlier in the war, continuously bad news over a long period. It was this moment that was chosen by Colonel Tod, whose finger was firm on the pulse of Colditz morale, for a talk by himself about his night in the trenches on 10–11th November, 1918, in which he described the uncanny effect of the sudden resumption of peace-time noises, "a man sawing wood", "the clink of a pail". These simple word-pictures, curiously calming and steadying, received a measure of satisfied applause whose sense seemed to be drawn out by the murmur: "just what one had always hoped to hear from one's own father about the war in Flanders" from one absorbed listener.

French chaos seeped deeper into British stamina when time-honoured quarters had to be shifted and squeezed to provide the thousand with living-space more suitable than the icy Chapel; and it was repeatedly intimated, in the furore and sweat of the moves, and categorized as self-evident, that the Prominente were "on the pig's back".

The Prominente had in fact done a stint of scene-shifting when they were being compressed into one room to make space for General Bor and his generals. It was undeniably however a light stint compared with the output and man-hours of the general run; and it was also true that the French flood had lapped only modestly at the Prominente door. In ones and twos French captains came to watch Dawyck at work or just to look at him. Dawyck was a fascinating figure to them. They had spotted with instant sureness in appraisal the quality of his seriousness. His romantic appearance, with the haggard, sunken eyes, was like some new property of that impression. They wanted to wrest his secret.

At first approaches they stood silent, inquisitive, even shy; but a bold compliment: "Le Captaine Binet était enthousiasmé de vos travaux"—sped soon in, and sweetly modest requests for loan of a paint-brush, and return of same with profuse, charming, thanking, led by tiptoe stages to an inevitable: "Quand vous aurez un petit moment—d'accord— j'y passerai". For Dawyck's visitors wanted above all to discuss.

"Il n'y a pas de couleur maintenant," said Dawyck, helpful. "Often when there is no colour one is depressed. And when one is depressed one paints the most gay and happy things possible."

Towards the end of this proposition Dawyck's French was not so clear as at the beginning, and the French captain (in his own language) replied: "Oh yes the camps are often just as interesting to paint in winter as in summer." Dawyck gravely nodded. The captain looked pleased; and an extraordinary discussion, launched on a misunderstanding which could only yawn wider and wider, developed with many expressions of agreement, pleasure, and esteem.

It was during this muddled February that Charlie Hopetoun began noticeably to overwork. He had as great a power of work as Dawyck and was very much more versatile. But Dawyck was slow, he took in a few things slowly, and always gave himself plenty of time. Charlie, in the circumstances of this Colditz winter, was too quick for his own good. He had just written and produced a play and now was producing Mr Priestley's "They Came to a City"; he was a master of humorous conversation who could be relied upon to switch on the instant from somnambulistic concentration to high-powered social affability and was in fact rarely allowed to stop talking. Now he turned his tremendous concentration and appetite for a subject to the study of philosophy. We especially discussed Whitehead, chief fascinator in Colditz of the intellectually inclined, perhaps because hypotheses such as that "mystical experience ingresses into physical experience" seemed to correspond significantly to occasions in the experience of prisoners. Unfortunately no standards, critical or disciplinary, were available. Notebooks could be filled, essays written. We might be intelligent as well as interested. But all that spun in a dangerous void. Eventually Charlie's physical system, weakened by the material privation, refused to tolerate the ungoverned strain that he had put on it. He fell ill and had to go to the *Revier* and abandon his projects and submit to the régime of an invalid.

When Charlie fell ill, Colonel Tod summoned John Elphinstone to discuss the general situation of the Prominente. There was nothing new to suggest that they were likely to be hunted down. Colditz in general still reckoned that they were lucky people "on the pig's back" and they themselves felt that it might be so and were scarcely disturbed even by a surprise call from a Mr Denzler, representing the Swiss Protecting Power, who was given permission to take the Prominente out to tea in a Colditz cafe. He did seem to hint—at nothing tangible exactly —and emphasised Swiss interest as if to reassure; but his twinkling pince-nez and avuncular sociability turned the edge of doubt.

Soon afterwards the castle was visited by a pooped-up German from the Wilhelmstrasse, a Colonel Baron von Beninghausen, with a mission to General Bor, essentially the same as all earlier approaches. But this time the terms of the offer to General Bor had been improved. He would be freed immediately *and anyone he cared to name would be freed* if he would order the Polish Home Army to cease fighting against Germany and to join with Germany to fight against Russia.

The Baron was also more pertinacious than his forerunners. Throughout three days he sought with unwavering suavity to breach the not less polite but impregnable "Nyet"s of General Bor. The Baron too, in the intervals of this main task, muddled about with the Prominente. Effusive to Dawyck, he professed to be anti-Nazi and "out to help". Dawyck tried to pin him down. The baron's fervour in currying favour did not fade—he merely deflected it to offers of subsidiary services such as getting George gramophone records from Berlin. Having seen all prospect of assurances about the fate of the Prominente skilfully dodged, Dawyck, cannily dubious, strode to Colonel Prawitt the Colditz commandant, from whom he could learn only that "Prawitt was trying to get the OKW to agree" that the Prominente should not be "handed over to the SS".

March went. A week of April went. Hostile armies were near the heart of the Reich. Surely now . . . On the first day of the second week of April the son of the American Ambassador to London, Mr Winant, was brought into Colditz from an ordinary camp in Bavaria where he had been a prisoner-of-war since 1943 when his Flying Fortress was shot down in a bombing-raid on Munster. This young airman, John Winant, was drafted at once to the Prominente room.

It was evening. The room lay in evening sun that came in aslant. The rectilinear shadow of an iron window-bar lay across a slice of earth-coloured German bread. The Prominente were bumbling through familiar occupations. Max was returning a packet of cigarette papers to a tin nearly full of soft-looking tobacco. George cruised in search of a record. Dawyck with unseeing care laid a wet paint-brush on George's open book. Michael (the Colditz Laundry Officer), asked by a brigadier for string to parcel his laundry, was removing the string by which his trousers were kept up. The brigadier puffed off grateful.

John Winant stood at the door, watching. He wore light trousers and a loose, zipping jacket. His hair was cropped and the sun made a fine powder out of it. He was in face and figure and in all else the Englishman's idea of an American college boy. Not yet the Prominentes' idea: they had not noticed him.

Bewilderment crickled in his eyes like breakfast-cereals. He advanced, and began to arrange private possessions on a top bunk and on a shelf above it, taking them one by one from an opened suitcase.

"Are you going to give us a concert, George?"

"Do you mind?"

"I shall mind if you don't, personally."

"Lovely! Well done!" said various Prominente.

A record started. Strings. Beethoven. A curious alchemy of sun and music in the squre room.

Afterwards the Prominente met their new member. They learned that he had gone to school in Switzerland; that when the war started he was at Princeton. He was quiet. They saw that he had charm and they felt that he was serious and independent. And that was that: Germans entered inexplicably and removed him.

The Prominente were undoubtedly a little put out. But very soon there was gunfire to intrigue them. Certainly something was coming nearer. The twelfth of April came. It was said that defences were being scrambled up in the town. It was said that the heavy gunfire, coming from the west, was less than thirty miles distant. These reports reached the Prominente. They were inclined to be sceptical about the defences and to pooh-pooh the "thirty miles" of the Colditz experts. But they agreed that the guns could be heard. It did seem to be a question how soon the attacking Americans would arrive.

The Prominente did not know however that that question was being propounded simultaneously by Colonel Tod. The setting was the Kommandantur and there the argument was taking a less academic turn. Colonel Prawitt told Colonel Tod that he had an order that the Prominente were to be moved. Colonel Tod pointed out that the Americans were at the gate and that therefore Colonel Prawitt should disregard the order. Colonel Prawitt regretted that he could not do so. The order had come from the highest authority. An escort was waiting. Colonel Tod warned Colonel Prawitt that he would be held personally responsible for the abduction of the Prominente and reminded him that the Geneva Convention obliged a detaining power to give twenty-four hours notice of any move and to state destination. Colonel Prawitt said that that was so but a division of SS had got into Colditz. If he refused to obey his order the SS would carry out reprisals not only against him but against the entire castle. Colonel Prawitt left it to be inferred that he in any case preferred to risk the hypothetical reprisals of the Allies to the certain vengeance of his own side.

This duologue was blown back later to the Prominente by John Elphinstone, whom Colonel Tod had summoned in order to apprise him of it and to obtain his view about a mooted plan to hide the Prominente in a deep corner of the castle. John had said incisively that he was sure that such a plan would be wrong. His chief reason turned on his conviction that the Germans at this crisis would be "pretty bloody". The castle was completely enclosed; there would be a breakdown search, the chances of not being found were infinitesimal, and it was quite probable that the SS would shoot ten Colditz "specials" for every one Prominent.

There was not much to discuss after these reports had come to hand. A gesture was made to the Prominente in the notion of a white towel that they would display at their window should they decide in spite of all to bolt for cover; in which case non-Prominente would rush about the yard and get in the way of the Germans. This semblance of initiative was bestowed with a sort of supplementary feeling that if the Prominente did try something nobody would blame them and jolly good luck.

An hour before midnight a German captain called Püpcke unclanked the Prominente door and gabbled from a paper. He looked miserable. Prominente offered him cigarettes. Nobody was able to cheer him up. The only person who might have done so—Charlie—had not yet been gabbled out of the sick-room. Püpcke's voice caught on several "Danke!"'s and he walked out broken, almost in tears. Could it somehow or other be he, not we, who was being ordered away?

Everybody liked the man.

Charlie came in. He was white and looked very ill. He had to pack.

Dawyck had pictures strapped to his back in a sling that he had made.

As to the room, a silent madman might have gone beserk in it. It was hard to leave letters. There was almost nothing personal that it was not hard to leave.

General Bor! Quite forgotten. He was marching out impeccable before his generals and juniors. A sudden wan catch of pleasure at sharing such fortunes with such a man.

Castle attempting its Van Gogh look. Walls light greenish-yellow. Potato-cobbles. Potato-faces. Prawitt switching boot. No good.

Prawitt mumbling to Dawyck. Promise. "Not broken my promise." Dawyck remote. Gaunt pillar of Border mist.

Calls from windows. No prisoner-of-war surprises. One nice little German surprise. John Winant? He. Merely came out of a cell. Merely locked out of it by German fat *Feldwebel* Gebhardt, having been merely for past four days locked in it. Now set to join party.

Püpcke, extraordinary thing, quite recovered, another paper, standing by wicket-gate ready for another gabble.

"BEIM GERINGSTEN FLUCHTVERSUCH . . ."[1]

The Prominente, ignorant of much and having been feeling confoundedly ignorant lately, *knew* that one.

". . . WIRD OHNE ANRUF GESCHOSSEN!"[2] they raggedly finished.

Püpcke this time did not cry. He smiled. It was a brave smile. He folded his paper. Smiled. Touched us to the quick. We went out.[3]

---

[1] Upon the slightest escape attempt . .   [2] . . . will without warning shot be!"
[3] Colditz was liberated 48 hours after the removal of the Prominente.

PART THREE

THE NIGHTMARE

Chapter Nine

The Midnight Bus Ride

IN front of the *Kommandantur* stood two ramshackle buses. To reach them we had to pass between a double line of soldiers; they were not part of the castle garrison and there was no friendliness on their faces. They looked greenish-yellow under the arclights, a black alsatian hung around their heels.

We bundled aboard. The escorting soldiers and an officer of the OKW followed. Colditz officers stood awkwardly in the background.

Then two motor bicycles started up with a roar and swung away through the gate. The buses rattled off. An armoured car, which had been waiting outside, followed.

We set off as if on some hellish holiday excursion, down the hill, over the bridge, and through the deserted streets of Colditz. Behind, mute upon its rock, squatted the tower, about to enter the next phase of its dismal existence. The church clock struck one—it was Friday the thirteenth of April.

The convoy took the Chemitz road and turned left on the East-West Autobahn. Nobody felt like talking, we sat passively, each with his own thoughts. The night air was cold, the seats were hard, and the smell of the *ersatz* petrol mixed sickeningly with the *Leberwurst* of the German soldiers.

Early in the morning we came to a large city through which ran a broad river. It was Dresden on the Elbe. A great moon, emerging from behind clouds, brought eighteenth-century buildings into stark relief and cast pink shadows on rococo walls. Then, entering a wider street, it became clear that this was not a city, only the ghost of a city. Dresden was dead, these walls were its bare bones. Only the facades were there; behind, as in a film set, was rubble. Three days before an enormous force of bombers had passed this way: Dresden had been gutted, thirty thousand Dresdeners killed.

We stopped for half an hour by a small park. Dawn came and instead of the expected orchestra of waking birds there was an awful unnatural silence, as if all the birds had died as well. Then, in the distance, a tram came clattering down the road. All lit up it lurched past us and disappeared round a bend. It was an early morning workers' tram, packed with silent people.

An hour later the buses turned down a side road that led through a dark wood. In a clearing was a cluster of small bee-hive huts, crudely built with sticks and hung about with rotten roofing felt. A few ragged figures, Russian prisoners, squatted forlornly about a camp fire. Suddenly through the trees a great wall of rock reared up. The buses, circling round its base, began to climb.

Then they stopped. The road was blocked with fallen masonry. We got out and were told to walk. Shouldering our luggage we struggled up a dolorous road: Dawyck clutched his canvases as if they were his sole link between past, present and future: Charlie, his illness at its height, was so weak that he continually stumbled and had to be supported. A German officer did not reply when asked for a stretcher.

Halting often we trudged up dusty scarps and through tunnels cut in rock. Then, at the end of a narrow defile approached by a wooden ramp, stood an enormous gate. It seemed to grow out of the rock into which it was built; from the heavy arch a gorgon's head stared down, birdlike gargoyles glared.

These huge gates did not open: a small side door led into a well of massive blocklike buildings: another door led up again on to a wide terrace flat and windy as the deck of an aircraft carrier. This was Festung Königstein.

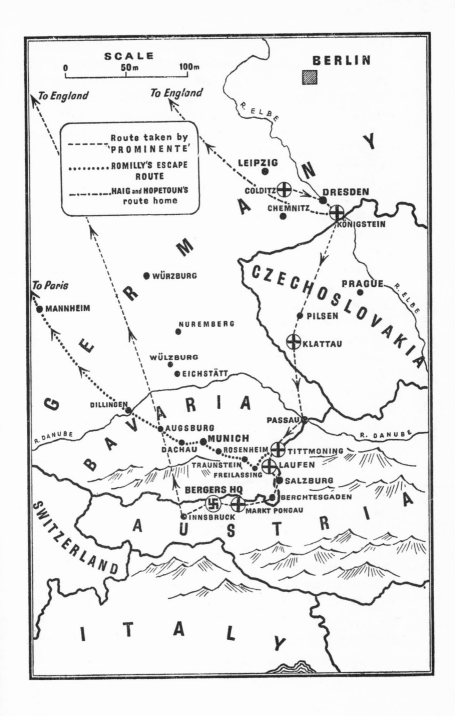

A German officer approached with "Please follow." A front door led into a spacious hall.

"No doubt you would like some breakfast after your journey," said the German, "but first you will be shown your rooms."

A soldier led the way upstairs and almost bowed us into a large, barely furnished room from which led other smaller rooms. John Elphinstone strode off, set and stern, to demand that Charlie be seen at once by a doctor.

We rejoined the waiting German and were led into a sort of drawing-room. It was furnished in the style of a hunting lodge; a log fire, round which stood a group of German officers, blazed at one end. The walls were panelled in a dark wood and hung with sporting trophies, a blackcock, roebuck horns, and a mountain hare, there was a chamois head above the door. An oil painting of Hitler hung at one end; as we entered an officer walked over to it and reversed it—face to wall.

On little tables coffee and rolls had been set. German officers conversationally approached. One of them, a Baron von Beschwitz, had known a family Dawyck had stayed with in Munich before the war; the improbable atmosphere developed into a sort of Junker cocktail party.

Suddenly the door was flung open; a German colonel entered with a grave face and held up a hand for silence.

"Meine Herren," he said, "Es tut mir leid, Ihnen mitteilen zu müssen, dass der Präsident Roosevelt gestorben ist."[1]

Germans and prisoners rose to their feet and stood with heads bowed in solemn and sad silence.

The Commandant, Oberst Hesselmann, took us out on to the terrace. On the ramparts of the fortress great seventeenth-century cannon, heavily ornamented with the Saxon cypher, stood pointing out into the beyond. Oberst Hesselmann, like a landowner showing off his property, indicated the view. The castle was set on a pinnacle of rock that rose straight up out of the valley plain; below, at the foot of 750 feet of vertical cliff, the Elbe

[1] "Gentlemen, I regret to have to inform you that President Roosevelt is dead."

curved in a perfect horseshoe. To the right was a toylike town with minature docks at the water's edge; beetle-sized barges moved slowly on the stream.

"Schöne Aussicht!" said the Commandant.

Giles, after this tour, asked for water to make tea. The Commandant seemed put out by such a request at such a time. Eyeing Giles, who was wearing his ragged old balaclava jammed down over his ears, he whispered to Dawyck:

"Is that really the nephew of Winston Churchill? He looks like an *alte Frau!*"

Dawyck explained gently that English people were very fond of tea.

The rest of the day was spent in a state of utter depression, endlessly walking up and down gravel paths in a back garden. We listened hopefully, but in vain, for any sounds of guns.

Next morning John Elphinstone was summoned by Oberst Hesselmann. There were orders for our immediate move.

John faced him grimly. On no account, he said, could Graf Hopetoun be moved. He must stay at Königstein, and someone else must stay to look after him.

The Commandant appeared willing to help in so far as he could. He said that the order for moving the whole party had come from the "highest quarter" and that it would be difficult for him to keep two back. John persisted. Finally Hesselmann agreed that one person should remain with Hopetoun until he was well enough to continue the journey. There was no point in telephoning for permission from Berlin, Hesselmann said, they would certainly forbid it; he would act on his own responsibility and hope that the military situation would develop too quickly for them to react.

John's half-formed plan was that he himself should remain at Königstein. But then he reflected that Dawyck, whose dysentery had broken out again, had a more valid claim. Reluctantly he put down his own hope and gave Dawyck's name to Hesselmann.

Leaving also Mittai, one of the two Maori soldiers who had

volunteered to accompany us from Colditz, the rest set off on a further journey.

The sun was shining brightly as we crossed the Elbe and entered Czechoslovakia. Now there were signs of approaching war: road blocks were being built by civilians and Hitler Youth, trenches dug outside villages. Air raids were frequent, bombers were attacking even small towns and low-flying fighters machine-gunning traffic on the roads; a guard was made to sit on the bonnet of the bus to act as air lookout. The gap separating the Americans advancing from the West and the Russians coming from the East was closing fast.

We drove southward through a country of woods and mountain meadows flowered with crocuses and cowslips; when we stopped, for a rest or during an air raid, it was tempting not to make a break for the trees and spend a day in the open air for the pure pleasure of it. Schemes to escape were irresolutely put forward and came to nothing; General Bor's view, asked and precisely given, was that we should more likely spend the day in a Gestapo gaol.

Late in the afternoon we passed through Pilsen, slick, shiny, and strangely undamaged—Central European rather than German in spirit.

Twenty-five miles further on, at Klattau, the buses drew up outside a large concrete barracks. We were led down bare corridors to a large barrack-room which was in the process of being evacuated to make room for us. Some Germans remained behind and slept at the far end but we were too tired to take interest in them.

Next morning we started early. Minatory conifers lined the route out of Czechoslovakia. We crossed the wide Danube at Passau and entered the military vacuum into which troops released from the collapsing fronts would soon be pouring. We passed lorries carrying V weapons—they were heading south.

In the late evening we came to a river spanned by a fine bridge emblazoned with great coloured coats of arms. It was the Salzach, beyond was Austria.

The buses stopped at an enormous blocklike building. John Elphinstone, who had been dozing, woke with a start.

"Laufen!" he cried. "Have we come all this way to fetch up here?" He and Max remembered the dreary days they had spent there when first taken prisoner. But Laufen was an Oflag no longer; a white notice board indicated in black letters that it was an "ILAG", concentration camp for civilian internees. The OKW officer ordered us out of the bus.

John Elphinstone grasped that the moment was critical. If we entered this place we should no longer be under the reasonably correct control of the Wehrmacht but at the mercy of less responsible groups. Peremptorily, as if he were in command of Germans and British alike, he refused either to leave the bus himself, or to allow anyone else to leave.

Other Germans had by now arrived and the order was repeated. Then John went white with rage, and began to lash them in their own language and style. On no account, he said, would his party stay in a civilian camp. Anyone who tried to make them would suffer for it after the war.

"Wir sind englische Offiziere," he said, "und müssen als englische Offiziere behandelt werden!"[1]

Giles felt a sudden terror that the Germans would seize on the point that he was a civilian. He begged John to insist that he was not left behind. John nodded fiercely.

The weight of John's anger and authority acting on German respect for the letter of the law had caused a waver. The Germans went away. They came back. There was a second encounter of insults. German confabulations hurriedly developed, telephone calls were made. Then scowling the escorting officer climbed back into the bus and slammed the door. We drove away.

Mile after mile, not a word was spoken. Far up the valley the climbing buses turned off the main road. A castle stood on a hilltop above a village. We crossed a bridge over a ravine and

[1] "We are English officers and we must as English officers be treated."

entered a courtyard. It was late, we were tired: wherever we had come to there could be no repetition of the previous scene.

We had come to the castle of Tittmoning, near the Austro-Bavarian frontier, inhabited by Dutch officer prisoners. Next morning, clearly visible from the window, was a great mountain range reaching up into the clouds—the Alps. Hazy on the distant plain Salzburg lay in a pool of gold.

The Dutch officers, staid, sedate, and in many cases elderly, could not absorb our anxiety. We visited their messes, they gave concerts; they were kind. But most of the time we stood about in depressed consultations on the nagging theme—our further move to the south. Anxiety fed anxiety—until one Dutch officer broke through our stagnant depression and helped to resolve our crisis. Captain Van den Heuvel, famed organizer of escapes, banished from Colditz for his many successes, was kicking his heels in Tittmoning. He had plans. He had not been idle here among his disciplined but more sedentary compatriots. He had reconnoitred an escape route and had constructed a hide, intending that both should be reserved for an occasion of great emergency. To him, our situation was such an emergency. Three people, he said, could attempt his way out, a descent down the castle wall by rope. Giles, who had known Van den Heuvel at Colditz, and had great confidence in him, wanted to go. Two Dutch officers, from among the few young ones in the place, were appointed to go with Giles. On the same night the other British Prominente would go to ground in the hide. The Germans would find evidence of an escape over the wall and would assume, it could reasonably be hoped, that the whole group had thus got away.

Chapter Ten

The End of the Reich

Giles Romilly

VANDY and his assistants had made a camera with which they took, developed, and printed unimpeachable passport-size photographs to be attached to the bottom left corner of the essential *Ausweis* (police-pass), also hand-forged. In such work, without which nobody could have moved a step, they were extraordinarily ingenious as well as thorough and accurate. Vandy also provided us with a plausible story. We were foreign workers—two Dutch, one French—employed on the inspection and maintenance of a complicated type of baking machinery. A letter from our employers, odiously realistic in its Teutonic script and style, supplemented the *Ausweis*, and specified that our duties required us to pass through many Bavarian towns, including Munich, where these machines were installed. The chief defect in our equipment was clothing; I had a converted beret and zipped corduroy jacket, which were all right, but my trousers were obviously military.

I was very much scared when it was intimated that I ought to be lending a hand in the making of a rope, by which we were to descend from the castle's ramparts; not through unwillingness to help but because I was certain that any bit of the rope that I had made would inevitably break and drop us, or one of us, into the moat. I had heard that the total drop was about ninety feet. Throughout the day that the rope was being made I kept myself sequestered. In the afternoon, fortunately, a concert of chamber works by Mozart and Schubert was being given by a quartet of Dutch officers. The large hall was cold and draughty, the great-coated audience small, smoking forbidden; listening in some discomfort to a performance of "Death and the Maiden" I suddenly heard a door creak as if embarrassed. There stood Michael. I knew who he was looking for and why he fixed me with a hard, meaning look. But I pretended to be in another sphere, utterly enclosed by the music; and Michael's feeling for concert proprieties was too acute to allow him to make a scene. Afterwards he told me that all of our group had been set to work on the rope. None of them had been too pleased about it. I did not want to look at the rope and did not ask what it was made of.

Then it was evening. Along one side of Tittmoning Castle there was a path inside and closely underneath the rampart. The path was a promenade for the Dutch officers who went to and fro in couples, smartly dressed, chatting seriously. But when darkness loomed the gate between this path and the main interior of the castle was bolted and locked. A sentry was posted on the gate and everybody had to be inside. We strolled with the strollers. A whistle blew, ordering return and preluding a camouflage of confusion and twilight as prisoners-of-war surged towards the gate, German guards acting as sheep-dogs. We then, jostling as normally as possible, edged sideward to a strip of shallow ditch scooped between path and wall. We reached it and lay down flat, head to foot, like a string of sausages. A small tree, growing out of the embankment of the wall, added its dark umbrella to our concealment.

Silence.

We waited for night and moon. We waited for about four hours. Cramps set in. It was cold. Movement and speech were forbidden. A cigarette could not be smoked. Discomfort apart, my nerves were subdued by confidence in the planning of Captain van den Heuvel, whose precise strategy governed every move.

It was Vandy and his assistant, a tall, youthful Dutch lieutenant, who scrambled to the tree and made the rope fast. Then the first of my Dutch companions crawled up the embankment and disappeared. I did not see what happened at the top, nor did I want to. There seemed to be shocking crashes as of boulders dislodged. The figures of the two Dutch organizers rose in vertical silhouette like shadows on a lighted wall. I got up to them, and in a moment—by what clumsy method and restraining help I could not tell—my legs were on the outside of the wall, hanging free, my hands were clutching its gritty top; my teeth held the handle of a tiny suitcase.

This had been as quick as an execution. I was facing inward towards the hands of the Dutchmen and the immediate safety of the castle. But going over the wall I had seen, riding high, a moon of brilliant power and size whose light reached far, far down to the base of the cliff on which the castle stood. In this light the cliff, curving slightly outward as it dropped, looked like the landscape of an alarming dream.

A new figure suddenly appeared on the ramparts within breathing distance. It was a man. He stared at me. He took in the two Dutch figures. He stood stock still, staring.

It was during the shock following this apparition that I noticed for the first time a tiny squarish hut perched like a bird-box on the rampart close to where we were and out of which the figure must have come.

"Was ist los?" he said. ("What's going on?")

The voice was neutral, interested, backward on the uptake. This was an undersized, elderly German guard, whose belt sagged, whose rifle seemed to be in his way. The way he stood, chin tucked into one shoulder, suggested a comfortable and wary sparrow, equipped to approach but not sure of its welcome.

These impressions, unexpected and verging on the fantastic, gave me an idea. Clamping one arm over the parapet I pushed the other hand over to a pocket and pulled out a packet of cigarettes and passed it to one of the Dutch officers while making a meaning gesture towards the guard.

The Dutchman offered the packet. The guard shook his head. Suddenly he sidled back to his box; vanished. There was nothing aggressive about his movements. He had not said another word.

We held a consultation on the parapet. The Dutchmen said that any second now the alarm would be given, there would be sirens, searchlights, dogs, shooting, road patrols; they said that there would be no point in going on as success would be out of the question, therefore I had better come back. Come back! I knew they were right.

"I don't want to come back" I said, feebly.

The helpers hesitated.

"If you are prepared to take a chance . . ."

I nodded.

"Well—good luck."

The handcase, freed during these parleys, was put back between my teeth. I got both hands on the rope.

The way to go down a rope, Vandy had told me, is to get hold of it with your feet as well as your hands. Like that you control your movement, you can go down slowly. Like that I meant to go. Unfortunately I did not succeed. While still getting the hang of the thing I discovered that my body (sheer deadweight) had begun to whizz. This scared me. Moon, castle, space, whirled in one bowl. The case flew out of my teeth. I heard it rocketing far down. My hands were being shaved as if by razor-blades, and the discomfort of this was so noticeable that only terror was able to persuade me to leave them where they were. Utterly ignorant how long I still had to whizz (fathomless miles it already seemed), shredded down to a prayer for survival, suddenly I felt a merciful bump.

I rolled. Silence. Then a hiss; out of a bush-clump loped, head down, my fellow-escaper, the first man down the rope. Quickly I whispered to him what had happened up above, and said that I was almost certain that the third escaper would not be able to appear. He had a luminous watch. We decided to wait five minutes. We waited. Nothing. The waiting made us palpitate; my companion had had longer of it and he was shivering. Released by the luminous hand, we shot away like startled rabbits.

The ground sloped upward as it left the base of the castle, and we had to get over a netted fence in front of a moonstruck cottage. But that was nothing. Scrambling beyond, abruptly we found ourselves on a road.

Holding a compass as tiny and miraculous as a wren's eye on his open palm, my companion took bearings and said that we ought to strike south, towards Salzburg.

We tore along the road, expecting that at every instant the peace of the night would be ripped by indignant furies howling for our recapture. We could feel them in our backs: paralyzing lights, lacerating dogs, shots pricking all over. In fact, the peace of the night amazed us. It was beyond reasonable hope. A long time passed, long ribbons of empty road rushed through our feet, before either would dare to believe in it. But suddenly we both stopped on a common impulse. It was true. In the whole night there was not a sound.

We set off again, going fast still but not so desperately. At a knot of roads on the edge of a village my companion stopped to consult the compass. While he was peering at it the compass vanished. Then we noticed a gridded grate in the road, exactly where he had been standing. There could be no doubt where the compass had gone. My companion, as he was more knowledgeable, was also more upset than I. He rallied, and made some expert gestures at the stars, with which the sky was crowded. We went through the village, our marching steps sounding terribly loud. The village never stirred in its sleep. Out in the country, a buoyant hopefulness surged through us.

Our companionship had started at the bottom of the castle wall. As fellow-prisoners we had not even met; and since the escape we had continued as intimate strangers, sharing nothing except the urge to keep on escaping. Now we relaxed. I learned his name—André Tielemann, lieutenant in the Dutch Colonial Army. We smoked. I felt for the first time that I had escaped. It was a glorious feeling. Every movement was a joy. I felt incapable of fatigue and was free of any thought of food or drink; my appetites were busy elsewhere, gorging themselves on fresh air, space, the beauty of the lake-like landscape. It was the night of 20th April. I remembered that this was Hitler's birthday. I did not know that it was his last.

On a high stretch of road, besieged by dark forests, my companion suddenly stopped dead.

"In certain situations" he said, "I am the commandant. We will now go and rest in the wood."

I am short. André, if anything, was shorter. He could not impose his will. I said that he was not the commandant. I disagreed vehemently with him that we ought to stop and rest. My view prevailed and we trudged on, silenced and surprised by our disagreement. It was the first of many.

As we were going through a village two uniformed figures came silently upon us. It was still the dead middle of the early hours. The patrolmen scrutinized us, blocking the road, and asked for papers. I produced mine silently, my spirit sinking. Suddenly I realized that André was chatting with the men. Gone was his languor; and he was performing with brilliant casualness, pocketing his false papers as indifferently as if they were bus tickets, shrugging and smiling, all in easy motions that I now covertly copied. Another moment, and cigarettes were being shared.

"What has your friend done to his hands?"

I quaked but need not have done. André said something in a tone that suggested that the point was really too trivial to have been raised. We were sent on our way with courtesies. As soon as we were well out of sight I hit André on the back and beamed. The encounter had inspired him with new zest; not only had he killed the suspicions of the patrolmen, he had also, as he now said with chuckles, got useful information from them.

"We must get to Traunstein," he said. "There will be a train going there from Freilassing, which is at the end of this road. From Traunstein we shall be able to go on to Munich."

Our confidence soared. It seemed that there could not have been any general alarm about the escape—or at least that it could not have got as far as we had. The false papers, having triumphed

at their first test, seemed now to be powerful protectors. We had
the cordial pleasure of acknowledging, each at the same time,
that we had begun to feel tired. I was feeling pain in my rope-
torn hands, which looked as though they had been ploughed up.
Light dawned as we trudged. On a misted field a peacock spread
its feathers like rain in a rainbow. It was early morning when we
reached the edge of Freilassing, having walked about twenty-
five miles.

Sirens were wailing. We took scanty shelter in a rough patch
of public ground full of natural dips and ditches. Townspeople
streamed to it and nobody took any notice of anybody else. The
noise of aeroplanes and the intermittent but persistent crumps of
bombs seemed to go on for an age. There was no defending fire.
A fatalistic spirit, an air of desperate holiday, reigned in the park.
We absorbed a bit of it and soon began to behave with a careless
confidence magnified by fatigue.

I had my hands disinfected and bandaged by a white-coated
Mädchen in a chemist's, who advised me to see a doctor in case
of blood-poisoning. She wrote down the name and address of
one, and André and I trudged along to his detached house in the
outskirts of the town. The doctor did an injection. He looked
strangely at us but seemed unwilling to put himself out to take
particulars; and we were too weary to bother. Back in the main
street we entered a bakers' shop where a depressed queue
shuffled forward with coupons. We had no coupons. When everyone had gone I pushed cigarettes across the counter. But the
door was opening again.

"Warte!" said a girl with frightened, friendly eyes. She
served her customer. Then she quickly produced a generous
amount of bread in exchange for the cigarettes.

We wandered into a restaurant and ordered the *ersatz* German
coffee, taking cheese and sausage from the suitcases to eat with
our bread. The room was full of listless people. It seemed as if
we could not be in danger from them because we were sharing
their experiences. When the sirens sounded again nobody
moved. André learned that a train was expected to leave for

Traustein at four o'clock. The bombing had made everything
uncertain. Time crawled. Finally we picked ourselves up and got
over to the station. André went to get our tickets. He was a long
time at the window, and when he turned away a clerk came out
from behind and escorted us through the ticket-barrier to a little
office on the side of the platform, where we were passed over to
a couple of security officers, in dark blue uniforms with silver
facings, by whom sat quietly two German police-dogs.

Our papers were in order, but we did not have the additional
train-travel permit required by foreign workers. It was suggested
that we should accompany the officers to the police-station and
we complied with the suggestion. There was a long, slow walk
through the town. The men were pleasant and glad to accept
cigarettes. The operations room at the police-station was up
some stairs. I sat down on a hard chair in the outer part while
André was ushered through to explain to an official who we
were, what we were doing, and why we had tried to travel on a
train without permits. Where I sat I could see André gesturing,
expostulating, leaning across the desk of the functionary. A good
many other things were going on. I was near the table of a
uniformed sergeant seated in front of a typewriter. He was being
spoken to by a lieutenant who kept moving about restlessly near
his table—neither of them taking any notice of me—and
gradually their two voices rose to a loud rasp; they were having
a private row. The lieutenant, closing right up to the sergeant's
ear, screamed:

"Sie lassen sich zu viel von Ihrer Frau leiten."[1]

The sergeant, infuriated, smashed his fists on the table with
such force that the typewriter jumped into the air. All round the
walls were notices with slogans exhorting the servants of the
Reich to be ever-watchful and to conduct themselves "with
highest discipline." André was still talking. We had been there
more than an hour. "Achtung! Achtung!" I suddenly heard. It
was the radio. It warned all military and police posts of the
escape from Tittmoning of two prisoners-of-war. It named us,

[1] "You allow yourself too much by your wife to be led."

said who we were, described us accurately, and concluded with peremptory warnings to look out for and arrest us.

Keeping fixed, as firmly as possible, an expression of bored indifference, I let my eye travel round. Not one man showed any sign of having even heard the message. The rambling business of the place droned on confusedly as before. Soon André strolled over to me with one of the uniformed men, who took us to the door and said, in a friendly way:

"Be sure to call at the *Polizeipräsidium* in Traunstein."

André had got travel-passes for both of us. I did not immediately ask him how he had done it because we were in a hurry to get back to the station. Fortunately the train was standing there. Tickets were handed over without demur. We hastened through. The train was packed, and an indescribable crowd surged about it. We wedged in.

It was a strange scene. Men, women, children, the uniformed and the civilian, ran together in a sticky mass like paints. The muzzles of rifles, leaning away from soldiers' knees, pointed a worn-out threat into the faces of tired elderly women. Those who had provisions unwrapped and ate into them with furtive care, as if to prevent their neighbours even from seeing what they were doing. It was a crowd of lost sheep and lost wolves. The train pushed slowly through the darkening country. Suddenly it stopped. There was a wild movement. The whole herd seemed to know, without any signal being given, that the train was not going to go any further. It was made clear, in cries and shouts above the stampede, that the rest of the line to Traunstein had been bombed.

André and I, holding fast together, were swept off in this melee. We stood still to take stock but as we did so the force of the crowd struck from behind like a powerful hose, jolting us forward. Willy-nilly we rushed on with the human stream. An old woman was lugging an enormous box. She dropped it. The crowd streamed over her; she fell and lay where she had fallen, helpless like a beetle. It was a crowd of the damned now, a Gadarene herd lashed by a mad devil. It was silent except for rushing feet. The silence of all those people, in louring semi-darkness, was macabre. Suddenly a clear voice just ahead of me, a clear and cultured voice, spoke in English. I looked. I saw a tall, gangling figure in an English kind of tweed overcoat, knapsack on back, striding at the right of another man.

I whispered to André: "That must be ——.[1] I've got to speak to him." I was insanely fascinated.

"For God's sake!" André hissed at me. "Are you mad?" He gripped my arm, refused to let go. He was right. I fell back. I grew calm. There was not one sensible reason for my certainty that the figure in the overcoat was the man I had said he was— a man whom incidentally I had never met; if he was, to have accosted him would have been beyond question the act of a lunatic.

This trek, with its tricks and hallucinations, brought us at last to Traunstein. Visions of urban comfort, which perhaps had upborne all these rushing feet, crumbled. Traunstein was a stunned wreck. After much wandering we noticed a dim red globe over a doorway at which people circled, bemused and questing, like bees at a gassed hive. We went in. The place seemed to be an emergency hostel for bombed-out people. It was only that day that Traunstein, a railway-junction on the line of German retreat, had met its end. The floors were littered with people in the last stages of fatigue. No questions were asked; there were no officials to ask them. We found an unclaimed strip of floor and claimed it, using our cases as pillows. The cold, stale heat of bodies was the only heating. It was a freezing night. We had neither blankets nor coats. I listened, in the waking intervals of clammy dozes, to miserable people whimpering. The one electric bulb, which somebody had shaded with a funnel-twirl of newspaper, seemed to shed a curious negative mercy, unearthly, not arranged by human beings, on this stranded, infinitely sad refuge.

We rose early and tiptoed out. We were stiff, aching, and

[1] An Englishman who supported the Nazis and was executed after the war.

chattering with cold. André, naturally more confident than I about encounters with authority, thought that it would be a good idea to wait till the *Polizeipräsidium* opened and call there. I felt sure that it would not. Eventually he agreed, as we were both longing to get out of Traunstein, and we set off west-north-west along the Rosenheim road. This soon became a four-lane motor-way not meant for pedestrians. The footpath along the edge of military-looking pinewoods disappeared. The woods were sewn with tank-traps, very white and new. Unshaved, with our little cases and obviously slept-in clothes, we felt unpleasantly conspicuous. We did not encourage each other. André was acrimoniously silent, as one who was being proved right, and I was nagged by a sickening feeling that perhaps he had been right. The road was uphill. The sun came out, a blessing, and there was still a wonderful lack of traffic. A white sign-post pointed down a little road to our right. "TITTMONING—22 km" I read, with horror. We had progressed in a narrow sort of boomerang curve, and only now were beginning to draw away from that castle. André, shuffling wearily with down-lolling head, had not seen the sign. I did not mention it.

What we needed was hot coffee. On a high corner, till then invisible behind the ridge of the road, stood a white-washed, large-fronted *Gasthaus*, the first since Traunstein from which we had travelled eighteen kilometres. We made for it. Inside were two or three tired-faced drivers, besides the proprietor and his wife. They all said "Grüss Gott!", the time-honoured Bavarian greeting, much more reassuring than "Heil Hitler!" There was no coffee, but there was beer and noodle soup and somewhere to sit. Nobody was inquisitive. The raftered room was spotless and it seemed to preserve, with the friendly manners of its hosts, the memory of a gentler, not-everywhere-quite-forgotten Germany.

We went on rested and restored. It was a mild afternoon. We were friends again. André described his interview in the Freilassing police-station. He had explained to the official that we had got separated on Leipzig Station from a third man, the leader of our party, who had carried our train-passes, a larger case of luggage, and most of our money. Sirens had sounded, our friend had dashed off, and gradually, waiting in vain for him, we had come to suspect that he had simply used the air raid as an excuse to disappear with our property. We had, naturally, reported the matter to a station-guard, who had promised to make inquiries. Meanwhile we had our urgent job and had felt justified in going ahead by train.

This was a wonderfully skilful story because the letters from our Berlin "employers" actually referred to a third man—the Dutch officer who had not been able to get over the castle wall. It showed too a perfect knowledge of the self-righteous German mentality which, no matter how depraved, cannot bear to be put in the position of appearing to penalize innocence. André had lovingly embroidered this theme.

I asked him how he had learned to lie so well. He gave the question some thought. Then "C'est parce que j'ai pris la connaissance de beaucoup de femmes," he said.

We spent that night in a barn, covered with hay—not quite so warm a covering as I had hoped. The barn belonged to a *Gasthaus*, and the proprietor himself took us to it. First we had a hot supper in his *Speisesaal*, where a good many guests sat at long tables. I felt sure that this man knew that we were not·what we were supposed to be. But he contented himself with a hard look and definite "Nein" when we asked if we could have a room.

The morning opened well. Then happy sensations of progress were overthrown by the onset of a really vicious blizzard. We were soaked and icily cold and our hearts failed as we battled against it. We waited at the side of the road. A lorry came in sight. We signalled. It stopped. We hoisted ourselves aboard.

It seemed extraordinary, almost unfair, to be covering mile after mile like this. There was a motley crew of passengers, all wet and cold and shrinking into themselves like bedraggled hens. A tarpaulin partly sheltered us. After a long time the lorry halted. The driver came round to the back and announced that he would be starting again in twenty minutes. He was a Pole. We clambered out and found ourselves in the main square of Rosenheim, the last real town on the way to Munich. The passengers seemed unwilling to let go of each other. André and I went off for a cup of coffee. When we came back the passengers were still gyrating. We all were united by a yearning for the re-emergence of the masterful Pole. There were uncomfortable mutters about a guarded bridge just ahead, where papers would be examined. Breezily the Pole marched forth. In a trice his protégés had packed themselves in, and now the tarpaulin was manoeuvred as disguise rather than shelter; for now it was not even raining.

The next minutes were anxious. We heard, but could not see, the trundle over cobbled streets, the lumbering turns left and right.

"Halt!"

We halted.

"Papiere!"

Rustling silence; then the easy, joky voice of the Pole.

"Los, los!"

"Los" it was; the lorry's gears grinded and we could hear the unmistakable hollow bump-bump as it passed over the bridge.

The passengers stirred, they relaxed, they looked almost blissful. Then, recollecting themselves, they assumed a stern blankness which denied to all the world that they had ever had cause for anxiety. We certainly had no wish to disturb any secrets.

Later the lorry stopped again. We stayed still, willing it to go on. The Pole came round and pulled back the tarpaulin with a look of purpose and finality. This was the end of the road for him. His destination lay down a side-turning. He obviously did not want us there. In fact, he suddenly seemed fed up with us; and our thanks fell lamely as we reluctantly climbed down.

We were on a pavement bordered by small, detached houses. It was a fine, warm evening, about five o'clock. The main road was a tree-lined avenue that ran straight for miles, disappearing in the congestion of a lengthy lateral smudge, an incalculably protracted bruise on the gilded skyline. This appearance was like sunset on a horizon of flat sea. But out of it rose spires and rods and darker fires. It was the great city, Munich, our goal.

What was André saying? He was pointing down one of the suburban side-roads. He thought that we ought to turn off and find somewhere to stay for the night.

We argued. André admitted that he was tired. I was possessed by the prospect of entering Munich. I said that I would not stop, whatever he did. I set off, and he followed with a sour shrug.

André's shoes were the rubber-soled gymnastic sort, strong enough, but not very pleasant for long walks. I saw the points of them as he limped along a pace or so behind. They were an accusing image of ache and weariness.

It was twelve miles into Munich.

We plodded into a thickening brew of workmen in blue denims wheeling homeward bicycles. This avenue traffic seemed like the hopeful augury of a great and civilized capital. But then it got dark. I ascribed to the fall of dark an unlooked-for atmosphere of desolation as the tall city closed about us. I could not believe that the city had emptied itself into its suburbs—that those outer crowds had been the end of metropolitan life, not its beginning. Yet there was no look of life in these unlighted streets. It began to freeze. We were lost in a ghost city. It had been quite a point for us that I had known Munich before the war. But now I could not recognize any landmark.

We had to find a tobacco factory and make contact with a Belgian employed there, a tried friend of the Dutch escape organization, who would be able—it was hoped—to hide, lodge, feed, clothe, finance, and generally keep us going. Somehow we did find this factory, and one glance at its dark bulk revealed that it had gone to bed. It was about half-past nine. André had a private address for the Belgian, only to be used if the factory had failed to produce him. We found this address—a number-plate on a post in front of a hill of rubble.

It was here that I began to feel guilty towards André. I had no idea where we could go, but was determined that we should go somewhere, and struck off as if sure of my bearings. We came to a desolate *Platz*, cold as Siberia. Suddenly there was a wail like an icy wind across the steppes. Hurrying figures appeared, weaving about the convex concrete, disappearing into the mouths of burrows. Down we went too. Walled with hard earth, the deep shelter had seats of concrete slabs and livid lighting that made people look terribly ill. A radio, askew like a gargoyle, rasped out the progress of the bombers, aggrandizing Munich's doom to ecstatic pitch. The listeners were apathetic, they seemed stunned. At the all-clear they rose in one obedient wave. It was slightly less cold down below, and we would have liked to remain, but dared not.

The in-and-out game went on till one o'clock. To us the peaceful silence afterwards was not a mercy. I went up and down a street knocking at doors. Nobody answered except once a woebegone woman, clutching a thin dressing-gown, who looked at me in fear and shut her door fast. Spotting a man diving into one of these doors, I accosted him, careless what I said or how. Shaking his head, as I tried also to get a foot inside his door, he pointed, saying something gruffly about, I thought, a soldiers' rest. I went back to the corner, where André was waiting, and then along where the man had pointed. I saw a ruler of light under a door. The door pushed open into a blast of sweaty warmth. It was true. Here were several soldiers. I pointed to André, who obviously was beyond speech. "Kranker Kamerad!" The soldiers nodded. They brought out a table and a bench. I got André on to the table. "Na, na!" said a soldier, looking at him, as if searching for some memory. Then he slumped round on his studded boots, went out of the room, and returned with a dark-grey blanket, which he slowly put over André.

"You will be all right till six o'clock," he said to me, uniting in one gesture the bench and a red-hot coke fire.

The soldiers retired to their dens. It was well after six when they woke us; when we left, thanking them, they still asked no questions.

The morning was cold, and it was still too early to go back

to the tobacco factory. We kept walking to try to preserve the heat of the last hours. I wanted to find out what had happened to Munich. André's vigour had returned, and he did not object.

I was especially looking for *Habsburgerstrasse*, a quiet, short, stately street, where in 1934, a schoolboy about to become an undergraduate, I had spent three months as a paying and (intendedly) language-learning guest in the residence of an elderly German countess. We got into *Türkenstrasse*, long and straight, and it was there that the sense of a contact with that Munich past came to life and brought with it a feeling of joy. Here on one side had been the *Studentenheim*, hive of serious student life; there on the other side, farther down, a velvety night-spot called *Simplicissimus*, entered with a shiver of pleasing sinfulness. *Türkenstrasse* was crossed at right-angles by equally straight streets, and I remembered how the sun, imprisoned at its changing stations by one or other of them, had caused conflagrations that seemed to consume the tall houses with blinding yellow fires.

Different agencies, since those days, had caused a less illusory destruction. I saw this. It was of a scale that I could not have imagined. But I knew my way now. I hastened to *Habsburgerstrasse*; and it was not until I stood outside the entrance of No. 5 and saw the flight of steps, approach of its once-happy bulk, leading to nothing, that I really experienced the destruction of Munich.

I was telling André, just as an excuse to go on staring at this socket of a ruin, horribly fascinating to me, how, when you pressed the outside bell for the Countess's flat, the big front door opened automatically, very slow and heavy. He was not very much interested. He pulled at me to go. We turned the corner into a short road leading to the *Ludwigerstrasse*, Munich's royal and friendly boulevard, beyond which lay the loved "English Garden". A vile voice screamed. Torpedoed out of my daydreams I saw with horror a jackboot personage in hideous liver-brown-and-red uniform, swastika on arm, gun on hip, facing me like an enraged animal.

It took all of André's skill to get us out of that. When at length we were dismissed, thrust on our way with gun-gesture and glares of malevolent ferocity, we were both trembling. André was furious with me. There was to be no more wandering about Munich. I was chastened, could not argue. In fact, however, we had to go on wandering about Munich. André was reluctant even to go in anywhere for a cup of coffee but he needed it so badly that finally we did.

We were at the factory at about ten and I waited outside while André went in to make inquiries. When he came out he was looking grim. He had seen the Belgian, who had appointed a meeting in the town at two o'clock. The Belgian had not been able to say much, because there were too many others about, but André had got the impression that our prospects were not good.

We both were worn out now. The disappointing meeting and the misery of this new wait sent our morale far down. André said that it would be madness to enter a restaurant and I felt obliged to accept his view. So it was trudge, trudge.

The rendezvous was a busy corner. The Belgian duly came, greeted me, and plunged into discussion with André (whom discussion always could animate). He was tall, fair, amiable of feature. I felt that he was embarrassed by us. It would be understandable. The war was almost over; why bother to escape now and endanger other people? He was passing things to André— money, food coupons. All too soon the discussion seemed to be over. André, still animated, was saying goodbye. I cut in, as the Belgian was about to leave, and asked if we were going to be put up.

"He cannot," André said. "He was bombed out, and in his new place he has had to take in the family of a German who is thought to be an agent of the Gestapo."

"Can he think of somewhere for us to stay?"

"No."

The Belgian looked at me with friendly understanding. I suddenly felt angry. Surely he could take the risk of putting us up? Or find somewhere else? Or do something more than he seemed to be doing?

I felt that André and I would not get through another night like the previous one. Here was this man, comfortably housed, fed . . .

André was shocked. He dissociated himself from my vehement pleas and said good-bye firmly to the Belgian while I was still vainly casting about for some way to get more help out of him.

There we were on the corner no better off than before. We had not run out of money before we met the Belgian and we could not use his coupons unless we went into restaurants.

We walked, with no real purpose, away from the centre of the city. At some point fairly far out we entered a *Gasthaus* which was in a state of unlimited confusion. People and luggage lay about the floors as if they were going to lie there for ever. André and I lay down. It seemed natural, like the desire of lost climbers to fall asleep in snow. There was no possibility of food or drink. Hunger drove us forth; and a harmless-looking civilian, whom we accosted outside, told us about a camp for foreign workers which was not far away.

This camp, a huddle of huts behind a pretence of barbed wire, stood in a corner of a rough field, apologetic and miserable, like a group of starved cattle. There seemed to be no German military: instead however we were met by a flabbergasting bureaucracy of the inmates, men scarcely less bedraggled than ourselves, who required us to fill in forms and asked suspicious questions. They were citizens of occupied countries, victims of the Nazi labour machine, who should have been our friends. They were pathetically degraded. They looked shifty and treacherous. The hut to which we were appointed was crawling with human wrecks ,who took no notice as the officials rapped out orders. We were allotted bunks (they were in three-tier sets) and a blanket apiece. As to food and drink you brought your own or went without. Men were hotting up bits and pieces over a fire, keeping a surly silence. We climbed on to our bunks, and were eaten all night by bugs.

As early as possible André and I fled from the gruesome spot.

We had both been prisoners for a long time; and this new, un-expected dose of prison mentality at its very nastiest was a shock which brought us sympathetically together again. Our quitting was really like a second escape, for we tiptoed out, terrified of waking the officials. We were very weak. But fortune or the solidarity of desperate resolution held out a hand. A *Gasthaus* (not the nightmare one of the day before) shone in our path. This one proved an oasis. It had coffee, as much as we could drink, and we drank to the smell and sizzle of a breakfast of meat and potatoes which soon were being got ready. Then came bread and cheese and beer. We were the only customers. We still had cigarettes; we sat speechless, loth to disturb the wonder-ful sensations of animal recovery.

Grown sensitive to the atmospheres of places, I felt here an innocent friendliness, a touch of loneliness too: the inn stood alone off a half-finished road, among a welter of sketchy roads, a no-man's-land outside an outer suburb. André, with his ease of manner, chatted with the host and his wife, who smiled almost like free people, not inquisitive, yet in some queer way appreci-ative. They seemed to agree, for our sakes rather than theirs, that it would be unwise for us to stay in their house; questions of registers, of police ... They alluded, casually but often, to a housing-estate a little way back that we could not miss. They had an idea that there were people there who would be glad to take in lodgers. As we rose, the man said, comfortably—"The Herren will soon be again with their families." His wife gave an inward, stricken smile.

We said good-bye. A few minutes later we knocked at a door and our prospects changed amazingly.

It was a door in one of the roads serving the housing-estate. "No. 32": no different from its neighbours; no special reason to pick it, we just did.

A gate and a short path led up to it. Everything looked *gemütlich*. The war was nowhere. We rapped at No. 32 as if calling on friends at home.

The door was opened by a woman. She had a pleasant face, neither pretty nor plain, a pleasant figure on the plump side, her hair was German-blonde, her clothes neat, she looked thirty years old. She readily agreed to take us in as lodgers.

Hugging the cold coil of a mattress with bright stripes, I staggered up narrow stairs on which linoleum glistened.

How quickly two beds were made, having first had to be put up!

The cold little bedroom had a window with two squares of coarse, clean curtain the size of a child's frock.

The woman was silent as she brought life back to it, moving quickly.

It was at this moment that I and my companion became independent of each other. Each suddenly was privately at home, improving the place with his own fancies, preparing his own important business, looked after, for so it felt, by two different women who happened by sheer accident to be one and the same.

There was a garden behind the house with currant bushes and an apple tree. The afternoon was mild, clouded pale sun, English sort of weather. Two deck-chairs were put under the tree, facing a discreetly protective toolshed. There André and I sat, two separate lords of the manor, basking, dozing, dreaming.

We did not move until dinner was ready.

The lady was married. Her husband was a sergeant in the Waffen-SS and he was fighting on one of the retreating fronts far north. The fact that he was in the SS was a worry to her. She knew, as every German did, that the war was about to end. She did not trust her neighbours. She was sure that one or other of them, as soon as Munich was taken, would report her connection with the SS to an Allied authority, in order to curry favour.

If her kindness to us had any motive, it perhaps was a hope that our gratitude would somehow stand in her favour, when denunciation began. This occurred to us. But we did not discuss it. She never asked us who we were or what we were doing.

It was just as likely that she was bored, fed-up, and willing to accept company as a gift from heaven.

With what in those days could an ordinary German, especially a woman, feel identified?

Frau Magda's life was like an empty shell. Her soul was empty. As to her husband, whom she had not seen for three years, she could indulge no warm hopes, cherish no expectation of homecoming and secure reunion. Her only definite feeling was this SS worry; and she would have made little of that if André had not taken it seriously.

André was a much better friend to her than I was. He made her go through everything in her house and destroy all tell-tale evidence. He spent a morning filing the "SS" out of a sword-hilt. Many of the sergeant's clothes had swastikas, which he persuaded her to pick out. For instance, there was a strange cow-brown cardigan, fastened in front by twigs latched over braided loops. The material looked like coarse wool, but was actually wood-fibre manufactured by one of those *ersatz* processes which the Nazis had so much developed. Magda gave it to me. It was wonderfully warm.

André helped her to peel potatoes. Food was a problem. Magda, who loved cooking, wanted us not only to eat, but also to taste the joys of her best art. But how was she to find ingredients? It seemed that the verbal description of some of her best dishes, with which she regaled us, was all that we would ever know of them. André, his German so much better than mine, listened attentively to these accounts. In the morning Magda went out to shop and to pick up gossip—of food rather than of war. She came back excited. The railway-line had been bombed and a *Wehrmacht* supply-train, on its way from Munich to the front, lay stranded not very far from where we were.

Outside, the whole population of the suburb seemed to be streaming one way. Approaching the raised tracks we saw hundreds of diminutive figures clambering over the helpless train. Looting was already highly organized. Many of the trucks were guarded by looters who pushed and kicked off competitors while their comrades passed stuff out to other waiting hands. Fights developed along the platform. Thwarted women screamed curses at the guard-gangsters. Cunning late-comers wriggled under or through bits of the train and boarded it from the far side. Then there were swaying fights inside the trucks. A man was hurled out. There was a silent, drawn-out, desperate tug-of-war with a frozen butcher's carcass. Carts and cars, brought as close as possible, shot off when loaded, obviously hurrying to return. There were many perambulators. The whole crowd was a middle-class, respectably dressed crowd.

Beset by opposition, the well-organized looters had often to cut their losses and drop things which then were fought for by housewives, children, and old and lame people. That was how we got some. We just had hands and Magda's big shopping-bag. We got sugar, flour, butter, pea-soup blocks (not much wanted by anybody), some lengths of *Wurst*, a round cheese as hard as cement which seemed to weigh a ton, several bottles of dark wine, and a carton each of tea and coffee.

The dinner that Magda cooked that day was unquestionably the largest, as it was also the best, that either André or I had eaten for five years. Nothing was done, thought, or said, except what had reference to it. We had the pea-soup, chiefly at my request: I knew it of old as nourishing stuff with a surprisingly good taste. Magda made an enormous pie. She did not ask us to admire this, as she despised its sausage-centre, but the pastry was more than good. What she did hope we would admire was her *Apfelstrudel*, a speciality she had previously described. We did admire it. It was memorable. We drank the wine, quarried the cheese, ate limitless bread fresh-baked by Magda, whose real ecstasy began when she discovered that the coffee was "echter Bohnenkaffee"—real coffee—unseen by German civilians since the first day of the war.

This episode put the seal on André's affection for Magda. The domestic side of his nature came to the fore. He was happy pottering in the house, doing little jobs for Magda, sitting in the parlour in his shirt-sleeves reading a newspaper. Indeed he looked very much at home.

There were still plenty of provisions: square meals stretched foreseeably ahead. Why go out? It certainly was the part of prudence not to. Magda was content. Yet I began to feel restless. I became the only thorn in André's comfort. He said I would bring disaster on us if I wandered. He got angry. I would have liked to heed him. I said that I would not involve him, whatever happened.

During the next few days I went back and forth on the single-decker, blue-and-yellow trams that linked our suburb, Mooseburg, to Munich. They were still the same trams, the old friendly irregular clank. I usually got out by the Gothic *Rathaus*, and from that busy point began to go over all the parts of Munich that I had known. I walked to the huge, severe cathedral, and went in by a side-door. The door opened into daylight. I was looking at a slag-heap range of debris. The brick tower and walls were a tremendous shell. An old woman, all black with long black head-dress, was stumbling on one of the heaps. She reached down suddenly and pulled out a small gilt frame with a girlish head haloed and painted in rich colours. She kissed it. She pressed it to her. She began to lament, looking up towards the unroofed sky. I went out quietly through that holocaust, where the little picture had been the only intact object.

Kaputt. Everything. Whole street-fronts, as if a giant had taken bites out of them—as if they were cake. (They had been rather cake-like, the Munich streets.) One thing was there though: the plaque in the wall opposite the *Residenz* commemorating the "fallen patriots" of Hitler's premature putsch of 1923. This was the spot where the putschists had been suddenly fired on. Hitler, very sensibly, fell down flat. In the pre-war years, after he had come to power, no German would have dared to pass by here without giving the Hitler salute. English visitors used to discuss whether they also should. Many did, just to be nice.

Now, as people passed, not one hand was being raised.

I went into restaurants. I did not dare to start conversations, but just looked at all the faces, thinking that the devastation must show there too. But they were all wrapped in stolidity.

Aproned waiters were stolid. Men with brief-cases ate business luncheons, cutting their *Fleisch*-coupons (joined by perforated strips) and handing them over with deprecating, prissy aversion as if they were tips. There was no unhappiness in these faces. They were empty, like fishmongers' slabs after closing-time, animation withdrawn into deep storage. They seemed to know that this day's business was done, this order finished. They seemed to wait for a new day, a new order. They seemed able to wait.

On one of these days there was a pretence of a revolution in Munich. Notices appeared on the *Rathaus*, on church-doors, calling citizens to unite for a reformed government. People collected, curious. Small groups argued on the *Rathaus* square. Handbills lay about. A helmeted policeman, unaggressive, peeled away the posters. There was no fist-shaking, no shouting. The groups melted. None of this was real to the Germans. It was not real to me. I felt curiously safe, peering about among them. I remembered the passion of discipline, the terrifying current of comradeship—love really—of the German soldiers in April, 1940, in Narvik. That had been real.

On the sixth day I set out for Nymphenburg, palace of Ludwig II. I had just a vague memory of lake, silver-blue rococo, pretty china. I was wandering along and got a sudden queer feeling of things going awry. Too many people in this peaceful outer district, too many of them hurrying. Irascible tones, orders rasped. Uniforms. Soldiers running. A soldier turned sharply, aimed his rifle. Crump! A fearful bombing had opened. It was here, whining into walls, chasing panicking people, crashing and sickening. But where were the aeroplanes? Suddenly I understood. There were no aeroplanes. This was artillery. Munich's time had come.

I pelted and dodged back towards Mooseburg. It seemed miles. Thankfully, as one reprieved, I panted into our quiet turning. It was absolutely, ominously quiet. I dashed into No. 32. Home! André and Magda were sitting together, tense. André was scarcely willing to speak to me. Magda told me that it had been announced that an American army was approaching Munich along the Frankfurt road. This army was rumoured to be about an hour's march away.

I sat down. Nobody spoke. Magda was white. I began to hear my heart beat. Was it possible? I could not sit. I got up and went out again, out through the little gate.

I had thought I remembered seeing one of Magda's next-door neighbours wheeling out a bicycle. If she would lend it! I knocked.

"Certainly!" said the neighbour. "But it is a woman's bicycle."

As if that mattered! A moment later I was outside, on the bicycle, pedalling towards the Frankfurt road.

Our north-western suburb was handy for the approach of the liberators. The high-level route was already thinly lined with Bavarian civilians. Soon a reedy noise, not quite a cheer, drew all eyes to the bend. A dark object came in sight. A tank. It travelled past slowly, unseeing and curiously gentle, like a blind man crossing a road. It was covered with flowers.

A lull. Then soldiers came walking. The nearest one was chewing a long stalk. They walked near or in the ditch, in ones and twos. They looked tired, unfeignedly and confidently tired. Not a word was spoken, not an order given.

The Bavarians fell back, awed to silence by this image of slouching power, as unaccountable to them as if it had dropped from another planet.

Military traffic thickened. Keeping with it, at some point nearer the city I dismounted, accosted a group of the soldiers, and breathlessly began to explain myself. The G.I.s gazed at me—dressed now entirely like a Bavarian—kindly, as at a local phenomenon to be humoured. I stopped explaining. They filled my pockets with satiny cigarette-packs and K-rations. What they really wanted to know was where they could get a drink. I was glad to be able to give some information. A lieutenant, smart in chocolate-brown, thinly elegant like his gold pip, wearing rimless spectacles, approached abstractedly, laid his hand on the shoulder of one of the soldiers, and whispered.

"This guy says he's British," said the soldier.

The lieutenant, without ado, asked me if I knew where he could find a certain Doktor "Blank Blank", for whom he had an address which was wrong.

"He's not a doctor," he said. "He's a Nazzy spy."

I knew nothing about the doctor. Feeling sadly useless again, I said good-bye and went on. I reached one of the two narrow streets, forking out from the *Leopoldstrasse*, which end at the *Rathaus*.

"WO GEHEN SIE HIN?"[1]

What was this? Well, it was a German, in uniform. He stood astride the middle of the road, brandishing a sort of knout. It was a *Panzerfaust*. More Germans, similarly armed, looked down from windows.

The truth touched me like ice. Diehard defenders! The American army had not reached this point yet.

I got down, stammered incoherences.

"HAUEN SIE VON DER STRASSE AB!"[2]

Thank you, thank you! Wildly I wobbled away, rounded the first corner (G.I. gifts searing my crammed pockets), and never ceased flying till an enormous detour had landed me in un-hazardable safety.

The next two days were full of frustration. The presence of the Americans made no difference to André's routine. He had settled down, and was perfectly content to wait till somebody took notice of him. He despised my impatience.

On the bicycle, now punctured in its front wheel, I scurried through suddenly merciless weather, searching everywhere for a helpful authority. As gradually it established itself, scouring out little lairs of desperate Nazidom, the American VIth Army covered Munich with black-and-white signs pointing the way to this or that headquarters. But there were a hundred false trails. Nobody knew what was what, nobody bothered. When I

[1] "Where are you going?"   [2] "Take yourself from the street off!"

stopped to consult military street-patrols, I often got engaged on the spot as an interpreter, questioning German civilians and scrutinizing German papers pronounced "fishy".

An elderly workman, halted thus, vented distraught sounds.

"He says he's sick," I explained.

"He don' look sick to me."

The patrolman waved away a medical certificate. Fresh bellows.

"He says he's only going home."

"O.K. Tell him go straight home stay home."

In these days Munich turned on itself. Ugly Germans tottered up from cellars staggering under the weight of huge Emmentaler cheeses. Every shop was ransacked. Wine ran down the floor, where a merchant behind his counter tried distressfully to protect some stone jars of Hollands gin, the only thing left on his shelves. The robbers went in and out methodically, expressionless, as if they were not daylight creatures, but sinister dwarfs risen from the city's depths.

These were dreadful sights, sadder than the destruction. The Americans, in their strange strength, never hurried, but waited to deal with everything in due time.

At last I found, in a pleasant outskirt, a white villa with a garden which was the headquarters of the 45th Division of the Sixth Army. Having once called there, I just went on and on calling until everybody in the place got used to the sight of me. Soon they seemed to expect me to stay to meals.

When I told André about this place he only shrugged. He did not want to come. But I by now had seen enough of the Americans to realize that secret principles of organization pervaded their informality. I felt sure that something would happen. I had just finished lunch there on the third day of my visit and was scraping a plate into a swill-bin bursting with fresh bread (sight at first incredible to an ex-prisoner) when a casual American voice said that a jeep was going to Dachau with one of their war correspondents—would I like to go along? I said I would like to.

"You better have some proper clothes."

I was given, and quickly pulled on, a suit meant for a vast G.I. The idea was that we would just be going there and back. But I knew that this was freedom. By the self-important silence of the war correspondent hunched in the front seat of the jeep: by the opulent fur at the neck of his military jacket: by the lordly fact that he proffered no help when the jeep (temporarily) broke down: by my own horrible discomfort in the back, invaded by icy wind and sleet: by the bumping progress of the devil-may-care contraption, by every sign and sensation, I knew that I was moving, not in geographical terms only, towards the frontiers of the German Reich.

Consequently, I was unprepared for Dachau. The jeep turned aside, scraped to a halt on a great concrete way. I got out, glad to stretch my legs, hilarious, light-headed with happiness: a state of moral levity.

The war correspondent had got out first. As I strolled over to him, he turned abruptly, brought a handkerchief to his face, and began to retch into it.

Behind him on the tarmac there were several mounds of refuse, miscellaneous stuff with a lot of rag of different colours. Possibly the mounds gave off a smell which had upset the correspondent. Reminding myself, and feeling a bit superior about it, that Americans were supposed to be obsessively sensitive about hygiene, I went nonchalantly to look.

The mounds were composed entirely of human bodies.

Do you know, when my eyes had informed me of this fact, it was still difficult to believe it? I saw hundred of arms and legs of spillikin sharpness. Some were angled and pointed like snapped-off chicken-bones; some had congealed into a spaghetti-like mass. The bodies with their indecipherable clothes were all mixed together in a neutral careless way that evoked the gestures of some careless happy occasion, the remains of a picnic, the airy litter of a popular holiday. Every mound was decorated with eyes. One near the top especially held me, it was bright and passive, less bright than the eye of a shot pheasant, more like a bauble. It belonged to the face of a young woman.

The SS had actually been at their job when the Americans caught them. This batch of bodies had just been gassed and was about to be incinerated. The contingents of the American VIth Army, who took Dachau, had never seen a concentration-camp before. Crazy with grief and fury, they kicked SS guards to death.

It was now only three days after that. The place still lay under a hush of horror. In silence we gazed at the gas-chambers, at their doors stamped with the cruelly friendly word "BRAUSE-BAD" (Shower-bath), at the cosy, incredible, stove-heated furnaces. Then we went into the barracks of the inmates, an enormous, low-ceilinged, twilit world, where bunks in tiers of six were crammed narrowly, like the shelves and overspilling recesses of libraries. Here thousands upon thousands of people, only less skinny than the corpses, crouched, crawled, stooped, absorbed in unfathomable occupations, utterly heedless of intrusion by strangers. One bit of the barrack had been cleared and pathetically brightened by a clerical, interdenominational group, with rags and buckles shaped into allied flags and emblems. Their representatives stood up and bowed and made signs of the cross. "It is homelike," they seemed to say, watching us with rapt, deferential eyes.

I was touched for the first time by a perception, but a very inadequate one, as to the real dimensions of this concentration camp legacy. Barbarous extermination was only one part of it. The day of liberation had been the end of that part. It should also have been the beginning of freedom. It was not. Nobody had rushed out of the gates. No prisoner had even asked if he could go. Such an idea did not occur to one among Dachau's fifty thousand inmates. Alive, they were paralysed. One day they might be free again, physically; they looked as if they could never again *experience* freedom.

There was an annexe of single stone cells, called the *Blockhaus*, where the Nazis had kept a few special prisoners, of whom

Pastor Niemöller was one. A ghostly noise came from one cell. An American major-general, a big and powerful man who was showing us round, stopped and slid open a square grill. Then a strange sight was seen. Seven figures in officers' uniforms, figures of ghastly thinness, rose towards the square of light, weaving and beseeching, a ballet of starvation. We looked anxiously at the general.

"That's militairry government," he said, cryptic, laconic. When he turned on his heel, the movements behind the grill grew frenzied, whispering voices rose to impotent clamour. One voice broke suddenly into German. I signalled understanding. The prisoner, pressing his face to the opening, said that he and the others were Yugoslav officers, that they had not done anything "unpatriotic", but had been locked up here (after the liberation) on the instigation of Communist prisoners who had secured positions of trust under the Americans. These Communists, he said, were also preventing any food from reaching them.

I translated to the general, who looked grim and sceptical, but agreed to accept from the seven a statement of their case pencilled on an envelope. He also bespoke by gesture that food would be sent.

This incident, which closed our five-hour visit to Dachau, was not at the time fully interpreted by me, nor, I am sure, by the American correspondent. It formed a sinister strand in a fabric of impressions whose least expected motive was its tentacular and poison-steeped complexity.

The correspondent now wanted to go on to Dillingen, to the VIth Army Press Camp there. His wishes, never gainsaid, were received by everybody as orders, with an extra touch of respect, endearingly sincere and humble, the plain American's tribute to an intellectual profession.

At Dillingen I felt for the first time the anxiety of my newborn freedom. The huge Press Camp, with its busy barge and bustle of correspondents, its time-racing typewriters and telephones, scared me. My five years of absence were like a deep shaft, I at the bottom, able to see the free people overhead, not able to make them see or hear me.

How exactly, in prison-camps, prisoners had learned to read the faces of other prisoners! How changeless the faces had been! Now, when a heavily-belted Negro correspondent, brushing by, gave me an odd, careless glance, I felt painfully nervous.

I met an old friend, Bill Troughton. We talked late. Delighted as I was to find him, our talk (or rather, my part in it) also seemed anxiously premature.

A more powerful antidote was the extraordinary kindness of the Commandant of the Press Camp, an American lieutenant-colonel. He gave me a safe-conduct letter, which referred generously to my escape and asked all US military authorities to help me to get home with utmost speed. He arranged for me to make the next lap on a mail-carrying aeroplane due to leave Dillingen first thing in the morning.

The aircraft, a tiny monoplane of a type nicknamed "General's Toy", took off about six. The colonel was up, spruce for the coming day. He came out to say good-bye and good luck, and to introduce me to the pilot, a youthful captain from the deep south, whose nonchalant drawl and smiling serenity made his machine seem more reliable than it looked.

We came down at Mannheim, several eventless hours later, and the amiable pilot discovered that I would be able to go on in a general-purposes military Dakota, which daily carried out an enormous circular flight, stopping all stations. It would call here; some time this same evening, had I not missed it, I would be in Paris.

I was not going to miss it. Back and forth I went, trying to keep everything in sight, running to greet every new landing, incessantly questioning the airport staff.

It did come, that Dakota, and I did get on it, stepping over a mass of people and freight. Nobody bothered, nobody asked for papers. We rose, then the big machine just rolled and rolled through the sky, for ever it seemed, with its indifferent untidy load. At the back there was a great heap of provisions, packages, and cans, and anyone who was hungry or thirsty went and helped himself. I drank a can of pineapple-juice which was exquisite.

Nine hours later a dark airport received us. Somebody gave me a lift into Paris, to the Hotel Scribe. Going in there was like coming late into the middle of a roaring party. There were faces I knew, faces not seen for years, faces merry, astonished, welcoming. Dazed, I gyrated in a haze of smiles, hands, drinks, cigarettes, glittering lights. Drink bore me up, and soon I was being borne along to a night-haunt, called "Ciro" I thought, and said to be the favourite resort of the "elegant elements" of the Resistance. It was a very, very *riche* place. Cinderella in the prince's ballroom could not have been more dazzled than I was, nor more amazed. The sumptuous tables, the muted music, the gold-collared bottles in buckets, the shiny pumps passing over smooth floor, the gloss and glitter and decoration, above all the menu—surely a Prospero had conjured the scene, for delight or merely relief, out of history's grimmest desert?

Beckoned to a table where M. Vincent Auriol with Mme Auriol and others of his family, all in evening dress, flashing with decorations, appeared benignly to preside over the throng, I was graciously welcomed and invited to drink champagne. M. Auriol and his beautiful wife said many kind, friendly things. Touched by their hospitality, I could only hope that through the novel aura of wonder and pleasure in which everything round seemed bathed, I was able to achieve, what had not been normal for five years, an appearance of being normally civilized.

I had never forgotten how much I loved France. The stress of the war's last weeks, so far as I had lived them, had kept different thoughts to the fore. But now this wonderful Parisian fairy-story, balm to the dull, stinging oppression of the past—balm instant and magical whose secret only France could have kept fanned this love.

The story did not end. It vanished. When I woke, after an enchanted sleep, the virtue of its memory seemed to have passed into me. I was happy, sanguine, and strong as I rose, ready for whatever the day might bring, and what it brought was a Scots

S.H.A.E.F. Captain with a ginger moustache, a terrier-sized man immensely active and befriending, who seemed to know everything about me (more, his manner said, than I knew) and also to delight in mystery. I followed him, his plans veiled under clues, to a large building, where by code-words, hushed lifts, and remote corridors, I was passed finally through a massive door and brought into a Presence. This achieved, the captain instantly withdrew.

A white-haired, majestic figure rose from a throne-like chair on the far side of a directorial table. The captain's methods had shaken me, I prepared to feel very small. Before me stood an American general. And the paraphernalia of generalship? It took quite seven minutes to realize that they had been nothing more than a concoction of the fervent captain. This General, his name was General Bradley[1], was a gentle, unassuming man with a charm which seemed to come from the depths of his nature. He had wanted to see me, he said, so that he could personally tell me the good news about the main group of my friends and companions, who were about to reach safety after various adventures. He was anxious because there was still no news about the fate of Dawyck Haig and Charlie Hopetoun, after we had left them in Königstein. Did I know anything? He thought that Königstein must have been reached by the Russians; but this was unsure. He asked me a great deal about my own journey. I tried to describe what was interesting, or at least objective. The varied pictures of Germany in decay, seen during my journey but not then separated from other things, became suddenly more distinct.

This long conversation was, for me, one of the most enjoyable I had ever had. I was quite under the spell of the General, whose personality seemed to magnify within itself a deep sincerity of manners present in all the Americans I had met, and also a curious visionary sympathy, looking beyond the clutter of underfoot fact. The General, standing looking out through his window, seemed to be looking far. It seemed to me that this must be the same kind of look as that which Roosevelt,

[1] Not General Omar Bradley.

supreme bearer perhaps of this American gift, had directed across the whole mortal globe.

I was glad to be able to reassure the captain, ahop outside, that the meeting had "gone off well".

The captain had booked me aboard a British Dakota, England-bound that afternoon, and had issued me with his own brand of pass, ink-scrawled on the back of an old *Luftwaffe* form, certifying me "permitted proceed to U.K.".

We had a jolly lunch. Bursting with beans, enthusiastically solicitous (though I must have been just one of his jobs) he rattled me out to the airport in a more or less incredible two-seater, whirled me through officialdom, pumped my hand as I mounted the steps to the standing aeroplane.

No luggage? No luggage.

So long! So long!

The allotted places were filled. This British Dakota was exactly the same as the American one in which I had got a lift to Paris. It was the same entirely. It was also entirely different. I found myself looking straight at a rectangular board attached to the cockpit door which listed, in legible black letters on white ground, a set of eight rules. I read the list. I read it again. I started to memorize it. The door behind opened, an officer in R.A.F. uniform came through, took a diffident one-leg stance with his back against the rules, and said tonelessly: "Attention, please. Just a few rules for your convenience and safety." Then he repeated the list verbatim. We, their objects, ranged in neat pairs, faced him as silently as a class. "Thank you," he said.

Safety-belts. That was Rule No. 1. (I had not seen any on the other plane, certainly none had been used.)

The officer looked in again and checked us over, all sitting silent and correct, contained in the belts. One minute later the Dakota roared, gathered its level run, rose.

There was no hope of seeing the coast, the English Channel, the white cliffs of Dover, or even grubby cliffs. The aircraft was browned-out. "No Smoking" was one of the rules. The flight began to seem very long. I got a blinding headache, could think of nothing, only long for the mercy of unthrobbing earth.

It was in this state that I did at last, after a torment of time, totter out on the tarmac of Croydon Airport. Goodness knows which way I thought I was going. An arm came out. There swam before me an elderlyish figure, some sort of trimly-cut uniform. A woman's voice. I listened. This was a voice with a re-minding, surely characteristic, by me almost forgotten tone; an English feminine voice, rich with the marvellous inflexible madness of zealous English kindness.

"Steady!" it said. "Would you like a boiled egg?"

Chapter Eleven

Wolves From Their Lairs

Michael Alexander

GILES went his way—we went ours. George Lascelles, John Elphinstone, Max de Hamel, John Winant and I went to bed that night and lay fully dressed under the blankets. At ten o'clock the door was locked. At eleven o'clock there was a tap outside and a Dutch officer came in, having unlocked the door with a master key, and told us that all was ready. We each took a blanket and a small supply of food and followed him up stone stairways and along endless wooden passages that creaked loudly with every step. At times he would signal us to stop as in the distance we heard the tramp of a passing guard. Our single file finally came to a halt in the deep recess of a window in the castle wall, which at that place was at least eight feet thick. The Dutchman got down on his hands and knees and, by the light of a small torch, began to ease a knife blade between the great stone blocks that formed the wall. A stone slid out and revealed the entrance to the hide, a hole just large enough for us to wriggle through one by one. The five of us crawled inside, took up the only possible positions, and began to take stock of our appointed tomb.

We were not in complete darkness—exposed electric leads brought in the current for a weak bulb. From the tiny entrance chamber a tunnel about six feet long and three feet high led to a vertical shaft three feet square and twelve feet high. To accommodate us all the only possible arrangement was for one person to sit on a stool provided at the bottom of the shaft, while another sat above him on a wooden plank that had been fixed not too firmly athwart the shaft; two people could lie in the tunnel side by side, while the remaining person sat with head bowed on the lavatory pail that had been installed near our point of entry. It was with misgiving that we listened to the scraping sound of the stone being cemented back.

Each place had its attendant disadvantages. It might be imagined that the recumbent positions were most sought after. They were not. The tunnel was not wide enough for two sets of shoulders and it was necessary to take up a semi-sideways position that soon became intolerably uncomfortable and claustrophobic, the more so in the knowledge that every movement was transmitted to the adjacent body. The perch up the shaft was the most nerve-straining, for not only was it hard and narrow, but it was also precarious and there was the double anxiety, which also applied to the person below, of going to sleep and falling off or dislodging a piece of stone by sudden movement. The lavatory seat was perhaps the all-round favourite, especially if a turn there could be put to useful purpose.

To give variety to our lives and relief to our anatomies we arranged to change places at regular intervals. The manœuvre for the change-over was as follows: 1. First recumbent man stood up in shaft. 2. Man on bucket took his place. 3. Second recumbent man sat on bucket. 4. Man on stool in shaft lay down. 5. First recumbent man (now standing in shaft) climbed to shelf in shaft. 6. Man on shelf got down on to stool. *Da capo*, every two hours—unless, as often and exasperatingly occurred, the bucket was wanted out of turn.

We passed the rest of a sleepless night sampling various discomforts and wondering how long we would have to spend in this intolerably ill-appointed hole. I wished I was out in the wide country with Giles—if in fact he had succeeded in getting away.

Dawn finally filtered through the chinks in the tiles at the top of the shaft. Then suddenly we heard a great commotion far away, a shouting and a chattering of voices and the distant sound of innumerable boots on cobblestones, clogs we thought, many of the Dutch wore clogs—this must be some sort of an emergency call-out. After a time there was more shouting, then more boots. After that, silence. The Dutch must now be back in their quarters and were no doubt discussing the event amongst themselves. We wondered what the effect had been on the Germans when our absence was discovered.

It had been arranged that in times of danger the Dutch would switch our light off from outside. The light went out that morning and for eight hours we sat in darkness without talking or changing position. We knew that after an escape it was routine procedure for the Germans to search a camp inside and we listened anxiously for unusual noises. Suddenly we heard muffled voices. Then there was a tap-tap-tapping as if the walls were being sounded. Casual tappings trailed along our private buttress; the thin entrance to the hide took a more determined blow, but Van den Heuvel, with characteristic expertise, had made it echo-proof.

For the rest of the day all was silent except for the drone of aeroplanes passing overhead.

On the evening of the second day the light was dipped three times—signal that the entrance was to be opened up. Then the stone was removed and Van den Heuvel peered in. He asked us if everything was all right, and quickly passed in a bucket of hot potatoes, and a piece of paper that he said would give us all the news. If all went well, he whispered, we might be able to emerge the next night to stretch our legs. The wall was hurriedly bricked up again and our fleeting contact with the outside world was over.

The news-sheet was interesting. We learned that Giles and one Dutchman had got away and that 3,000 men searching the district had so far failed to find them. The Germans had not at first realized that a successful escape had been made, but later in the night a patrol noticed that a wire on the perimeter had been cut. The prisoners had then been counted and it had been discovered that seven Dutchmen were missing from their beds. This had not seriously worried the Germans, who had merely remonstrated with the Dutch for being so unreasonable as to go in for escaping at this late stage of the war. It was not until early next morning that they discovered that our beds had been occupied by five Dutchmen.

The bulletin also said that the Allied advance was slow and gave no estimate of how long it might be before the castle was relieved. Our food, therefore, was carefully rationed; a biscuit-tin larder contained chocolate, bread, cheese, and dried fruit; a crudely effective immersion heater, made of a dried-milk tin with the blade of a knife as conductor, could boil water to make tea. We had each brought in small luxuries provided by the Dutch canteen, such as bars of nougat, chewing gum and raisins. We decided to pool our resources and each produced his treasure from his pocket. John Winant pulled out an enormous globe of garlic with a proud, "Look what I've got!" and before anyone could snatch the foul thing from him he took a great bite at it; from then on our sharing of it was involuntary.

Competing with the smell of garlic was the chloride of lime in the lavatory pail. The Dutch had not realized that this was dangerous in an enclosed space and had it not been for the action of Max, who was something of a chemist, in preventing the use of a further supply, we should probably all have been gassed. At least, so Max said.

Life was lived in terms of our complicated two-hourly changes of position. Round and round the circuit of seats, shaft one, tunnel one, shaft two, tunnel two, pan. The nights were cold the days were hot and stuffy. The only book was an old Tauchnitz edition of Oscar Wilde's "De Profundis" which George had brought in; this was not a work which anybody else would have felt like reading at that time, even had the light been bright enough.

On the morning of the third day the light went out and we

heard a distant tapping noise which, though small, was sufficient to shake us out of the almost foetal state into which we had lapsed. This tiny sound continued sporadically throughout the day and seemed to be getting nearer and nearer. We tried to visualize what was going on outside. Was it possible that the plot had miscarried and that another search was going on inside the castle? Would relief arrive before they found us?

On the fourth morning the knocks started early, they were stronger now and increasing in intensity; there was a determined regularity between each blow as though someone was wielding a pickaxe and hearts began to beat in painful expectancy. The crashes came louder and louder and soon the hole was reverberating with the ring of metal on stone. We froze in our seats. Then suddenly the wall caved in like a rotten tooth and light and dust came flooding into our stone womb. It was a Caesarean operation with a vengeance! There was an outburst of hysterical shouting from without, a bloodhound leapt forward barking, and pistols and machine guns were poked into the hole as we emerged shamefaced and embarrassed into the world.

Out in the passage were grim-faced soldiers in the black uniform of the S.S. We were made to stand with our hands behind our heads and in this position to pass down a double line of S.S. men, pistols at the ready. We were hustled out into the courtyard where the rain was pouring down in cataclysmic torrents. The sullen sky threatened retribution. We were confronted, outside the Kommandantur, by Hauptmann Klau, the Abwehr Officer, white-faced and shaking, his rage mixed with relief that we had been found. A rigid hand gestured meaningfully across his throat. It was only later that we grasped it was the loss of *his* head that he was referring to rather than ours: he had apparently just been condemned to death over the telephone!

The Commandant, a retired Regular officer, was quieter. He told us that there was an order that, if we escaped, the Commandant, the second in Command, and the Abwehr Officer of whatever camp we were in would be answerable with their heads. The Commandant did not seem to care, he had just had the news that his wife had been killed in an air raid. He was like a man already dead.

We never learned how they had come to find us. It was thought that a certain Dutchman, who was known to be a German stool-pigeon, had got wind of the plot and had betrayed it, in spite of the fact that very few Dutch officers knew we were still in the castle—even the Dutch General thought that we had escaped.

Our departure from Tittmoning later that day was from our point of view as triumphal as could be expected under the circumstances. The route out from the castle over the wooden bridge was lined with imported S.S. men, rifles and sub-machine guns rampant: some even had taken up strategic firing positions behind rocks in the ravine below. The German officers who, in spite of Giles's continuing absence, had now recovered much of their poise, turned out to see their embarrassing guests off the premises. From now on, it was indicated, we should be allowed no liberties whatever.

The fact that the Commandant at Tittmoning clearly thought that he was in the greatest danger of losing his life as the result of our disappearance made it apparent that, in spite of the catastrophic condition of Germany at that time, someone with the power of life and death was still interested in our existence. The extra five days gained by our entombment did not then seem much to our advantage. Although we were still protégés, as it were, of the German Army, which we regarded as not wholly irresponsible, it was by now obvious that they were acting under direct orders of other and more sinister authority. The next move, we thought, should bring us nearer to the source of the trouble.

It was with no pleasure that we found ourselves back again in Laufen, where certain disquieting arrangements had been made for our reception. For our better protection and to deprive us perhaps of the argument that we were British officers and as such should be in a military camp, barbed wire barricades had been

rigged up in the passages and in the entrance hall, isolating us
from the civilian prisoners, and in fact creating a prison within
a prison. We were taken to a room high up in a remote wing.
Next door were General Bor and his staff who had been moved
two days before from Tittmoning.

Supervision was strict; all communication with the civilian
prisoners was forbidden. From our wired-up window we could
see them circulating in the court-yard far below. A simple plan
was worked out. We put a message inside a matchbox and
dropped the box out of the window, hoping that it would fall
into helpful hands.

In this message we said who we were, and asked that a matchbox containing a reply should be left under the single tree in the
exercise ground. We were lucky. At our first outing an answer
lay ready. It was signed "Felix Palmer" and gave sufficient information to reassure us that our contact was reliable. He was a
Major in the East Surrey Regiment, he wrote, captured while
working for Military Intelligence in Norway. In Trondjheim
when the Germans arrived they had arrested him one day before
Germany was officially at war with Norway, and on this nicely
observed technicality he had escaped serious trouble. He wrote
that he had known Giles Romilly on the Wülzburg, when both
were interned there. Now at least we were in touch with friends
and felt more at grips with events.

In the next matchbox we asked whether it was known how
long we were to remain at Laufen. Answer came that it was
thought that we were likely to stay—the prisoners' schedule for
football in the park had been altered for some days ahead to
enable us to exercise at different hours.

Next day the *Abwehr* officer, a smooth-cheeked, pink-faced
young man wearing a very small pistol, told us that we were to
receive a visit from an important person. This proved to be
General Gunselmann, commander of the Munich Area, beefy as
a butcher, red-tabbed and gold oak-leaved. We were introduced.
John Elphinstone put on his best military manner and in clipped,
tight speech expressed indignation at our treatment and cir-

cumstances. He used his only available weapon, a threat that if any harm befell us the General would be held personally responsible—"nach dem Krieg"—"after the war". General Gunselmann, somewhat taken aback, gave his word of honour that we would not be moved from Laufen, though he showed pained surprise that we should apparently prefer to run the risk of being overrun by the Russians than to remain "safe" in German hands. It had not occurred to us that it would in any way be awkward to be rescued by the Russians, though perhaps we anticipated this more happily than the Warsaw Poles, who had sinister precedents to remember. General Gunselmann in fact issued orders that the Poles were to be handed over to the Americans, should the Russians look like arriving first.

That day we had a second visitor, the Swiss Minister Dr Feldscher, who had been given plenipotentiary powers in dealing with PoW matters; accompanying him was our old friend and visitor at Colditz, Mr Denzler. Drinking coffee in our rooms, Dr Feldscher assured us that he was taking especial interest in our prospects. He showed us a stern letter from the British Foreign Office that warned "whoever it might concern" of the direct consequences that would follow if anything happened to us contrary to the usages of war.

At this meeting we were introduced to the leaders of the respective interned groups. The British leader was a tall thin man who had been Attorney-General of the Channel Islands. He told us that most of the British inmates of Laufen came from there. The American leader, Mr Gompertz, bald, with pince nez, made a charming speech, and offered to send supplies of food and cigarettes from his store. Before leaving, Dr Feldscher confirmed our suspicions that the orders for our movements had originated with Himmler. We learned that Berlin was beleaguered and that it was almost impossible to deal directly with the Heads of State concerning our future. But, judging by the General's promise and the Commandant's confirmation, it looked as though we were likely to remain uneventfully where we were.

Understandably, in the circumstances, precautions against further escapes were rigorous. We were not allowed into the shelters during the frequent air raids unless we signed a parole, extra guards had been brought into the camp, and an officer was always in attendance. One of these officers-in-waiting, the Laufen second-in-command, told us a strange little story. He had served with the army in Denmark when his name had been discovered on a list in possession of a captured British agent. He was summoned to appear before the commanding general to make an explanation. Fortunately for him the general's adjutant shared his anti-Nazi views and persuaded the general to take no action. This officer kept apologizing for the strict security measures but said that he had no wish to lose his head at that late stage of the war if it could be avoided.

It was now a fortnight since we had left Colditz, and even if the Germans' promises proved false there was a continuously diminishing area to which it would be possible to move us. From our windows we had seen troops fixing long metal boxes containing high explosives beneath the bridge over the river Salzach; Americans or Russians must soon arrive from the north or east, and it could not be long now before American tanks would come rolling across the Bavarian plains from the direction of Munich. Our money was on the Americans as the Russians still had the barrier of the Danube ahead of them. But there to the south was the great wall of the Alps dominated by the Watzmann, snow-capped guardian of the south-western approach to the Redoubt. In an hour or so we could be whisked away out of reach of rescue and the game, whatever game it was, would begin again.

The matchbox telegraph still worked. Twice a day we went out into the small park for exercise. The Germans seemed to be more on the lookout, so we abandoned the too obvious tree and now left the matchbox lying casually on a grassy bank.

One morning the box contained unpleasant information:

"Bus new to Laufen parked behind walls. They seem to be trying to keep it hidden. Rumour you are to be moved."

Our newly acquired sense of security was immediately shattered. We wrote:

"Do everything possible to sabotage transport or otherwise delay departure."

Transport was at a premium, if the bus was damaged it would take time to repair it or find another.

That evening a late-extra news flash was delivered in a loaf of bread. "Sabotage attempt unsuccessful. Double guards on gate. Understand bus now filled with petrol. Trying to contact Swiss. Good luck."

At an unusually early hour next morning a guard entered the room with a shout of "Aufstehen!" Almost before we had finished dressing strange things began to happen in the courtyard. There was a loud blare on a klaxon, the gates were thrown open, and two cars drove in at some speed, a black Mercédès Benz and a smaller Opel. We were hurried downstairs and as we stepped out into the courtyard the black bus of the messages drew up as if it had been kept secretly in the background until the last possible moment. From the Mercédès stepped a tall figure in a long black leather coat almost to his ankles, he wore the insignia of a colonel, and his cap bore the deathshead emblem of the SS Totenkopf Division. From the other car came a major in the blue uniform of the Luftwaffe; with close-cropped moustache and rimless spectacles his face somehow looked familiar. George Lascelles whispered: "Don't look now, but isn't that our old friend Himmler?" We remembered that he was said to be somewhere in the area. The other occupant of the Opel was a hard-faced blonde wearing trousers and smoking a cigarette through a long holder.

These sinister visitors said no word, but as we came out our so-called "Himmler" gave a meaning tap to his holstered Luger. We were herded into the bus. As well as an escort of soldiers, came a beautiful girl we had not seen before, with a face as sad and soulful as Alida Valli's. Nobody seemed to know why she was there. Though seemingly so sympathetic in appearance she would exchange no glance of friendship nor accept a proffered cigarette. It was almost as though she regarded us as the tangible agents of her country's downfall.

As the bus moved off we felt that the apron strings that had kept us attached more or less reassuringly to the Wehrmacht had been cut and that we were now in a different sort of company, a more malignant world of purely arbitrary hostility. But suddenly, as we drove out through the village, we saw, crouching behind a kiosk, a familiar figure wearing an enormous grey trilby hat pulled down over his eyes. It was the faithful Mr Denzler. As we passed he gave us a conspiratorial wave—at least our departure had been noticed, a lifeline was still out.

The convoy, which included the Mercédès and the Opel, set off southwards towards the mountains, glum and forbidding in the early morning light. Salzburg was not far away. We drove straight through, past the bombed cathedral and the splintered Domplatz and out under the old stone arch and on to the Autobahn. We soon reached the mountains and were curving up through fir trees. The country was magnificent but its effect oppressive. Then, like a warning finger, stood a signpost inscribed in gothic lettering BERCHTESGADEN. This, we thought, must be journey's end. High above, atop a great pointed mountain, was the Führer's impregnable headquarters, the Eagle's Nest, approached only by a lift running through the heart of the mountain.

The little town of Berchtesgaden still had the air of a holiday resort in spite of the large amount of military transport parked in the streets. With its hotels, cafés, and shops selling carved wood objects it invited the tourist to stop. But we hurried on —out through the other side and into the mountains in what seemed a more westerly direction.

The road was now crowded with vehicles of every sort moving in both directions; it was clear that even in the Alps a military situation was developing. One of the reasons for the resulting traffic jam became suddenly clear. Along the road, *allegro vivace*, a detachment of Hungarian cavalry, in full manoeuvre order, trotted by. Brown uniformed, forage-capped troopers, handsome, dark, determined, rode loosely at ease. An unusual bugle cried in the cold air. They passed our stationary bus, casual yet controlled, in a cloud of steam and a smell of sweat and saddle-soap. They seemed to be on the march to an earlier war. Was Sarajevo down the road? Were Bosnia and Herzegovina still marked on their maps? Salzburg, we learned, was threatened; these horsemen were its appropriate defenders. Innsbruck, ninety miles or so to the west, had fallen—evacuated Innsbruckers were doing their best to make their way to Salzburg, while Salzburgers were already panicking out into the mountains along these roads. We were in the middle. Mêlée.

The convoy was only able to make the slowest progress. Overtaking was impossible on the narrow road; to one side was a wall of rock, to the other a precipice. Late in the afternoon we entered a wide valley in which lay a huge encampment of huts surrounded by barbed wire. We turned off past stilted sentry boxes. A notice board carried the name Markt Pongau.

There was still a touch of winter in the Alpine air. It was a grey damp afternoon and a sullen mist hung about the valley. There was an unhealthy asylum air about the place; the inmates seemed to limp or squint or bear some other mark of physical deficiency. From among the huts rose a tall tower, like the chimney of an incinerator. George Lascelles suggested that we were in a concentration camp of the good old-fashioned sort; a number of wounded S.S. men loafing or limping about in dirty black battle-dress did not allay our fears.

The Mercédès, the Opel, Alida Valli—all had vanished.

We were left to linger among a motley throng, remnants of a number of different German units, S.S., Luftwaffe, and some pantomime Mongolians (pro-German Kurds?) with long drooping moustaches, who looked incongruously ill-dressed in German field-grey uniforms and black boots. There was a group of elderly reluctant-looking peasant Volkstürm and a squad of boys who could not have been more than fifteen years old. One of our guards pointed at them and said sarcastically: "Germany's last line!"

Beyond the wire at the end of the compound we noticed another group wearing khaki. They were Poles, smart in British battle-dress. A small red-headed figure detached itself. George Lascelles said: "Good God! That looks exactly like Johnny Graham. He used to sit next to me at school!" We went over to the wire. The small redhead *was* Graham—an officer in the Scots Guards, he had escaped from various places and had recently been picked up near the Swiss frontier. He had pretended to be a private soldier and had thus been sent to Pongau which was, he said, a sort of international Stalag—non-officers' camp. The "incinerator", we were pleased to hear, was only a water tank. Shortly afterwards one of the Polish Generals discovered a nephew among the prisoners; he had not seen him for six years and a touching greeting took place through the wire.

We were housed in a dismal hut that had been wired up while we waited, and went to bed that evening with anything but a sense of high adventure.

Next day we were taken out for a walk in the surrounding mountains under a large escort that included two officers. Climbing the hillside we left behind the almost overpowering sense of material squalor and spiritual degradation that war had brought to the valley bottom, and entered another level of existence among the flowering meadows and peacefully grazing cattle. Escorting Germans vied with each other in pointing out notable views. The best, over a wide gorge through which raced a roaring torrent with a waterfall, was marked up with a notice board naming it as an official Aussichtspunkt[1] and, after warning the out-looker not to leave litter lying about, announced that it had been put up by the "Verschönerungsverein".[2]

Shortly after our return we had a visitor.

From the hut we saw the arrival in the compound of an enormous black Mercédès Benz. It contained, apart from two black-

---

[1] Lookout point.   [2] Beautification Society.

caparisoned figures in the front, a portly figure propped up on pillows in the back. With awe in his voice a German officer told us that this was *Obergruppenführer* Gottlob Berger,[1] General of S.S. We too knew of Berger—that in 1944, over the heads of the army generals, he had been put in charge of all matters relating to prisoners of war—that it was he who held our fate in his hands. General Berger advanced towards the hut followed at a distance by his bodyguard. He entered alone, smoking a large cigar, and swaying as if slightly drunk. We stood up. He airily waved us to sit down.

In appearance the *Obergruppenführer* looked more like a successful character actor of the Sydney Greenstreet–Francis L. Sullivan school than a man of war, and we were glad to note that his eye was more venal than fanatic. His glance darted round the room, sizing up our individual reactions to his presence, as if we might have heard unfavourable reports about him and were bearing overt malice. He took the initiative by saying that we had no doubt heard that he had once been head of the S.S. in Prague. He looked round furtively, questioningly—nobody in fact had heard—then sanctimoniously he informed us that this had been against his wishes and that after three months he had requested a fighting job from the Führer. We did not speak. We did not have to.

The General seemed to have further things on his mind. He began to speak of the difference between the Waffen S.S., who, he said, were primarily soldiers fighting alongside the rest of the German army, and what he called the Gestapo S.S.—the S.D. or *Sicherheitsdienst*—the security force on which the Nazi regime depended to maintain its power. It was the Gestapo S.S., said Berger, who were responsible for concentration camps and mass

[1] Gottlob Berger, S.S. *Obergruppenführer* and General of the Armed S.S., was born in Swabia. He was the link between Himmler and Rosenberg, the Minister for the occupied Eastern Territories, during the early stages of the Russian campaign. As from the 1st October 1944 he was Chief Commissioner of Prisoners-of-War, and thus in charge of Colditz. He was sentenced to twenty-five years hard labour by the Inter-Allied Tribunal in the "Wilhelmstrasse" trial at Nuremberg, but was recently discharged.

murders. Because he disapproved of these activities he had asked to be transferred to the Waffen S.S.

After this ceremonious whitewashing the *Obergruppen-führer* seemed relieved and began to play the host. Were we short of anything? What could he do to make us comfortable? Cigarettes? He made an expansive gesture that suggested whole crates of them. Crates of whiskey, it seemed would also be made available. It would not have surprised us had he suggested unlimited female companionship.

General Berger then became more serious; he embarked on a long and theatrically declaimed speech of explanation and justification of Germany's part in the war. The phrase "Rote Virus" was his *Leitmotiv*, the red virus that would insidiously attack the sinews of Europe like syphilis.

Then, throwing up his hands, he announced dramatically that the situation in Germany was catastrophic; as Chef des Kriegs-gefangenenwesens—Head of Prisoner of War Affairs—he regretted that he was no longer able to guarantee our safety.

The *Obergruppenführer* then made an astonishing statement. He had recently flown into Berlin in a Fieseler-Storch aeroplane, which had landed him in the centre of the city almost in the middle of the fighting. He had had an interview with Hitler, he said, and had been given his final orders. Our fate had been discussed.

General Berger then produced his bombshell. He announced that he had received a direct order from the Führer that we were to be shot. It was not difficult to imagine the strained nerves and twisted face of Hitler, the spitting out of this pointless order, "Erschiesst! Erschiesst sie alle!"

It was now known in Berlin, said Berger, that this drastic instruction had not been carried out, and as a result he himself had been proscribed. His wireless set had intercepted a message from Martin Bormann at the Führer's Headquarters to Gauleiter Giesler, the recently appointed Reich Defence Commissioner, that he, Berger, was, as the Party jargon phrased it, "to be made sure of for all time".

Following on his defection, our execution, Berger said, was to be carried out by S.S. Führer Ernst Kaltenbrunner. Berger said that he himself had bearded Giesler, a diehard to the ultimate degree, in his Munich office, and that they had had a violent dispute. When Giesler was looking the other way he, Berger, had appropriated the list of our condemned names from his desk.

Kaltenbrunner, a notoriously ruthless personality, would now be looking for the opportunity to carry out his orders. He was known to be somewhere in the mountains. To forestall any attempt at abduction Berger was providing, he said, a special escort with orders to defend us against all comers. He then gave his orders. We and the escort were to leave at eleven next morning accompanied by a representative of the Swiss Government, with General Berger's personal *laissez-passer* through to the American lines.

"Gentlemen," he cried, with a gesture that contained both pride and pathos, "these are probably the last orders I shall give as a high official of the Third German Reich."

Before he left we asked if we might take some extra orderlies with us. The *Obergruppenführer* replied: "Obviously!" and seemed surprised that we had not assumed we might be allowed as many servants as we considered necessary. Thus we were able to take Johnny Graham and the Polish General's nephew.

Next morning a big American car with C.D. plates and a Swiss registration number arrived outside our hut. From it stepped a dark young man as elegantly dressed and as charmingly casual as if he was just dropping in for a drink. He introduced himself as Werner Buchmüller, and said that he was to accompany us through to the American lines.

In view of Berger's warning it seemed that the earlier we left the better. We were all ready to go when it was discovered that the buses had disappeared. There were no others. The bus drivers, who were civilians commandeered for the job, had decided to disappear before the war came too close.

In the late afternoon, after incessant efforts by Mr Buchmüller, two lorries were procured; a notable achievement at the time when everyone was looking for mobile means of retreat. With a powerful sense of relief we helped to drape them with enormous Swiss flags that Mr Buchmüller, with the finesse of a prestidigitateur, produced from the boot of his Buick.

Darkness was already descending into the valley as we quitted that sorry place. With the dark came a certain sense of anxiety that our flags and our company, which included an S.S. medical officer (emissary of Berger), and the escort armed even with anti-tank weapons, could not entirely allay. In this country of conifers there was an atavistic feeling in the air that after dark the wolves emerged from their lairs. Herr Kaltenbrunner, with his scarred face and hectic eye, we knew to be a wolf, and a vicious one at that. At that stage of the break-up of Germany all the robber chiefs who could get there would be lurking somewhere in these mountains each with his private band of desperate retainers. Any of them might well think that personal possession of our group would give them a bargaining counter for their lives or in the last resort an opportunity to indulge their *Schadenfreude*. Berger was lucky—so far it was he who, if he included a joker or two, held the royal flush.

We drove over the high passes that connect the Salza and Inn valleys, on the lookout all the time for possible abductors, and beginning to see Kaltenbrunner around every corner. Once we were followed by an S.S. lorry for several miles. As it was about to overtake us a Polish officer foolishly tossed a whisky bottle out of the back of our truck which smashed on the road just ahead of it. Luckily its occupants did not seem to notice.

At about midnight the lorries suddenly stopped. There was an exchange of shouting and we saw in the dim rays of the headlights the figure of an S.S. soldier waving a gun and signalling us to turn off to the right. We left the main road and climbed up into the mountains and through a small hamlet. Beyond the village we turned up a rough dirt track and entered the dark courtyard of what seemed to be a large farm. Military vehicles were parked around the walls. There was no sign of life. Then there was a shrill whistle, and some guttural shouts, a door was thrown open and a shaft of light shone out. An enormous man, dressed in S.S. black, came out. He wore the insignia of a sergeant-major and looked like a cunning prize-fighter who had retired to become a butler. In a particularly unpleasant mock-butler manner he bowed us into the house.

The scene in the dimly-lit upstairs room was a surprise. Perhaps we had expected an austere military-looking head-quarters with maps and desks. This room seemed, to heightened sensibilities, almost fantastic, a stage setting for the cave of a robber chief. It was a long, low hall dimly lit by lamps and candles; in the foreground stood a long table spread for a feast such as prison-conditioned eyes had not seen for a long time. Cold meats ("viands" was a word that immediately suggested itself), game, smoked fish and crystallized fruit lay among bottles of French wine, Scotch and American whisky, and the liqueurs of every country in Europe. An S.S. officer, slapping backs and saying, "England gut!" gestured us to eat and drink. The Poles, who up till then had been impassive, almost blasé, became interested. We started eating with enthusiasm and helped ourselves liberally to the liquor. The room began to take on an even more improbable appearance. Beyond the table, on the floor, about twenty S.S. men, boys almost, lay sprawled like retainers on a Saxon hearth. They were half undressed and seemed too tired, or too drunk, to be interested in our presence.

Achtung! A sudden very loud shout from one of the officers. If you were not used to it the German military custom of giving every order as if frenzied with rage could be very disconcerting. This particular bark preceded the entry, through a side door, of an already familiar figure. It was General Berger. He was wearing a white mess-jacket that on his plump form gave him the appearance of an American business man on vacation at Palm Beach. His face was shining, his eyes were bright. He had the look of a man who had just had a much needed shot of dope.

Berger passed a podgy hand to each in turn and said that he was sorry he had not been there to greet us in person. It was clear, however, that he had timed his entry for maximum effect and had waited until his guests were in a receptive state of mind. For he then proceeded to make a speech. The tenor of his message was not new. There had already been veiled suggestions in the German press that the Americans and the British should join them against the Russians. This idea the *Obergruppen-führer* now tried to put over in his most rhetorical prose. "England and Germany", he said, "blood brothers of the same Aryan stock, should now settle their differences and unite in arms against the common enemy." Then there was more about the "Rote Virus" most of which we had heard at the earlier meeting.

As a peroration the General said that he had heard what Mr Churchill had said about the S.S. troops and how they would all be shot at the end of the war. "Your Mr Churchill says we are all assassins," he said, pointing towards the soldiers on the floor, who did not seem to be taking much interest in his declamation. He called one of them up, a good-looking youth of about eighteen, and patted him on the shoulder. "This is Karl," he said, "does Karl look like an assassin?" Karl certainly looked more like an eager boy scout.

At the end of his performance General Berger clapped his hands, and at this signal a white-coated orderly entered the room ceremoniously bearing a scarlet leather case. The senior member of our party was asked to step forward. John Elphinstone moved towards the table. Berger held out the box and, as John held out his hand to take it, snapped it open. In the box, resplendent on a couch of red velvet, lay an enormous automatic pistol about the same shape and size as a Colt ·45. This splendidly flashy weapon was inlaid with ivory and enamel, its squat barrel was elaborately chased with golden oak-leaves in high relief. On the butt was the enamelled monogram of the S.S. and a small plate engraved with Berger's signature. He was making this offering, he said, as a proof of his good wishes for our safe arrival in Allied hands. The pistol, presumably a modern and more lethal equivalent of the jewelled sword, had, he said, been given to him by the Führer himself. The case also contained a clip of very live-looking bullets. The orderly now returned with another box. To each of us was presented, as consolation prizes, a cigar of more than Churchillian proportions garaged in a thick glass tube. They were good cigars, said the *Obergruppenführer*, and demonstrated how they would light without being drawn.

It was not until five in the morning that General Berger finally bade good-bye. Returning to the buses the giant sergeant-major managed us as efficiently as the doorman of an expensive nightclub, his odiously confidential expression indicated that he was used to handling important, if unsteady, persons in the early hours of the morning. We drove out into daybreak.

Along the main road were positive signs of military activity. Road blocks were being prepared at the precipitous curves; on the cliff side were piles of boulders, held in check by ropes and wires, ready to be released against an advancing enemy; engineers were laying explosive charges under the bridges and culverts. In the absence of fixed defences the "Great Redoubt" seemed something of a myth.

The Americans had apparently advanced beyond Innsbruck and were forcing their way up the Inn Valley. An S.S. division, the last fighting troops in the Western Alps, was slowing them down with an earnest rearguard action.

Soon we entered what was obviously a forward area. Exhausted-looking, sweating troops were preparing reserve positions for the guns, transport was continuously moving back. There was no shooting; it was almost as if they were waiting for us to go through. Then, turning a bend, we saw ahead a river with a stone bridge. Covering the bridge, backed by the mountain road and commanding a fine field of fire down a valley, was an 88 mm. gun, its slim, wicked-looking barrel waiting for the first approach of enemy armour. Those who had fought in North Africa or Italy knew that these elegant guns, capable of a rapid rate of fire, could penetrate any tank likely to be forming the spearhead of an advancing army. The gun crew, stripped to the waist, were working frantically to improve their position. None of them looked over eighteen. They watched us with a curiously detached air as we sailed past, immune under our neutral flag, towards our friends who were their enemies, towards our salvation and their probable destruction. In a contrary way it was hard not to wish them luck, at least with their lives.

We drove across the bridge and towards the widening Inn Valley. In a meadow to the left was an old wooden barn. Creeping towards the barn were two figures carrying rifles or submachine guns. They were Americans. We cheered. Round the next corner was a troop of three American tanks. A dusty steel-helmeted figure was peering out of the turret of the leading one. A raised hand and a slowly swivelling gun signalled us to stop. Mr Buchmüller nervously stepped out of the Buick and flourished papers. Our credentials checked, the American impatiently waved us on; it was almost as if he resented our presence in his game of war.

In the next village was the squadron to which these tanks had been scouts. Tanks were parked in the village square, their crews, slung with every conceivable weapon, were standing around smoking and chewing gum. A little white church shone in the morning sun, a few villagers stood uncertainly watching these surprising visitors. Most surprising of all, even to us, were the negro soldiers, who seemed to have come from another planet.

The American soldiers gave us chocolate and bottles of wine taken out of their tanks. They were the spearhead of the 53rd U.S. Division, whose headquarters was at Innsbruck about thirty miles down the valley. They were anxious to know what German forces we had seen and were relieved to hear that we did not think they were likely to run into much opposition up the valley. They said, laconically, that they were way ahead of their main body because the officer in charge of them, the gentleman we had met further up the road, was anxious to get a name for himself.

While we were chatting our German drivers had taken it into

their heads to go for a stroll. They were promptly arrested, and were only released when we explained how necessary they were to our continued journey.

The Americans told us that after they had found a number of their compatriots murdered they shot all S.S. troops, never making them prisoner. No doubt resulting from this policy they had found piles of dead German soldiers with their uniform jackets missing and S.S. tunics lying round about. It was assumed that the S.S. were murdering their fellow-soldiers in the Wehrmacht and wearing their uniforms to avoid being identified if captured. Luckily the S.S. doctor, who accompanied us, had by this time and at our suggestion removed his badges.

Since we were now in the American controlled area John Winant, who had hitherto been completely retiring, began to assume an air of responsibility. Our Swiss friend had suggested that we follow the Arlberg route into Switzerland, where he would see to it that we had a few days' amusement before returning back home. The proposal was entirely attractive but Winant seemed to think that it was our duty to report as soon as possible to the American H.Q.

Thus it was that we came to Innsbruck.

Innsbruck was all gold in the morning sun. At the crossroads in the Maria Therese Strasse American military police in their snowdrop helmets and spacemen boots casually flipped the traffic by. Groups of G.I.s, heavily armed with Leicas, sauntered along the sidewalks in the style of Gary Cooper. The citizens, looking at the shops or sitting in the cafés, seemed already to have adapted themselves to the new climate of life.

Seeing our C.D. plates, a fat singer from the Vienna Opera asked, falsetto, if we could help bring his mother from Berlin.

At the American headquarters on the hilltop we found that another group of "Prominents" had recently arrived after being released from a castle down the valley. Standing out in the sun on the terrace were Paul Reynaud in plus-fours, the square thick-set figure of M. Daladier, General Gamelin, the wizened

General Weygand, and Colonel de la Roc, founder of the Croix de Feu, the French semi-fascist Action Party. There, also, was Jean Borotra, the veteran tennis champion, for once without his famous beret. A small dog belonging to the party bounded up and investigated us. It was called back by one of the "Prominent" wives, who had apparently been allowed to join their husbands in captivity. We imagined the arguments they must have all had according to their degree of attachment to the Vichy government, in their comfortable, if enforced, confinement.

By this time cameras were clicking frantically and reporters were busy with pencils and pads. An American officer, Tony Drexel, who coincidentally had been in the same house at Eton with John Elphinstone, led us off to his mess canteen for a late breakfast of spam served with pineapple, creamy coffee, and the whitest, lightest bread we had ever seen. It was difficult to believe that we could actually eat as much as we liked. Outside, loud over the sunny barrack square, the Andrew sisters were harmonising their hearts out on the public address system. "Way down South in Birmingham. Way down South in Alabam. That's where my heart belongs."

Next morning the German drivers and the S.S. doctor were provided with civilian clothes and were sent on their way home. Mr Buchmüller departed to Switzerland, General Bor and his officers to a concentration area at Murnau. The rest of the Prominente travelled in an open truck to Augsburg, to the headquarters of the American Seventh Army where, as they arrived, a British major said curtly: "You're very dirty." An American colonel, more intelligent and more practical, indicated the washroom.

General Patch, the American Army Commander, had arranged that the two royal ex-Prominents, George Lascelles and John Elphinstone, should be flown in his personal aeroplane to Paris, in order to be presented to General Eisenhower at Versailles. This kind and flattering plan was nevertheless a little worrying because George, hitherto the most resilient and imperturbable of our party, had begun for the first time to feel the strain of the recent events, and he did not feel well enough to face such a triumphal whirl. John felt that perhaps it was his duty (since obviously it was not George's) to explain this to General Patch; yet at the same time John felt that he could not.

A solution came in an unexpected way. The Americans, after dinner that evening in their H.Q., told John that they had a surprise for him, and they beckoned him into a room where there was a telephone with its receiver off. As John, at a sign, picked up the receiver, he noticed at the farther end of the room a group of American colonels, craning curiously. He said: "Hullo!" A voice that sounded as if it was only two feet away answered: "Hullo! This is Buckingham Palace," and asked if it was speaking to the Master of Elphinstone. John saying yes, there followed a silence after which he heard, for the first time in five years, the voice of his aunt, the Queen. She had learned that day that John was safe, but had been surprised and delighted when told, a little later, that she would actually be able to speak to him.

When the Queen asked about George, John said that George had a bad cold, and that therefore he wondered if it would be possible to arrange for them to come home directly and quickly. The Queen said that she would speak to the King.

Next day George and John were flown off in General Patch's aeroplane, not to Paris, but to Northolt, where they were met by an equerry and John's three sisters and were driven straight to Buckingham Palace. George was collected by his mother, the Princess Royal, and John was left to recount their adventures at a family dinner party that night with the help of unstinted champagne which had no special effect on him, he was surprised to note, although he felt in very good form.

The others, meanwhile, after hospitable American entertainment in Augsburg, were staged aerially homeward and landed on a sunny airfield in Sussex.

Chapter Twelve

Out of the East

THE Fortress of Königstein had appeared horrific to the Prominente when they first saw it. As their small figures zig-zagged up its affronting rock, Dawyck Haig, whose thinking was always pictorial, and often silent until picture had been translated into symbol, that represented that gloomy approach as a "journey of penance and torture . . . a road to Calvary".

Yet Königstein, pinnacle as it was, and mighty in stance above the Elbe bent like an iron bar, was not unreservedly horrific. Internally it had a different character. The Prominente, on the morning of their entry, had been in no state to appreciate that. If they had been, however, one memory at least might have presented itself to their minds. Two months earlier a French Général de Corps d'Armée, General Flavigny, a man of monkey-wrinkles, sheepskin collar, and a complexion of blistered mahogany, had appeared in Colditz. This general was *sympathique*. Previously, he had been interned with a lot of other generals, and in Colditz his caustic observations to the effect that he had had enough of living with those old men "qui causent toujours de leurs ma-la-dies, quoi?" had been popular. He had been amusing, too, about the overwhelming politeness of certain interned Italian generals, who, he said, "prenaient le vent". Where, we had asked him, was this senior and extraordinary retreat? General Flavigny had then pulled out a snapshot. It was a castle at the head of a wooded hill. It was Königstein.

The Prominente never glimpsed those generals. The generals were there. But they did not come out. No hobbling figure emerged to chat tetchily of his "ma-la-dies" and to impart thereby a cosier tone to the nightmare-like unreality of the thirty hours in the fortress.

Dawyck Haig and Charlie Hopetoun did see, however, the more agreeable, the almost vacuously idyllic, aspect of Königstein. It began to steal on them, like Prospero's music, as soon as their fellow-Prominente had been made to vanish. First they experienced new sensations of peacefulness. They were two people together. They liked each other and they could begin to sound their liking. There was plenty of food, cooked and served by Corporal Mittai (one of two Maoris who had voluntarily accompanied the Prominente), and he also looked after them in other ways. The din of Colditz, the guards perpetually stamping in the Prominente passage, the general German and prisoner uproar of that place, had suddenly been whisked into oblivion. They were once more in touch with their own beings, which seemed almost palpable. Morally, as well as physically, these first days in Königstein were the beginning of a period of building up and healing which might have been wholly cloudless, but for the recurring anxiety that the Prominente situation might catch up with them again.

For the bonds that held them comparatively safe in Königstein were weak. It was only "Graf Hoptetoun" who, as a result of John Elphinstone's insistence, had been warranted unfit to travel. Even that status was shadowy since it depended, not so much on any medical certificate as on the power to act (which might at any time be taken away) and on the courage to act well of the Königstein Commandant, Colonel Hesselmann, who had told John that he would not telephone to Berlin because he knew that permission to keep Charlie would be refused. Dawyck's hold was yet shakier. He was where he was because "Graf Hopetoun" could not be left alone. He was there to watch over Charlie; and it was only a Prominente quirk that Charlie in fact, within a few hours of their stay, had made a notable recovery, while Dawyck the overlooker had fallen violently ill with dysentery, and had become so appallingly haggard that his appearance scared Charlie his patient.

In this situation the two of them were moved from their prisoner-of-war block to a spare room at the bottom of a tower in which Colonel Hesselmann had sumptuous quarters. In this room there were beds with linen sheets, romantic nineteenth-century oil paintings, better food from the Colonel's kitchen, and a window looking on to a pretty garden in which the Colonel's children, a dark boy of twelve and a fair boy of eight, played. The contemplating of these ordinary and pleasant things was so enlivening, to Charlie and Dawyck equally, that they felt that they must be lucky, and that rescue was imminent.

In the evening, after dinner, they climbed the tower stairs to an arched hall leading into the Commandant's private rooms. Colonel Hesselmann had invited them up for Schnapps. Dawyck during this visit scarcely spoke. Was he unawake? Far from it. Like successive negatives, his eyes recorded the lines of the pretty china in the cupboards, of the log fire and the light from it flickering on the walls, of the little boy in dressing-gown who came in after his bath to say good-night, of the highly strung, quick-moving face of his host, and of a personal atmosphere that to him spelled "life", "humanity". Dawyck, whenever he drifted away from his pictorial anchorage, readily made irritable judgments which were less expressive. Charlie had to do the talking. Dawyck merely noted that Hesselmann's conversation was *gemütlich*, that intense subjects were (rightly he thought) avoided, that some of the topics were *too* trivial, and that Frau Hesselmann elaborated these with unnecessary detail.

This gentle evening inaugurated several modes of fellow-feeling between the two Prominente and the Hesselmanns. Frau Hesselmann, a high-bred, handsome woman with dark hair raised high in the old-fashioned mode of some *Gräfin* in her matronly phase, busied herself with the welfare of Dawyck as an invalid. Dawyck admired the Colonel's manners, his knowledge of the castle's antiquities, his grace of mind, distinction, and understanding of beauty; the Scot in Dawyck, conceding so much, was nevertheless not yet prepared to feel sure about Hesselmann's *character*. Charlie, on the other hand, who for five years had fought and despised every German trick until to him all Germans had become creatures of horror (not hate, it was not in him), had summed up in favour of Hesselmann unhesitatingly. He was sure that this man would do almost anything to safeguard him and Dawyck. Consequently, for the first time, Charlie felt *protected*. Just to check, though, he nipped over to consult the French generals, and they gave Colonel Hesselmann an unimpeachable chit. "Très correct."

Dawyck's system of checking was characteristically different and far more slow. Whenever he and Charlie called on the Hesselmanns, which now they fairly often did, he carefully observed Charlie, knowing his revulsion from Germans, in order to gauge how far their host was "getting across" to Charlie. After ten days Dawyck cautiously concluded that Hesselmann *was* making headway. Dawyck also perceived more profoundly, through his dark interior lens, that the Hesselmanns, in this relationship with Charlie and himself, were trying to get their own bearings; their curiosity was not separable from their readiness to help.

Suddenly, on a clear and unmistakable issue, Colonel Hesselmann rejected a direct order from Himmler to move his two prisoners south on the track of the rest. As an extra cover, chiefly to pacify the friendly but teetering Abwehr officer, Major Sieber, who quaked for want of "proofs of illness", bags of dried fruit were cooked by Charlie and eaten by Dawyck until his insides became even more fluid than they had been already.

It was Hesselmann who thus proved decisively how much he was willing to stake. The Prominente nightmare receded. As to that, Charlie and Dawyck felt for the first time free at heart. The Germans in Königstein were no longer human instruments to be clung to at all costs. They were human beings. Charlie and Dawyck began now to take an unwary, receptive, and healthily dispassionate interest in them.

They listened without prejudice to the outpourings of "Porky", the old Abwehr major: how his love of German morality and culture had bamboozled him into an admiration of Hitler and how that had turned to horror. Curiously, by their

disarming of the "Prominente" threat the Germans had also
revised, in their own disfavour, the power-balance between themselves and their two prisoners. It was they now who, despite
sentries at door and window, sought to propitiate and to win the
good offices of Charlie and Dawyck, often with placatory gifts
of surreptitious bottles of vermouth.

The Commandant was in fact bracing his spirits to meet a
momentous and unimaginable responsibility. He had confirmed
that Königstein was nearly certain to fall inside a Russian opera-
tional zone. Russians? On this great rock it scarcely seemed real.
But the vacuous idyll was in truth ending. A furrowed and preoccupied Colonel Hesselmann sloughed off his grace, distinction,
understanding of beauty; was not sociable. Dawyck and Charlie
perceived all the same that he had not forgotten them, and
that his schemes and dispositions took them in some way into
account.

Charlie and Dawyck had already exchanged social calls with
the allied prisoner generals—General Bourret, the senior of the
150 French interned generals, General Winckelmann, the Dutch
Commander-in-Chief, and the Dutch General Forst van Forst.
They had strolled the ramparts; Dawyck had painted. The Elbe
Aussicht, stupendous but not at all subtle, had begun to bore
them; and there was a certain danger on the ramparts from
sociable French generals who could not know that they had
already heard, from other French generals, the story of the escape
of General Giraud; that they had already and frequently ap-
plauded the collective cunning of all assisting French generals in
having engineered, at the spot from which Giraud was to descend, the elimination of a German sentry, on the pretext that he
spoiled their view; that they had indeed memorized (if since forgotten) the exact length of string that had been collected, the
precise position of the buttress which had been the *point de départ*,
and the overall method of construction of the chair in which
General Giraud had been lowered.

On an evening as they warily strolled, hoping not to be way-
laid anew by this story, the tall figure of Hesselmann's second-

in-command (that Major Baron von Beschwitz with whom in
Munich Dawyck had exchanged pre-war bows) loped suddenly
towards them, glasses swinging at his neck. The major was out
of breath as he beckoned them back towards the Hesselmann
tower, and there pointed upward. They climbed the tower stairs.
The Commandant was on the telephone. He was speaking crisply
to a German garrison and was giving it permission to surrender.
This was repeated. Colonel Hesselmann's command included that
of a number of garrisons outside the castle. His orders were clear,
his voice was without a tremor, his nerves were wholly under
control. Beschwitz dashed in, his glasses still round his neck, as
if he had just thrown himself off his horse outside. Beschwitz
brought in hour-by-hour reports of the progress towards Königstein of the Red Army. The last, the dustiest and the most glass-
agitating of his bulletins was: "5 miles away. Early tomorrow
morning." Also: "Burning, Raiding, Out of Hand."

The Commandant wanted to know whether he could count
on help by Dawyck and Charlie, as representatives of Russia's
allies, to protect the German women, of whom a motley hundred
or so had gathered under the umbrella of the fortress, against
Russian soldiery. On that point, the French generals had come
out with some sort of benevolent undertaking. There was also
some lesser organizational business. Dawyck received the key of
the food store and agreed to distribute as necessary.

Charlie asked the Commandant why, since he had a car, he
did not get his wife and children away through a gap to the
Americans. Hesselmann waved this off. His wife was determined
to stay with him, he replied, and he was determined to stay at his
post; apart from which, he feared S.S. ambush.

Hesselmann then dropped his voice. Hidden inside the castle,
he said, were the Saxon Crown Jewels. He had them stowed safe
and secret in twelve suitcases. They were valued at three million
pounds. He had received orders to destroy them. But he did not
wish to do that. He would like to hand them over to Dawyck
and Charlie for them to take back to England.

"I would like the Saxon Crown Jewels to be carried by you

as a present to the British Nation and to the British Royal Family," the Colonel declared.

Charlie and Dawyck thanked him for the sentiment; the offer, they felt, would prove impracticable. Hesselmann, however, seemed to feel that he had made his point. He was full of a nervous vitality that the crisis of the evening appeared to have called out. Less formally, and as if for good measure, he tossed in the matter of the Dresden pictures. They also were in the fortress, he said, some upright in wooden structures like gramophone cabinets, some in roll-up canvases. It was his wish that the pictures too should be carried to England. A tapering hand sketched transport.

At this point Charlie and Dawyck, stirred simultaneously by a feeling that something had become due, rose, and returned under the minute with a small transportable packet of coffee, which they presented to Colonel Hesselmann as a "token present for your wife and two sons". They then engaged him in a short chat about German atrocities. Could never have happened with decent people in power, the Colonel said. What made him nervous, he confessed, was the possibility of a war between England (plus America) and Russia on German soil. Then he sprang up and quickly came back with a satchel out of which emerged, for Charlie and Dawyck, a bottle of vermouth.

Next morning, following the proclamation of the general cease-fire on all fronts, the French Generals formally invited Charlie and Dawyck, as representatives of Great Britain, to a little ceremony to introduce the running-up of a French tricolour flag and a Union Jack. This was done. Shortly afterwards, however, a Russian fighter aircraft, lurching like a solitary drunk across the top of the fortress, fired a burst that hit a Frenchman in the knee. The French then took down their flag and ran up a hammer-and-sickle.

That was a side-show. The entire Königstein population was soon on the ramparts watching out for the Russians, who were seen first in ones and twos advancing across the landscape. As they came closer, small and disreputable-seeming parties could be seen poking into haystacks and firing shots through farm windows, attended by a rabble of liberated Russian slave-labour. Farms were burning. One party got into a boat and pushed across the river below the ramparts. On the Königstein battlements, white flag already rampant, the Germans watched fascinated.

A rout poured up the Königstein ramp looking approximately, Charlie thought, like a French Revolution mob marauding across an aristocrat's garden. Suddenly Charlie, horrified, saw the two small Hesselmann boys tearing down merrily towards the gate in sheer interest to meet the approaching rout. As he watched helpless Charlie saw two Russians, grinning and guffawing, pick up the children, set them on their shoulders, and carry them back into the castle.

Above, the German troops were drawn up. Colonel Hesselmann stood waiting. A big Russian officer, very calm, gave sharp, short orders. The German soldiers, who had gathered that they ought to take out all their personal possessions as they would be going a long way, at first by barges down the Elbe, were ready with trolleys packed with everything that they owned. The big Russian gave an order, and the Germans under Colonel Hesselmann went out like a parade, escorted by drunk and dishevelled Russian soldiers. German women watching them go stretched out imploring hands and wept hysterically. Siberia! The word flew from mouth to mouth. In his own room, in which he had stayed unnoticed, an elderly German major shot himself.

There still were batches of Russians inside, turning things upside down, charging all ways like wild cattle. A German woman would flash by, flash back, dodge in and out through doors, Russians galvanically in pursuit.

Charlie and Dawyck had rammed three German girls into cupboards in their room. Knots of Russians kept lounging and gyrating that way. Two Russian officers, conspicuously drunk, detached themselves and drifted towards Charlie, who was looking out from his ground-floor window. One of the rammed-in German girls broke cupboard and popped up by Charlie at the window. She could not resist. At once the two Russians quickened purposefully towards the entrance of the tower. Charlie, alarmed especially for Frau Hesselmann, who was upstairs in her drawing-room, barred the doorway.

"Our quarters! No!" he objected in pidgin German.

This was not well received by the Russians. They forced their way past, lurched up the stairs, disappeared.

Ten minutes later Charlie heard appalling yells. He bounded up and rushed into the Hesselmann drawing-room. The two Russians were sitting at a little table. Frau Hesselmann was lying back in a chair, moaning and holding her head as if she had been struck. The Russians rose and embraced Charlie.

"Wein! Wein! Wein!" they said.

"Do pull yourself together, " Charlie then said to the moaning, rocking Frau. "Spoil them. Get some wine." At that moment a German maid looked in, saw the Russians, and plunged into hysterics. Charlie urged the now outmoaned Frau Hesselmann to get rid of the maid and to fetch the wine herself.

Frau Hesselmann, who had sensibly taken this advice, returned shortly with a bottle and three glasses. She filled the glasses and handed them to the Russians. They, however, would not drink. They demonstrated, by mime, that it was necessary to produce a *fourth* glass. Frau Hesselmann again complied. Immediately the Russians, with much politeness, helped her into her chair, filled her glass, clinked their glasses with hers, and drank her health. This left them tipsier. They pointed meaningly at a watch on Frau Hesselmann's wrist: she told Charlie that the watch was not valuable except sentimentally, since it had been her husband's wedding-present. Charlie asked her to pass it to him, she did, he put it in his pocket. Hell broke loose. The Russians leaped from their chairs and unfixed bayonets and flourished them before Charlie.

"Do give them the watch!" begged the much-put-upon-hostess.

One of the two Russians, after handling and fondling the watch, used his bayonet to open it, smashed it, burst into tears and handed it back to Frau Hesselmann.

A ruse at last discouraged the mercurial guests: a filthy potato soup served, at Charlie's suggestion, in response to their requests for *Fleisch*. The guests spat out the soup. Then they left.

It was clear by now that the entire Hesselmann plan for the protection of German womankind had gone awry. The indispensable and missing factor was the failure of the 150 French generals to redeem the pledges that they had given, or were held to have given, to stand epaulette to epaulette against Asian lust.

How could this have happened? Had "ma-la-dies" kept all from the field of honour? Dawyck called to remind them of what had been pledged. It was not yet too late, he said, if they would come out.

"Ah non!" said a general—and nodding heads of other generals confirmed that he spoke for others. "Ah non! Maintenant nous sommes les victeurs."

With the Commandant embarged "for Siberia," and all his men too, there did not seem to be much more that could be done.

But Colonel Hesselmann had not in fact gone far on the way to Siberia. He had not even been on a barge. Nor had his men. There had been no barges. It was two hours since the Germans with their trolleys had been marched out of the fortress; within three hours of that departure they were all back inside. As men, they looked the same. But they did not have their trolleys. Nor were any of them wearing either the boots which they had been wearing or any other boots, only stockings.

These few hours of fantastic turmoil could not leave in their wake a bland and immediate calm. All the Russians pelted out. But it was not watches alone that they had broken, nor only the treacherously exposed flank of the defence of German virtue that they had disrupted. Their primitivism had played havoc with settled habits of mind. Mittai, the devoted Maori soldier, emulating their drinking, absorbing their appetites, had fallen suddenly foul of a pent-up rage, whose charge almost certainly had been accumulated by his long captivity, and he had hurled himself at Dawyck in an assault that might have even proved mortal, if

Mittai had not in fact had a civilized heart. At a late point, Dawyck standing non-resistant, the rage in this friendly man suddenly gave way.

Colonel Hesselmann fell ill. Charlie and Dawyck, whom now no sentries detained, went down into the town, scrounging up odds and ends of British soldiery for, as was hoped, the imminent trek home. The Russian regular troops, that were stationed in the town, were incomparably superior to the roughnecks of the castle visitation. They asked Charlie and Dawyck whether they needed anything—food?—medicines? clothes? They would not allow them to leave the area, however, only answering politely that they had to wait for orders. Charlie noticed that guns facing west were being emplaced.

These were frustrating days, seeking a westward contact vainly, yet they were not unpleasant. It was fine, and Charlie and Dawyck had tea in a farmhouse with Polish girls in pretty dresses, one of whom had been in Auschwitz and was an artist in whose presence Dawyck felt an affinity, as she in his. Charlie met a nineteen-year-old Polish girl, who had been brought to Germany as a foreign worker, and there had been branded on one thumb. Charlie felt his old *deutschfeindlich* revulsions rising to choke him. He could scarcely help remembering how he had tried, only three days earlier, to protect German women. He went straight back to the fortress and exploded the story of the branding in the face of one German woman whom he had thought to be decent, even good. Cowering from his vehemence this flustered Frau cried "But she is a Pole!" Charlie went quickly away.

One morning two American airmen, who had been a few days in Königstein, borrowed tommy-guns and motor-bicycles and tore off importantly like dispatch riders, along the Chemnitz road. Soon it was happily clear that they had got to Chemnitz. Charlie, walking down in the town, saw with joy an American military policeman piloting an armoured tank force. He and Dawyck were given two hours to get ready. There were things that Charlie wanted to clear up—legacies of their strange uneasy weeks—Corporal Mittai (astray in the town somewhere), odd-men-out British troops that he had collected, the Hesselmanns, the ——. He was chivvied away. "Ah, you do what you're told!" said the American commander, who however gave Charlie his word and gave it as the word of an American officer, that he would come back next day to fetch the left-over British troops and the Hesselmanns. He did both.

The mysterious processes of American organization at last bore aloft Charlie and Dawyck, lorry-wise, on a lovely spring afternoon, through hedgeless, houseless miles of cultivated country. At a flat and lonely crossroads there was a Russian traffic control, manned by Russian policewomen. Placed on the road stood a long farm table with, as centre-piece, two pink china-glass vases. At one end rose, in the open country, a full-length looking-glass on a swing-bar; at the other end a grandfather-clock. Charlie smiled at the policewomen. They did not smile.

The French generals riding in the U.S. task-force camions sat bolt upright, five in a row, with grey-white eyes, like Black Sambos. At Chemnitz there was the hospitality of a U.S. Divisional Commander and there were waffles for breakfast; then an aeroplane journey to Brussels, Dawyck miserable with dysentery, and travelling with them the Dutch General Forst van Forst, of whom the last that Dawyck and Charlie heard, as they walked on the Brussels airport towards an England-bound hospital aeroplane, were the general's frigidly indignant efforts to order the U.S. pilot to produce an aeroplane that would carry him on at once—"I am the personal aide-de-camp of Queen Wilhelmina"— to The Hague; and the lazy, floating tones of the pilot inquiring—"Where the hell's The Hague anyway?"

They landed in Gloucestershire on a green field. Kind British hospitals, one for Dawyck near Swindon, one for Charlie near London, were ready. Stuck fast on the fly-paper of British hospital-tape, Dawyck and Charlie, pacing far-apart rooms alone, rooms that seemed to their captive eyes to be cells, summoning their last energies to summon doctors (German Commandants), reconnoitring escape exits from buildings that they felt sure were prison-camps, at last broke clear, hours having been to them like years: Dawyck to near-by friends, a walk by a chalk stream, English church bells: Charlie to the meeting with his wife—telephoned by a friendly sergeant, when she had not yet known that Charlie was in England, she had sped to the hospital—from whom he had been involuntarily separated for more than five years.